7/13

Thirteen Months, Fourteen Days The Journey

My objective is to portray the everyday struggles a GI goes through, trying to stay alive while being so far from home and the ones he loved.

Company B of the Twentieth Engineers was initially a combat-engineer company. However, most of the assignments received were that of a construction-engineer company. Being engineers, our mission was not to seek out and destroy the enemy. Our mission was to build and maintain Vietnam's infrastructure.

Many of the names of the individuals appearing in the pages to follow have been changed due to the fact that I remember their actions but not their names. The stories of the incidents portrayed are actual happenings.

Again, I salute all those who served in Vietnam and especially to those who gave the ultimate sacrifice. Your country called, you went, you served. Some returned bruised and broken, some returned whole, some returned not at all. To all I say, "Welcome home."

The Draft

17 January 1969, 6:30 a.m.

Not a word had been spoken as Grandfather drove the fifteen miles from our home to the draft board at 7 High Street, Belleville, Illinois. As we approached the three-story buff brick building and entered the parking area, the silence was broken. "Well, son, you know you have done everything possible to avoid going and failed. The time has come for you to accept the fact of being drafted. I had to go as well as your dad and your uncle Raymond. You are an American above all. I think you need to realize that when your country calls, it is your patriotic duty to go and serve. And if you lose your life in defense of your country, this is a price you must be willing to pay for liberty."

My grandfather had served in WWI, my dad in WWII, and my uncle in the Korean War; fortunately, none had gone overseas. Grandfather was assigned to Portland, Oregon: Homeland Security. My father was on a troopship to the Pacific Theater when the war ended. My uncle went to Alaska, also Homeland Defense. I assuredly would go to Vietnam. My registration for the draft was prior to the lottery. Your number was assigned numerically as you registered on your birthday. The first person to register that year was number 1, the second number 2, and so forth. As my birthday was in March, I was the sixtieth person to register, so my number was 60. I had registered on my eighteenth birthday five years earlier in 1964. I had received a deferment as I was going to school. I graduated in May of 1968, and then the fun began.

"Fill out the form, sign the bottom. Get on the bus," barked a heavyset lady behind the desk just inside the door. It was 7:15 a.m. The bus was full.

"Remember who you are," said my grandfather as he put his arm around me and gave me a hug, one of a few I had ever received from him.

My father and mother had divorced some nineteen years earlier. Until I was sixteen, my mother and I lived with my grandparents who were actually my father's parents. My father had met my mother, who was working in the cafeteria at Kelly Field in San Antonio, Texas, when he was taking flight navigation school. She was a Mexican Native American. After the divorce, my grandmother didn't want my mother to take me back to Texas, so she convinced my mother to live with them. Until the divorce was final, my mother and I lived with her brother, Manuel, in Chicago. After about a month, Grandma, not being able to stand it any longer, came to Chicago on the train and took me back to East St. Louis. My mother lasted about three and a half weeks before coming and taking me back to Chicago. I went back and forth between Mama Grandma and Mother like this for about six months, then we finally moved back to my grandparents' for good.

The bus arrived at the Mark Building in St. Louis, Missouri, just before 8:00 a.m.

"OK, you boots, off the bus. Line up behind the white line. Time for a recheck. Yeah, that's right, another physical."

There were many, many busloads of young men there that morning; over eight hundred draftees in all. Soon we were all lined up behind the white lines, dressed only in our Skivvies.

Several doctors walked up and down the ranks, checking everyone.

"Is there anyone that has a physical problem that would keep them out of the service?" a doctor asked. Immediately I raised my hand.

"What is your problem?"

"Sir, I have a bad knee," I replied.

"Come with me." He motioned as he moved toward a small exam room. "Lie down on the table and hold your leg straight up toward the ceiling. What is the problem with your knee?" he asked as he twisted my leg this way and that.

"Sir, it pops, cracks, and hurts all the time," I answered as he continued to move my leg in odd directions.

"What do you do for a living?" he questioned.

"I am a carpenter, and I lay floor tile."

"Your knee is fine, but I must admit I have never ever seen anyone with calluses on their knees like you have."

By noon, all the physicals were completed. After lunch, 1:00 p.m., the next step was the written test. One hundred questions, two hours to finish. Only questions answered in sequence were counted. If a question was skipped, however, it was also counted as wrong. I managed to complete

96 of the 100. As the time period closed, we were given a short break as the tests were graded.

"William E. Mattatall III," called out a navy recruiter as he entered the room.

"Here," I replied.

"Please come with me. I would like to talk to you."

We entered a small office off the break room. "You know you are going to Vietnam, right?" he opened. "You did pretty well on the test, and I would like to give you an opportunity. I see you have gone to carpentry school for four years. How long have you been a carpenter?"

"Seven years," I replied.

"Well, with that much experience, I can offer you an E-5 rating right away if you join the navy as a Seabees right now. Just sign the dotted line. Of course, you will have to give us three years."

"Sorry, sir. I don't want to go at all, let alone for three years. I'll just take my chances with the draft."

Again we were lined up along the white line. This time, there were about ten officers talking to each draftee individually. My turn came. A Major Mayer spoke with me.

"How much college education do you have?"

"Sir?" I asked in amazement.

"How much college education do you have?"

"None, I went to carpenter apprenticeship school, but no college."

"Well, you had better go, son. Of the ninety-six questions you answered, all were correct. You achieved the highest score of the day. Never before has anyone not had at least one wrong answer."

5:00 p.m.

"Listen up, everyone!" shouted a red-haired sergeant above the noise of the break room. "Go to room 116. There you will find a series of white lines painted on the floor. Line up thirty men behind each line."

After everyone entered room 116 and were behind the white lines, twenty-five to thirty MPs entered the room and stationed themselves around the room, each carrying an M16 along with a .45 automatic pistol holstered around their waists. As a young captain entered the room, the MPs locked and loaded the M16s. I could see the hair on the back of the neck of the fellow in front of me stand on end. *What are they going to do now, shoot us all?* I thought.

"You will now take the oath entering into the United States Army. I will read the oath. When I am finished, I will drop my hand and everyone will take one step forward crossing the white line. This will complete the swearing-in ceremony. If anyone, and I repeat, if anyone refuses to step across the white line, you will go directly to a federal prison for five years. NO TRIAL, NO NOTHIN', just straight to jail. Got it? If anyone resists, they will be shot for treason right on the spot. I am going to give you a minute to think about it."

As the moment passed, the words of my grandfather came to mind: "You are an American. You are a patriot. It is time to serve your country."

I decided in that moment everything I had tried to keep from going had failed, and from that moment on, I would do the very best I possibly could.

As the captain finished reading the oath, he dropped his hand, and needless to say, everyone crossed the line.

"Back to the break room. Wait for the buses to take you to your new homes. That is, everyone except Mattatall. The feds need to speak with ya!" shouted our redheaded sergeant.

Again I went to the small room off the break room. There sat two FBI agents. *What now?* I thought.

"Bill, is it?" started the smaller of the two men.

"Yes?"

"Tell us about the weapons charge that is in your file," said the other.

"What weapons charge?" I queried.

"April 6, 1965, Belleville, Illinois, you were picked up on a weapons charge," he answered.

"That April morning on my way to work, a semi making a right hard turn had sideswiped my car. The policeman taking the accident report noticed I had part of a shotgun in the back window of my car. It had belonged to my great uncle. I was restoring the relic and was to drop it off that evening to have the triggers and hammers brass plated as well as the body chromed. The gun was inoperable, but I was still hauled off before a judge. He fined me $50, reading an ordinance stating any firearm needed to either be locked in the trunk in a case or have every screw removed." My reply was accepted, and I was allowed to continue on with my army career.

8:00 p.m.

"OK, you boots. Off and on. Smoking lamps out. Let's go, let's go, let's go. Buses are here. Time to be a soldier. Everyone with a red ticket on the five buses out this door. Everyone with the yellow tickets out that door."

The redheaded sergeant seemed glad that we were leaving and he could go home. All red tickets led to buses going to Fort Leonard Wood. All those holding yellow tickets were on their way to Fort Benning, Georgia. Those holding blue tickets were off to Fort Pork, Louisiana, and the green tickets were off to Fort Dix, New Jersey. I had drawn the red and would soon be on my way to Fort Leonard Wood, Missouri, a mere three-and-a-half-hour drive from home.

The day had started out clear and at about thirty-five degrees. The temperature, however, had dropped during the day. Freezing rain and sleet had moved in. The three-hour bus ride landed us at Fort Leonard Wood at zero dark thirty. Actually we arrived at 12:35 a.m., four and a half hours after leaving St. Louis. As the bus crawled along the icy highway, I began to reflect on the events that led to this most tragic day.

On 26 August 1968, I had reported to the Mark Building for a predraft physical. After the physical, the written test was given along with a hearing; an ear, nose, and throat; and a spit-shine test. I was told, "You're a prime candidate." These words came from a red-haired sergeant with a thin build. He had completed his tour in Vietnam and was back in the States counting his days to freedom.

"Go sit at the red table. I will tell you when you can go."

I had been sitting at the red table along with others for about a half hour when along came an MP.

"OK, OK, OK. Gimme your undivided attention. All you guys at the red table, out the door and on the buses. You all are going to Fort Wood."

I instantly jumped up. "Wait a minute. Wait a minute. I just came for my physical. I haven't been drafted," I stammered.

"Yeah, yeah, yeah," he replied, "and I've got prime land in Florida I'd like to sell you too. Get on the bus before I kick you up there." Not knowing what to do, I started for the bus.

"Hold it! Hold it!" came the shrill voice of the red-haired sergeant just as I reached the bus door. "Where do you think you're going?" he replied. "You haven't been drafted yet. Go home and wait. We'll call you soon enough."

1 September 1968

"Billy, I want you to go out to California and meet your cousins. You don't know when you might have the opportunity again," counseled my mother. My cousins she referred to were the offspring of her oldest sister.

They were all my dad's age. Several of their children who were my age lived with their grandmother, my aunt Janie, in Arroyo Grande, California, ten miles from Pismo Beach. There was also a young girl who lived with them named Carla. My mother and aunt were secretly planning to get us together. Aunt Janie convinced Carla to write to me. After several exchanges, I decided to go to California and meet everyone, including Carla.

As I departed the plane at LAX, my eyes began to burn and it looked as if a fog rested just above the skyline. My cousin Nate was there to meet me along with his sister Bobbi and a whole bunch of young girls.

"I'm Linda, your cousin Bobbi's daughter," said the first.

"I'm Rosa Linda, Johnny's girl," said the second.

"I'm Jovenita, your cousin, too."

"Me too. I'm Rosa Linda, Nate's sister."

"I'm Yolie, Nate's girl, and this is Carla!" shouted Linda.

A very good-looking young lady stepped from behind the rest. She was about five feet seven, had long auburn hair, an olive complexion, a beautiful figure, and a wonderful smile. As the hour's drive from the airport to Nate's home passed, I was surrounded by all those pretty girls and was the center of attention. *Surely I'm dead and have gone to heaven,* I thought.

Most of the night was spent talking about our families. However, I thought it strange that all these girls named Linda of one sort or another were all related. Aunt Janie's youngest girl, Rosa Linda, was the same age as her brother. Johnny's daughter was also named Rosa Linda. Linda was the same age as the two Rosa Lindas. She was Bobbi's girl, Rosa Linda's niece and Rosa Linda's cousin.

The next morning, we left for Aunt Janie's. Arroyo Grande is near Monterrey, California, about 180 miles north of LA. The whole family was gathering there to meet me, Louisa's boy. It was the Labor Day weekend. People came from all over everywhere. The house was literally wall-to-wall with people; sleeping bags covered every inch of floor space. There were camping trailers and tents. Even the barn was full.

I had a wonderful time. However, it didn't take long to learn that Carla and Richard, Nate's son, had been dating in the past, and I soon learned I was an intruder. Linda came to my rescue. She was a dark-eyed beauty even though she was my second cousin.

"Come on, Billy, I'll show you around. Let's go to the beach."

We spent the weekend exploring the caves along the ocean, watching the seals and whales along the small islands near the beach. Tuesday came much too quickly.

Nate and I had become fast friends in the short few days we were together along with my cousins Johnny, Joe, and Tito.

"Billy, you need to come spend more time with us."

"Yeah, why don't you come spend a month? Next month we'll all go hunting together," Johnny interjected.

"That's a great idea," said Nate.

"Yeah, Billy, you should come. We'll have a great time," said Joe, smiling.

"You can stay with me and Manuel. Linda and Catherine would love to have you," pleaded Bobbi.

"We could go to Frisco." Linda giggled. "You told me you have always wanted to go to Frisco. And who knows, you said yourself you'll be drafted soon."

"It's settled," Nate replied. "You come back, and we'll go to Utah deer hunting. Season starts October 1."

The plane ride home was long. I kept thinking of the absolute great time I had had and only if Linda weren't my cousin.

The next few weeks seemed to fly by knowing surely that the draft was imminent and the usual six weeks' interval between your physical and induction was quickly coming to a close. I gave my two weeks' notice at Lindberg Acoustics and was off to LA.

28 September 1968

My mind drifted to the events of the year as the three-hour flight passed. How Alberta, my girlfriend of five years with whom I was engaged and almost married, became weary of waiting for me to grow up and married someone else; the end of my four-year free ride when I graduated from carpentry school and lost my deferment and the experience of the actual physical.

Reality returned as the pilot announced, "We are approaching the Grand Canyon and have been given permission to fly through the canyon to give you a bird's-eye view."

Wow, I thought as the spectacular view passed before my eyes.

As the plane settled into its final glide pattern, steadily losing altitude, my mind shifted to the Labor Day weekend a few weeks earlier and what a great time I had.

"Hey, dude! I really missed you. I'm so glad you're back!" shouted Linda as she ran up and embraced me, her dark eyes shining. Bobbi and her sister Catherine were waiting for us at the baggage carousel.

With baggage in hand and on our way, "Where are we off to?" I questioned.

"You can stay with us tonight, and Linda can take you to Nate's in the morning," answered Bobbi.

"Tell me everything you've done in the last four weeks and just how many new girlfriends you have," teased Linda.

We talked most of the night after arriving at Bobbi's. Manuel was glad to see me and asked about Mom and my stepfather, Ted. Linda spent the night telling me the names and characteristics of all the cousins and just how everyone fit into the family.

"Well, you haven't answered my question. How many new girlfriends?" teased Linda, this time a bit more seriously. Everyone had long since retired for the night, leaving us alone.

"No new girlfriends," I replied.

"Not even one?"

"No, not even one." I did not tell her how I had struggled with my feelings over the past month. How beautiful she was. How there had been an instant bond on our first eye contact. What a great time we had the few weeks before. How I would soon be off to war and, most of all, the fact that she was my second cousin. How I had finally decided to return and let fate take its course.

I startled awake at the sound of Bobbi's voice, "OK, you lovebirds, wake up. It's morning. Breakfast is ready. Nate and the guys are waiting."

I felt more than a little embarrassed as I shook the sleep from my eyes. Linda and I had fallen asleep on the family couch during our long conversation. After breakfast, we were off to Nate's in South San Gabriel.

"Think about me . . . think about us," Linda said softly as we pulled into Nate's drive.

"I will," I muttered with almost a tear in my eye.

"Hey, Billy, how ya doin'?" yelled Johnny. "Are you ready? We goin' to have a good time."

Nate had bought a new GMC truck the day before, fully equipped, camper and all. There were five trucks in all with a total of sixteen men ready for the adventure. Our truck, Nate's, was first with Nate, Johnny, and me in the front and Tito in the camper. One of Nate's best friends, Ralph, drove truck two. Along with Ralph was Charlie, whom we later called Crying Charlie as he was homesick the whole trip. My cousin Joe, Rudy, and Benny followed in Rudy's truck, pulling a four-wheel drive scout.

El Viejo or Ambrosea was the captain of truck four, a man who seldom left camp. Along with him was Leo, a huge fellow with a mustache that reminded me of a walrus, and Ambrosea's son, Alahandro, who pretty well kept to himself. Bringing up the rear were Johnny and Joe, two brothers who came strictly for the meat. Ralph Jr. rode with them as well as Chris, a friend of Johnny's. Ambrosea pulled an old, old, old jeep behind him.

The morning passed as we loaded the vehicles. The jeep and the scout each contained four cardboard boxes each containing four one-gallon jugs of wine, thirty-two gallons total. Each carried five cases of beer, 240 bottles in all. I, a teetotaler, thought, *What kind of a mess have I gotten myself into?* I later learned that anyone who couldn't control their drinking wasn't invited back. Being a nondrinker along with being by far the youngest on the trip, I was instantly put on the planning or governing committee who had to vote on and OK anyone wishing to come along. Nate, Cousin Johnny, Ralph, Benny, and I were the committee. The morning and the afternoon passed as decisions were made and tents, cooking gear, even the kitchen sink, were loaded.

"Oh! Finally I think we're all done. Ralph, is the highway through the pass open yet?" asked Nate.

"Yeah, the winds are dying down. The road will be open at five. If we leave at four, we'll be just in time," answered Ralph.

The plan was to leave at 4:00 p.m. and drive to Las Vegas. There we would pull the one-armed bandits until 6:00 a.m. and, finally, drive the final four hours between Las Vegas and St. George, Utah.

5:00 p.m.

"Are we ready? Billy, you drive first so I can sleep awhile. Wagons, ho!" shouted Nate as we all cheered and the caravan was on its way. We reached the pass at San Bernardino a little after 6:00 p.m. The road was open. It had been closed the whole day due to high winds.

As we proceeded through the canyon, the shoulders and medians were strewn with Volkswagen Beetles, house trailers, and tractor-trailers that had been blown off the road by the wind. Some were in the ditch, some on their sides, and some were even upside down. We had traveled about a third of the total distance of the pass when the wind began to blow again. The CB crackled, bringing the news that both ends of the pass were again closed. However, those in route had to continue and exit the pass. The wind came so strong Nate's truck became all but impossible to handle.

"Billy, you need help with the wheel?" said Johnny, seeing the truck being blown so fiercely it was tilted at about a thirty-degree angle.

"I can hardly keep it on the road, John," I gasped.

"Let me help ya," Johnny said, grabbing the wheel in an attempt to keep us from being turned over.

"What's goin' on? Where are we? Who's driving? What's happenin'?" The rocking of the truck being plummeted by the wind had awakened Nate from his nap.

"The wind's goin' to blow us over. Me and Billy both can't hardly keep her on the road."

"Eeeho, look at that! Careful, guy, careful!" exclaimed Nate.

A semitrailer in front of us began to fishtail. The trailer swished back and forth across the road like the tail of a great dragon. The driver braked, trying to regain control of his vehicle, putting us in peril of being wiped off the road by the trailer.

"Slow down, slow down! OK, OK. I think we're going to make it. Watch the trailer. Here it comes again!" shouted Nate as large beads of sweat formed on his forehead. As the trailer passed in front of us, a gust of wind hit it, pushing the trailer completely off the pavement, causing the tractor to turn sideways in the roadway.

"Oh no! Oh no! We're dead!" shouted somebody.

"There's no place to go. We're going to hit the trailer," Johnny stated calmly.

At that instant, the trailer uncoupled from the tractor sliding off the road, turning over several times, spilling boxes and cargo all over the creation. We negotiated the tractor and were able to exit the pass without harm.

"Welcome to Nevada. Drive at your own risk" stated the sign at the Nevada border.

"Just what does that mean, 'drive at your own risk'?" I asked.

"There are no speed limits here. But if you drive recklessly, the fines are really steep," Johnny answered.

"Wow! Look at all the lights!" I shouted with joy as we entered the Strip.

"Billy, stop at the Golden Nugget. We'll play a few slots then go eat."

As we entered the Golden Nugget, I stood in amazement. I had only seen one or two slot machines in my whole life, and there were five hundred or even one thousand in this room. I played a couple of dollars in one of the nickel machines with no luck.

"Hey, Billeeeeeee boy!" called Leo. "You can't win nothing on them nickel machines. You gotta play the quarter ones if ya want to win the big money."

First quarter hit two cherries and paid three quarters. Second quarter hit three plums and paid six quarters.

"Come on, guys, let's go eat, I'm hungry," yawned Nate, barely awake from his napping. We walked across the street to the El Cortez Hotel. It was customary to eat at the El Cortez as they featured a twenty-ounce T-bone with all the trimmings for $4.75.

Adjacent to the restaurant at the El Cortez was a small gaming room full of slot machines. As I was sitting waiting for dinner, I could see a rather, or should I say, extremely, large twenty-five-cent slot machine. I kept looking at that machine, and it kept looking at me. I am six feet tall, and it was quite a bit taller and wider than I. Finally, the temptation overcame me. I pulled one of the ten quarters out of my pocket just as it was about to burn a hole through my pocket. I inserted it in the huge machine. It took both hands and all my strength to pull the lever, which was as tall as my head. The tumblers began to whirl. They continued for the longest time. Finally, the first tumbler began to revolve slower and slower and eventually came to a stop, 7. The second started its descent, and it stopped, 7. Then the third came to a rather abrupt stop, 7. A larger red light on top of the machine began to flash. The thing began to make all sorts of loud unforgiving sounds. The payoff tray began to fill and, almost immediately, was overflowing, spitting quarters all over the floor. When it was all said and done, I had hit a $100 jackpot.

After supper, we went back to the Golden Nugget and gambled the night away. At 6:00 a.m., we were on the road again, heading for St. George, Utah. As the new highway through the canyon hadn't been built yet, the drive to St. George was a four-hour trip meandering through the mountains.

St. George in 1968 was a small town barely more than a single main street of businesses, with mostly older homes clustered around. The St. George Temple stood out as a beacon dominating the skyline. The temple was built shortly after the western migration of the Saints from Nauvoo, Illinois.

We continued northward to Pine Valley, a beautiful valley at the foot of Big Pine Mountain. "Looky there," I squealed as seven does crossed the road in front of us.

Camp was made in the nearby state park.

Trainee Barracks

Fort Wood Sign

"Hey, guys, let's have a meeting. We've been here two days and haven't seen a buck," called Ralph.

"I saw one just this morning right here in camp, a six pointer," replied Ambrosea.

"Why didn't you shoot it, old man?" jumped Joe.

"I came for a trophy," snapped Ambrosea.

"A trophy, a trophy, old man, just what do you call a six pointer?" stammered Joe.

"If it ain't a ten pointer, I ain't shootin' it, ya snot-nosed kid!" bellowed Ambrosea. "I know you, Ralph, Nate, and the others want to go to the other side of the mountain to New Harmony. There ain't no deer there, and I ain't goin'," continued Ambrosea.

"Fine. You can just die here, old man. We're goin'!" yelled Joe.

The next morning, all of us except Ambrosea and his son drove the twenty miles around the mountain to New Harmony, which was just a handful of houses. On the very edge of town was an apple orchard that was partially fenced in by an extremely high fence. A dirt road running along the orchard led to an excellent campsite. The early settlers had built a concrete and stone sluice to bring water from a spring some eighteen miles away near the summit of Big Pine Mountain. Big Pine Mountain rose behind us, first rather gradually, then turning into a series of stair steps. Each step was ten to fifteen feet tall and about one-fourth of a mile wide.

Three quarters of a mile from camp, I found an excellent spot on one of these steps where I took up my relentless vigil. The terrain was rocky with a moderate covering of scrub oak and the odd pinion or cedar tree scattered about. Off to my right, a dry creek bed wandered down the mountainside, crossing in front of me about seventy-five yards away. As the creek came down the mountainside, it was mostly hidden by brush except for a ten-feet-wide clearing, leaving a clear view of the creek bed. At the upper edge of the clearing was an extremely large ponderosa pine. The spot I chose on one of the steps was about three feet tall, allowing me to sit on it with my feet on the ground below. There was a small cedar tree directly in front of me, which I could just see over.

I had barely sat down to enjoy a container of Hunt's pudding when I detected a movement along the creek bed that was partially obscured by low scrub oak. Shortly, a doe emerged into the clearing. She continued following the creek bed, totally obscured by the scrub, emerging again where the creek bed crossed in front of me. That was just the beginning.

That day, I counted no less than 104 does and fawns traveling down that creek bed.

At about 2:00 p.m., a huge set of antlers come ambling above the bushes. I could see spots of brown through the brush. My heart began to race, seeing such a big buck on the first day. I considered taking a shot through the bushes but resolved to wait until he entered the clearing. I waited anxiously. The big buck passed behind the big pine at the clearing edge. In another second, I would have a clear shot. Seconds passed, then a minute, then two; no buck. He never did enter the clearing. Finally, just before dark, I dropped a spike buck, the only other buck I saw all day.

Before going back to camp, I went and looked behind the pine. At that exact point, there was a fork in the creek. The big buck had saved his life by taking the right fork, remaining out of my line of sight.

The next morning, I returned to the same spot. The whole day passed, and only four deer came along the creek bed. At about 10:00 a.m., I was just sitting there enjoying the world around me when a doe with a fawn close behind appeared in the clearing. Instead of continuing along the creek bed, she made a left turn and began walking right toward me. I sat there motionless, thinking she will see me any second now and bolt. She just kept coming until she passed right in front of me between my rock seat and the small cedar I was sitting behind, which was no more than four feet in front of me. As the fawn approached, she stumbled over a stone and crashed headlong into my right leg. Without even a glance, she righted herself and trotted briskly after her mother.

The rest of the week went rather uneventfully until Thursday afternoon. My cousins, friends, and I were at camp having supper. It was about an hour before dark. A rather plain-looking olive green Chevrolet came rumbling and bumbling down the dirt road, pulled right into our campsite, and stopped. Two men in business suits emerged and asked, "Is William Mattatall in the party?"

I acknowledged. One of the men pulled an envelope from his breast pocket, smiled, and said "Congratulations. Greeting from your uncle" as he handed me the envelope.

I opened it, which to my surprise contained my draft papers. After composing myself and with a lot of jeers from my compas, I asked, "How in the world did you find me?"

"Your draft papers were sent to your home. Your mother called the local draft board and told them you were in LA and gave them your cousin Bobbi's phone number and address. The papers were then delivered to

Bobbi's. She told the agents that you were in Utah, deer hunting. With the help of Nate's wife, Consuela, we learned of your general whereabouts and were given the assignment to find you. When we finally arrived in New Harmony, we just asked where all the Mexican Indians were camped. Being as there were sixteen of you, it was pretty easy."

Saturday came very quickly. We were all ready to go home. Nate kept complaining that the mesquite was bothering his allergies and making his eyes water.

"He can't fool us. He just misses his wife, Consuela." Johnny laughed.

"Well!" jumped Nate. "What is that I see in the corner of your eye?"

And poor Crying Charlie, he had been a basket case since Tuesday. He had tried all sorts of ways to go home. We arrived at Nate's at four thirty. Everyone was there; all the wives, kids, brothers, sisters, friends, even strangers, were there to welcome us home. Nate's home was all decorated, and a big fiesta ensued. With every one of the guys being able to play some kind of instrument, singing and dancing went well into the night. And there to meet me were Manuel, Bobbi, Catherine, and Linda. I was barely out of the truck when Linda whisked me aside.

Immediately, all the guys began to tease me, especially Leo.

"Washy dishes, Billeeee boy. You gonna get it now."

Linda's eyes were shining, almost as if they were on fire, as she pulled me aside. "Well?" she asked.

"Well what?"

"Did you do what I asked? Did you think about me? Did you think about us?"

"I did," I answered. However, I didn't tell her that she was just about all I could think about as I sat behind that cedar tree day after day. As the night melted away, I knew I had been smitten.

Linda was enrolled at East Los Angeles College. During the day while she was at school, one of the other cousins would come and get me. I would spend the day seeing LA. Linda would always meet us wherever we were, and we'd go off for the evening on another adventure.

"Hey, Billy, let's go to Frisco next weekend!" exclaimed Linda. "Julie, a friend, has a brother who goes to Berkeley. She'll pay for the gas, and we can stay in the dorms. This is your chance, Julie is a cutie, and Sarah, her sister, wants to go too. She is even better."

"What? Are ya trying to get rid of me already?" I snickered.

"No! No! No! No such luck, buddy. I just want to show you off. Dad said we could use the Chevy."

Manuel had a 1964 Chevrolet that he had practically given to us while I was there.

Friday Morning

The Chevy was loaded: three girls, me, and Simon and Garfunkel. I had installed an 8-track player under the seat. Away we went, jamming all the way to San Francisco.

We spent two very exciting days in Frisco. I saw my very first hippie at Haight-Ashbury. With each passing day, Linda and I grew closer and closer. Originally, I had planned to stay for two weeks. Four blissful weeks passed.

"Billy," said Bobbi one morning at breakfast, "you need to make arrangements to go home. Today is October 28."

I made reservations for the 12:35 a.m. flight, LA to St. Louis, arriving at 6:00 a.m., St. Louis time on 1 November. I called my brother and asked him to pick me up at the airport. Bobbi made a special candlelight dinner for just Linda and I that last evening. Not a lot was said as we ate. The drive to LAX was also quiet. Manuel, Bobbi, Catherine, and I said our good-byes as we entered the terminal.

"We'll leave you here, Billy. Linda wants to say good-bye alone."

Bobbi gave me a big hug as well as Catherine, and Manuel took my hand. "Thanks for staying with us. You have really helped our Linda. Be safe. *Vaya con Dios.* Above all, come home." With that, Manuel turned and walked away.

After checking my baggage, Linda and I walked to the gate, holding dearly to each other. As we approached the gate, passengers were just beginning to board. I turned to Linda, not knowing what to say. Tears were streaming down her cheeks. I could no longer hold the tears back.

"Billy, please don't go. Please don't go," Linda sobbed as she pounded my chest with her arm.

"You know I have to go."

"I know, I know, but I want you to stay. Please . . . Please come back from over there. Think about me. Think about us. I don't want you to go. I love you."

"I love you too." Our tears intermingled, a soft kiss, and I was on the plane.

The three-and-a-half-hour flight home seemed as if it would never end. The events of the past five weeks played over and over in my mind.

The moonlit walks on Santa Monica Beach with the incoming tide gently lapping at the shore. The evenings spent on the fishing pier watching the moon come up, the joy of just being together. How much I cared. How I didn't want to leave. Emotions overwhelmed me, and the tears continued to flow.

"Sir, are you OK? Can I get you something?" asked the flight attendant.

"No, thank you. I'm fine."

"She's a pretty girl. I saw you at the gate. If I can get you anything, just let me know."

The plane landed just before six.

"Hey, Bill, over here!" called my brother Ray.

"Hey, Billy."

"Hi, Sue." Sue was a girl I had met through a mutual friend when she hired me to install new floors in several rooms in her home. We had dinner on occasion and had a casual, friendly relationship.

"Where's Mom?" I asked.

"Well, she said if you couldn't come home for a few days before you left, she couldn't come and see you off," Ray replied.

"Wow! My own mom. She's tough. Oh well, let's go."

With that, Ray handed me an envelope with an official business return address. I noticed the envelope had been opened. The letter was from the draft board granting me an additional sixty-day extension, allowing me to tie up loose ends concerning my business before I left.

Upon returning from the hunting trip, Manuel and Bobbi suggested I write and petition for a deferment as I was a business owner. Manuel thought I could get a one-year deferment to prepare my business for my absence. I wanted to be on the next flight back to LA, but I knew that sixty days would pass all too quickly and I would just be prolonging the agony.

Boot Camp

When we arrived at Fort Leonard Wood, we were escorted to barracks.

"OK, boots, I'm Sergeant Simmons. This is my barracks. My room is at the end of the hall. If the door is open, you can come in. If the door is closed, do not disturb me. This will be your home while you are in processing. I expect you to keep it clean and tidy. You will now follow me across the parade field to building B23."

B23 contained several classrooms. After a lot of hurrying up and waiting, we entered a classroom. It was 2:37 a.m.

"OK, recruits, quiet down. You are now in the army. You all have the rank of E-1. Your first command is to take the paper on the desk in front of you and write a letter to your mother. Believe me, we don't want them to worry."

After the letters were written, signed, sealed, and delivered to the sergeant, we were allowed to go back to the barracks.

Several days were spent there with absolutely nothing to do.

"Hey, guys, we could use a little help in the mess hall. Any volunteers?" asked a young PFC.

We were all so bored everyone volunteered. As we entered the back door of the mess hall, the mess sergeant, seeing the number of us, all but swallowed his cigar.

"I need ya all to peel some potatoes." He took us over to a washtub full of potatoes. It wasn't long before we had made a game of the chore and were peeling potatoes assembly-line style. The mess sergeant was amazed at the speed and quality of our work. He brought in two more washtubs full. "How 'bout these, guys? You did such a good job on the first tub." In minutes, the additional tubs were done. "Wow, I can't believe it. You guys peeled a week's supply of potatoes in less than an hour. You all will get a double portion of dessert tonight." Seeing the mess sergeant smiling so as we left really made me feel good.

The next afternoon, we were loaded on buses and transported to building C-3-3. As the bus stopped, a drill instructor rushed on board.

"I am Sergeant Grey!" he shouted. "You will get off my bus now! Now! Get off! Get off now!"

We all jumped up and scrambled for the exit. There were three more DIs waiting to ambush us as we exited.

"You boots, move, move, move! I said MOVE! What is your problem, boot?" asked one of the three.

"No problem, sir," I replied.

"Do I look like a sir? Do you see these stripes on my arm? I AM A SERGEANT! I am your sergeant! Do you understand, boot?" he screamed in my face, banging the bill of his Smokey Bear hat against my forehead. "Do you understand?"

"Yes, Sergeant."

"I can't hear you!" he screamed as his nose practically touched mine.

"Yes, Sergeant!" I screamed at the top of my lungs.

"That's better. Line up."

"Gentlemen, I am Sergeant Graeve. These are Sergeants Cook, Knoweles, and McClain, and this is Master Drill Sergeant Grey. He is in charge of your training. You are in Company C, Third Battalion, Third Brigade, Fifth Army. For the next eight weeks, this will be your home. Remember the numbers on the corner of the buildings. They all look alike. Repeat after me, C-3-3. I can't hear you."

Everyone screamed, "C-3-3!"

"That's better. Sergeant Grey."

"Gentlemen, I am Sergeant Grey. I will be your mothers, daddies, your brothers, and sisters. But I am not and will not be your friend or your sweetheart. My job is to take you mama's boys and turn you into mean green fighting machines. I do not fail. I have never failed, and I will never fail. I do not do windows, and no breakfast in bed. As your name is called, line up along the sidewalk. There are 192 of you. You will be broken down into four platoons."

Sergeant Graeve began calling names starting with the letter *A*. Cook was next and then Knoweles. I was in Knoweles's unit, Third Platoon. McClain was next.

"Gentlemen, I am Sergeant Knoweles. Follow the rules. Do what you're told, no problems. Foul up, and I will be your worst nightmare. Leave your gear on the sidewalk, line up in rows four wide behind Second Platoon."

We marched over to supply, about a half mile away. There we were issued two duffel bags full of field gear; a helmet (pot) and liner was placed on our heads, a laundry bag and bed linen stacked on top. We were then marched back to the barracks. What a time we had, trying to carry all that stuff. There were pots and pans, tent parts, linens all along the way back to the barracks.

"OK, you boots, line back up on the sidewalk behind your gear. Each platoon will be billeted on the corresponding floor. First Platoon on the first floor and so on. When I blow the whistle, I want you to run as fast as you can with all your gear to your floor. Are you ready?"

With that, Sergeant Grey blew his whistle, and a mad rush of gear headed for the door. All four drill sergeants yelled and screamed at the slower ones, banging the bills of their hats against the trainees' foreheads. We barely made it through the first-floor door when the whistle blew again.

"OK, OK, you guys, as you were. Back to the sidewalk. Line up! I thought you guys were boots. You are the sorriest, and I repeat, the sorriest bunch of ragtag mama's boys I've seen in twenty-three years in the army. Now we are going to try this again, and you will make it to your rooms. Do you hear me?"

"Yes, Sergeant!" came a unison response.

"Now when I blow this whistle, don't you dare disappoint me! Don't you dare make me look bad in front of the other master DIs in these surrounding buildings."

With that, the whistle blew. A blur of bodies rushed for the door. Up, up we went. All the way up, I kept repeating in my mind, *Don't let the whistle blow. Please don't let the whistle blow.* Two steps from the top, just a little bit further—*tweet!* "Oh hell!"

Back down the steps we crawled. By now we knew the procedure. Line up on the sidewalk. Another tongue-lashing. Try again. We didn't even make it to the door. Back to the sidewalk.

"OK, you babies, I see you can't do this. Just go to your rooms."

The three flights of stairs might as well have been Mount Everest. The stairwell was totally covered with bed linens and equipment. Upon reaching my room, an equipment inventory revealed I'd only lost my laundry bag. Going back to the stairwell, there were plenty from which to choose.

3:45 a.m.

"OK, ladies, off your butts and on your feet. Formation in five minutes!" cried Sergeant Knoweles. A blast of cold air greeted me as I exited the building to the all-too-familiar sidewalk. Six inches of snow covered my boots.

"Gentlemen," called Knoweles, "we will now march over to the exercise field." The field was several blocks away. One of the DIs called cadence as we made a disastrous attempt at marching. No one could keep in step. Recruits were running over the recruits in front of them, tripping over their own feet. Fourth Platoon couldn't keep up. We began to run as we reached the exercise field. The night air was cold, crisp, and dark—very, very dark. The run totaled three miles and lasted just short of an hour. I noticed while running it would be easy, then very difficult, easy again, then difficult. This continued for the entire run. "Line 'em up. Ten-hut! Forward march." We were off to the mess hall.

Twenty minutes passed as we stood outside the mess hall in the cold, waiting for our turn. Everyone, being hot and sweating, were shivering intensely by the time we entered the warm building.

"What is that?" exclaimed Robert Cribley, a recruit from San Diego standing in front of me.

"That, my friend, is SOS," replied the specialist 4 behind the serving counter. "Toast, generously covered with sausage-laden gravy. Scrambled eggs on the side, hash browns topped with a banana or an orange."

The stuff tasted a lot better than it looked, or just maybe we were starving. After breakfast, it was back to the barracks.

The Haircut

7:00 a.m.

"Formation, Third Platoon, you know the procedure."

"Company, ten-hut!" barked Sergeant Grey. "I would like to introduce you to Captain Lippard. Company Commander Captain Lippard."

"Thank you, Sergeant. Welcome to the army. How do you like it so far? Just a few more rules: every morning, 0700, you will form up right here fully dressed. I'm not a big fan of spit-shined shoes. High-brush shine will do. However, you will be in the uniform of the day, which will be fatigues until further notice. Now if you foul up, you will be asked oh-so-gently to assume the position. The position, in case you are wondering, is the front-leaning rest. Everyone take this position just so you will be familiar with it. Hands on the ground, up on your toes, arms fully extended, back straight. Now everyone give me ten push-ups. Sergeant Grey!"

"Yes, sir! Everyone on your feet. We will now march over to the barbershop for your first GI haircut. Captain Lippard doesn't like skinhead cuts, soooo count your lucky stars. Ten-hut! Right face! Forward, hartch!"

The few blocks to the barbershop were another marching disaster. The barbershop consisted of a barrack with twenty chairs running the length of the building. At each chair, there was a front and back door. Everyone was lined up in front of the twenty front doors. As their hair was cut, they exited the back door. The barbers' trimmers were attached to vacuum hoses. In seconds, there wouldn't be a trace of your once-beautiful hair. The whole procedure would take about thirty seconds. The line moved steadily forward. The fellow in front of me had hair that hung below his shoulder blades. As he sat in the chair, the barber spoke to him.

"Well, son, how would you like your hair cut?"

"What do you mean?" replied the recruit, looking at the barber rather strangely. "I thought everyone had to have short hair."

"Oh no!" exclaimed the barber. "All the other guys wanted their hair that way."

"Really? Now you're just joshin' me."

"Oh no, really. I'll cut it any way you want. It would be a shame to cut all that pretty hair off."

"Come on," replied the recruit.

"No, really, your wish is my command."

"Mmmmmm. If I leave it this long, I'll stand out, so maybe I need it to be shorter, but not too short. So how about trimming my hair just above my collar, that way it won't be too long and it won't be too short."

"You've got it, pal." And with that, the barber turned on the clippers and cut a three-inch-wide swath right down the middle of the fellow's head, leaving a patch of one-half-inch-long hair in the clipper's wake. "How about that, sonny? Short enough for ya?" laughed the barber.

"But, but, but! I thought! You told me! Ohhhhhh! Oh no, man! Not my hair!" exclaimed the recruit, mouth open gasping for air with great tears welling up in his eyes. Seconds later, he looked like everyone else, short hair and all.

At lunch, we noticed that the recruits from the other companies had really short haircuts, especially the guys from Company B. They were all skinheads. Cutting all of your hair off takes away your identity. It was surprising how all of Company B looked exactly alike.

The 0348 ritual went on for what seemed forever. Every morning, at the 0700 inspection, the same guys would show up half dressed or with shoes not shined or untied shirt tabs hanging out. The DIs loved it. They had a favorite mode of discipline. "Drop and give me twenty," or "Drop and give me fifty," they would command, almost giggling. Every morning, those same few guys would be doing twenty to fifty push-ups.

"Mattatall!"

"Yes, Sergeant Knoweles."

"Well, y'all been here a week now, and tell me who do you think should be trainee platoon sergeant?"

"Well, I think Johnson would do the trick. He's the biggest guy in the platoon."

"So you wouldn't want the job?"

"Naw, I wouldn't know what to do."

"So Johnson it is. However, I want you to be a patrol leader. Deal?"

"Deal."

As a patrol leader, I had a unique privilege, which was to go to the PX (army convenience store) and pick up personal hygiene items the patrol members needed. This also gave me a license to buy whatever junk food I thought I needed at the time. This was great as I am the king of the junk food junkies, and as usual, my alligator ego overcame my hummingbird brain. It became a game. After supper every day, I would go to the PX and load up on candy bars, chips, etc. I'd walk right past the DI sentry at the barracks door, pockets bulging.

Now these were the after-supper rules. One must run from the mess hall all the way to the door handle of the barracks, or the guard-dog DI would make you do twenty to fifty push-ups if you stopped even a foot short. I would sell the candy bars to the other recruits at a profit. I would even take special orders.

By the third week, everyone had a cold from running three miles in the morning then standing in line waiting for breakfast. Both sides of the sidewalk were covered with yellow phlegm that guys had coughed up. One evening, as I ran back to the barracks, I began to cough violently and stopped ten feet from the barracks' front door.

"Mattatall, I am ashamed. You of all people stopped short? Drop and give me twenty-five."

"Yes, Sergeant." As I dropped to the position, my heart began to race. *What have I done?* I thought.

That evening, on my daily trip to the PX, I had a real yearning for a Coke. Knowing I wouldn't have time to drink it there, I took a short fat empty twenty-ounce cup and shoved it into the pocket of my field jacket to see if it would fit. It was just so perfect. I filled the cup with Coke, snapped on the lid, paid the cashier, slipped it into my pocket, and was on my way. As I counted off the push-ups—"One, Sergeant, two, Sergeant"—I just knew the lid would pop off and my clandestine operation would be discovered. *Please don't come off! Please don't come off!* I repeated in my mind over and over again. Somehow the lid stayed on, and my secret was safe.

Fourth Week, Day 2

"OK, boots, time for your shots."

It seemed as if we were getting shots once a week. This was to be the last go-around. The medical building consisted of rooms on either side of a long hall.

"OK, boys, listen up. These shots will be a little different than those you have had in the past," instructed the medic. "There will be a medic in each doorway. As you pass by, you will receive a shot. These shots are administered using an air pistol. There is no needle involved. The serum is forced through the skin by the air. Each pistol shot will inject four different serums. Do not, AND I REPEAT, do not move your arm. Any movement will cause the air to gash open the flesh, which can be very painful, usually requiring stitches."

All went well until a rather obese fellow jerked his arm sideways as the shot was administered, causing a four-inch-long gash, spurting blood everywhere.

Fourth Week, Day 3

Rain had fallen most of the night, leaving everything and everyone a little soggy. We marched over to building 183 to learn the nomenclature of the M14, M16, M60 and the .45-caliber pistol. This would be the start of our weapons training. I had never before heard that word *nomenclature* and was a little confused at first but soon learned the meaning of the word.

"Take a ten-minute break," instructed Sergeant Grey. "All those wishing to smoke, on the parade field out the back door. Everyone else, on the gravel out the side door." It was about 1000; along came Sergeant Knoweles.

"Ten-hut!" Everyone on the parade field quickly came to attention. Some dropping their cigarettes, some in their mouths, some not knowing what to do with them.

"Sergeant Knoweles," replied Graeve, "why on earth did you call those nice young men to attention?"

"Well, Sergeant," replied Knoweles, "I guess maybe, just maybe, I have this feeling or sixth sense or something."

"Recruits, remove your field jackets, fold them up, and place them on your feet," replied Graeve. "Sergeant Knoweles."

"Yes, Sergeant Graeve?"

"Do you see what I see over there, second row?"

"I surely do, Sergeant Graeve," replied Knoweles, licking his chops. "You there, I believe it is Ronald Ingram, isn't it?"

"Yes, Sergeant," Ingram acknowledged, his voice trembling.

"Why don't you come right up front here with us?" Graeve insisted. As Ingram came forward, I noticed his shirttail was hanging out and his belt buckle was unbuckled and hanging astray. Upon coming forward, the sergeants began an inspection and found his shirt was improperly buttoned and his pants were unzipped. "Well, Ingram, we are sooo pleased with the way you are dressed that we are going to promote you to platoon sergeant for the day," snickered Graeve. "Call your platoon to attention."

"Ten-hut!" yelled Ingram.

"Good, good," replied Graeve as the group came to attention.

"Now have them assume the position." Knowles chuckled.

"Outstanding," Graeve replied as the group moved to the front-leaning rest position.

All the noisemakers over in the gravel began to murmur, "They are going to make those guys do push-ups in the mud."

"Next command," instructed Knoweles.

"Tell 'um to low crawl," commanded Graeve.

Ingram gave the command. The group began to crawl around in the mud. This went on for several minutes.

I sure was glad my name wasn't Ingram. Every man in the group was covered from head to toe. From that day forward everyone made sure Ingram was in proper uniform.

Fourth Week, Day 4

At 0700, inspection was completed, and Company C was loaded up into four waiting school buses. As the buses ambled along the blacktop, the seven miles from our barracks to the rifle range, Sergeant Knoweles educated us on the agenda for the next several weeks.

"Every morning, you will be bused to the rifle range. Every evening, you will MARCH back."

The first day was spent teaching the dos and don'ts of the rifle range. The march back to the barracks was very, very long. Day 2, however, was an entirely different story. Sometime after lunch, one of the recruits stood up and, without provocation, leveled his M14 on one of the training towers and opened fire. I guess he didn't like the C rations we had for lunch. Several DIs quickly congregated on the fellow, disarmed him, and whisked him away, never to be seen again. Luckily, no one was hurt. The instructors bailed out the second he pointed his rifle at the tower. The tower however, was DOA, receiving a full twenty-round clip of M14 ammo.

The last day at the range, training complete, we began the long walk home. Sergeant McClain took the lead. I believe he was a marathon runner. As we moved along, he quickened the pace. The increased pace at the front caused the two platoons at the rear to be almost continuously running to keep up with Fourth Platoon running steadily. When the company would come to a road crossing, the front of the column would stop. This would cause a slinky effect, with the guys at the rear of the column crashing into those in front, knocking them down like dominoes, rifles, packs, and gear flying everywhere.

After the second mile, guys in the Fourth Platoon began to pass out due to the stress. By the end of the fifth mile, guys in the Third and Fourth Platoons began to drop like flies. Finally, the barracks were in sight. Two more blocks, and it would all over. The street we were marching down was lined with Quonset huts on both sides. A goodly number of the huts' inhabitants had gathered at the curbside to watch the parade go by. One of the spectators made a derogatory remark. A member of the Second Platoon quickly responded with a hand gesture (the bird).

"Company, halt!" bellowed Sergeant Jones, Company C, first sergeant. "Assume the position, rifles on your hand."

The minutes passed, not a word said, 160 to 170 soldiers in the middle of the street, front-leaning rest, with rifles lying across the backs of our hands.

"You boots ain't never going to learn, are ya? You have disgraced me and my staff," Sergeant Jones addressed us in a low-key monotone voice. For forty-five minutes, he admonished each and every one of us. Finally, one fellow couldn't handle it any longer and passed out. Then another and still another until they were dropping like flies. Again the medics came and were hauling guys away by the wagonload. Finally, Sergeant Jones released us. Never ever was another word uttered or jester made, good or bad, to a passerby while we were in formation. The pain in the shoulders and the upper arms was excruciating. My body began to shake violently as my extended arms tired. I kept getting tunnel vision and had to fight it off as I was a patrol leader and had to set the example. The weight of my rifle lying across my hands became so heavy I couldn't move my hands. Upon reaching the barracks, I collapsed in total exhaustion.

Fifth Week, Monday

"Company, ten-hut! Sir, the men are ready for your instruction," First Sergeant Jones acknowledged.

"Gentlemen, this week you will be introduced to war," suggested Captain Lippard. "You will march over to supply and draw the necessary field gear. You will then board buses and report to the bivouac area. You will each be issued a half tent. Don't get excited. You will buddy up, put your two halves together, and be in business. Are there any questions?"

"No questions, sir," replied First Sergeant Jones.

"Hey, Johnson, what do ya think is gonna happen?"

"I don't know," he answered as we were leaving the bus at the bivouac area.

"Gentlemen, our first exercise will be hand-to-hand combat, bayonets attached. I will demonstrate." Sergeant Knoweles then demonstrated the proper procedure of attacking the enemy. Scarecrow-type figures were used.

"Patrol leaders, come forward. You'll be first. Remember: step forward right foot, thrust, jab, withdraw. If, and I repeat, if you have penetrated your enemy, withdrawing the bayonet will be difficult. You will more likely have to put your foot on his chest to remove your bayonet. Any questions? OK, on my command. Step forward! Thrust! Jab! Withdraw!"

My first attempt was pathetic. My timing was off; as I thrust, I completely missed the target. My forward motion carried me headfirst into the midriff of the practice dummy.

"Mattatall! You're supposed to stick the dummy with the bayonet, not your head. Now try again."

After several more attempts, I finally got the hang of it. The week played out with our platoon learning various tactical techniques.

Having two guys in a tent was a bit cozy, but we managed. Carroll Carr was my tent buddy. I was glad he was on the skinny side.

"Gentlemen! Gentlemen!" called Sergeant Jones. "Tonight will be your last night out. I know you all will be glad to get back to your nice, warm beds. After all, it's the middle of February. It snows every other day. Y'all have done well. Tonight you will go through live-fire training. You will low crawl one hundred yards negotiating barbed wire. There will be simulated incoming rounds. These will be quarter-pound sticks of TNT detonated in the pits. There will be live machine-gun fire thirty-six inches above you head. Rise up during the exercise, and we'll send you home in a box. Understand?"

"Yes, Sergeant," came the unison reply.

The training started with each man crawling out of a ditch. The first barbed wire fence lay five feet in the designated path. We crossed the field of fire five at a time, each of us about five feet apart. Carr was to my left. As I rolled on my back to crawl under the first fence, it was then that I saw the red tracers of the machine gun directly over my head. Fear took over to the point of not being able to move. It took several minutes talking to myself to regain my composure in order to go on. By the time we reached the end of the hundred-yard field, Carr and I were laughing and joking about the ordeal.

"Hey, Carr! Let's go back and do it again."

"Yeah, this is cool!" We then turned around and crawled back toward the starting point.

"What? Are you guys totally nuts?" complained a recruit as we passed him going in the opposite direction.

"Was that sweat all over his face, or was he crying?"

"I don't know," I replied. "But he sure looked nervous. I hope he doesn't rise up." As we reached the start, we once again turned and headed toward the finish.

At about the midway point, there lay a pit directly in my path. As I approached, I could see Knoweles and Graeve manning the machine gun that was sitting on an elevated deck. I swear I saw Knoweles grinning like a bear in a honey pot. *Kawhamm!* The pit exploded as I crawled around the left side. The concussion ripped at my helmet, the strap cutting off my air. The ringing in my ears was deafening. I teetered on the edge of consciousness. My head felt as if it was several times too big for my body. I was barely able to crawl to the finish line.

At the close of the exercise, our company boarded buses and was taken to a remote area.

"OK! OK! Listen up!" yelled Graeve. "You ladies will get off my bus! You will go into that tent! You will stow your gear and your weapons by patrols! Your weapons will be picketed by patrols! You will retrieve your poncho and your sleeping bags only! I repeat, ponchos and sleeping bags only! You will then form up in front of the tent! You have thirty seconds! Now get off my bus! Now! Go! Go! Go!"

Seconds later, we were all in the tent. The interior was hot and moist. A glowing potbellied stove located at the tent's center provided the heat.

"Third Platoon, ATTENTION! Right face! Forward, march!" called Knoweles.

Third Platoon came to attention, turned right, and moved forward. We had finally mastered the art of marching. We proceeded to a large plowed field. The moon was full and waning. The air was crisp. The temperature was somewhere in the twenties. The snow-covered field crunched as we walked.

"Third Platoon, halt! Dress, right, dress! At ease!" came the commands from Sergeant Graeve. "Take your ponchos, spread 'em out on the ground. Now sit down on 'em. No boots on the ponchos. Now, take off your boots. Put 'em at the top. Spread out your sleeping bags! Get into your sleeping bags. Snap your ponchos together around your sleeping bags! Keep the snaps to the right. Now take your field jackets off, fold 'em up, place on your boots, use 'em for a pillow! OK, that done, strip to your Skivvies! Fold up your clothes, put 'em under your sleeping bag but on top of the poncho. Your body heat will keep 'em warm during the night so you will have warm clothes to put on in the morning. Any man not removing his clothes will be eligible for an Article 15 court-martial. Is that understood?"

"Yes, Sergeant!" as we bedded on, in, and around the frozen plowed furrows.

The DIs came around and covered each man with an additional poncho. Every hour on the hour, one of the DIs would wake a man. He would have to dress and pull a fire watch in the warm tent for an hour. Then it was back to the cold field and going through the whole ritual before again being able to sleep. At 4:00 a.m., it was my turn. As I awoke, I noticed that I was totally covered by an extra poncho. Four inches of new snow had fallen. At the end of my fire-watch assignment, the DIs had me stay in the tent as new falling snow prevented me from returning to my sleeping bag. Knoweles had personally brought in my bag and poncho when the additional snow began to fall.

Week Six

Training continued with the introduction to the pugil stick. Now the pugil is a wooden rod about one and a half inch in diameter and six feet in length. Each end is covered with a six-by-twelve-inch cylindrical-shaped pad. Opponents would form in groups of two. The pugil was used as a staff with each opponent trying to knock the other off his feet by bashing the head, pushing and thrusting the midriff with the padded ends. The pugil stick resembled a giant Q-tip.

"Matty, you're a patrol leader. I want you to show 'em how it's done. Pair up with your platoon sergeant, Johnson!" snickered Knoweles. Now Johnson was six feet eight tall and weighed about 230. My six-foot-one and 180-pound frame wasn't much of a match.

"Don't worry, Matty, I'll take it easy on ya." Johnson grinned.

I raised my pugil to the defensive position only to find myself falling flat on my back. I quickly sprang to my feet. "I thought you said you'd take it easy on me, big fella."

"Sorry." Johnson grinned as his pugil crashed into the side of my head, knocking my helmet off, breaking the chin strap.

"Ohhhhhh," I groaned, slowly returning to my feet. As I righted myself, my stick went instantly to his groin. A look of surprise came over his face. A second strike came quickly to the right side of his head followed by a third strike to the left side of the head. With the fourth blow striking him in the midriff expelling his tidal air, Johnson's six-foot-eight, 230-pound frame struck the blacktop with a thud. I stepped back, trembling, knowing a parry was sure to come. None did. Johnson was out cold! The previous blows to my head were too much, I couldn't right myself and, finally, fell in a crumbled heap on the blacktop training field.

"Aww-gh," I groaned as my nostrils burned from the ammonia-based smelling salts. Johnson was also brought to. He had a large bump on the back of his head, a result of his head striking the ground. For the next week, I sported a large peach-shaped abrasion on the right side of my face as well as a long one-inch-wide scrape running under my chin almost ear to ear, left by the chin strap as my helmet left my head.

As the training continued, no one would pair up with either Johnson or I. Everyone claimed Johnson was too big and I was too nasty.

Sixth Week, Friday Afternoon

"OK, boys, training's over. Platoon sergeants, back to the barracks. There will be a formation at 1530 hours. You might want to clean up!" snapped Sergeant Gray.

"Ay, Matty, what's up?"

"Don't know, Carr. Guess we'll have to wait and see." The platoon was abuzz as we marched back to the barracks.

1530 Hours

Wheet-wheet! The whistle blew. Company C exited the building in a mad rush, lining up by platoons in the parking lot in front of the building.

"Aten-hut!" came the command from Sergeant Gray.

The entire company came to attention in one smooth motion.

"Well, Sergeant, you have done an excellent job with these young men!" replied Captain Lippard.

"Thank you, sir!"

"Gentlemen!" continued Captain Lippard, "I am sure you are wondering why you are not still training today. At 1600 hours, all of you who wish to will receive your first pass. It will be good until 1800 hours on Sunday. For those of you who have not yet learned the army way, that is SIX PM! Now if you are not back in your building by 1800 hours, you will be counted AWOL, and make no mistake, we will hunt you down like a dog. Sergeant Gray."

"Thank you, sir! Your pass is good for a fifty-mile radius from the front gate. Are we clear on that?"

"Yes, Sergeant!" came the reply.

"Company dismissed!"

Another mad rush from the parking lot to the building as most of us rushed to change from our OD uniforms to our Class As. The bus station was unusually full that afternoon, but there was room for everyone. A bus ticket to St. Louis was $10.30. I called prior to the bus leaving, and a friend's father was there to pick me up when the bus arrived in St. Louis just before 8:00 p.m. (2000 hours). The weekend passed much too quickly. Sunday evening, 1800 hours, I was back in my room at C-3-3.

Week Seven

My cough had become much worse as the weeks progressed due to the morning ritual of running three miles followed by a twenty-to-thirty-minute wait in the cold at the mess hall door. I had a low-grade fever most of the time. Somehow I could go all day. However, once the sun went down, the fever would elevate followed by severe chills. I would go to bed early and somehow be able to answer the bell the next morning. Week 7 was devoted to training for the five-event PT (physical training) test that would take place at the beginning of week 8 as well as reviewing for the proficiency test, a fifty-question test on how well we had learned to be soldiers.

At the end of week 7, passes were again issued. I was on my way home for the weekend. This time, however, I went to the family doctor Saturday morning. The fever and chills were so bad I needed help. I refused to go to sick bay as I knew for sure that I would be recycled and not allowed to graduate basic with my company.

"Son," stated Doc Eisele, "you have a very bad case of walking pneumonia. You are a very sick young man and need to go to the hospital right away."

"Listen, Doc, I can't do that. This is my last week of basic training. I am not going to be recycled and do basic all over again."

"I see your predicament. I'll tell you what. I will give you as heavy a dose of penicillin as I can in shot form as well as a prescription that you can take this next week. I will do this only if you solemnly promise me that you will be here in my office next Saturday morning and only if you promise that if this gets any worse you will go to sick bay. This is a very serious situation. Deal?"

"Deal," I replied.

The shot felt as if my hip was being filled with concrete. Sunday brought a chipper day with fever not plaguing me as badly as it had just the day before. By Monday, I felt much better.

Week Eight

"Gentlemen! Well, your basic training is officially complete. This week you will practice for the PT test and the proficiency test. Thursday is the big day. First will be the proficiency. Here we'll see just how much you have learned in the last seven weeks, then after lunch we will go to the PT field for the big test. You will be tested in the following events. Sergeant Knoweles, if you will."

"My pleasure, Sergeant Graeve! The first event will be the low crawl. To max this event, you will need to crawl fifty yards in twenty seconds. Event 2 will be the run, dodge, and jump. In this event, you will have to run around the barricades, jump across the ditch, then back across the ditch, around the barricades, and back to the start. Again, in twenty seconds. Number 3, the horizontal ladder, forty-five rungs in sixty seconds. Most of you know how difficult this can be. Event 4, the one-man carry. Piggyback your partner forty yards in forty seconds. Your fifth and final event will be the mile run. That's one mile in six minutes."

The mornings of the next two days were spent reviewing the nomenclature of the different firearms. Tactical procedures, all that we had learned in the last seven weeks. The afternoons found us at the practice field low crawling, running, jumping, with the final event of the day being the mile run. My time in the previous runs had been very consistent: five minutes, twenty seconds. The results were always the same. The run consisted of four laps around a quarter-mile track. I would lead the pack for the first three laps. There was a Native American fellow. I would almost be a lap ahead at the end of three. He would be maybe fifty feet ahead of me. At the beginning of the last lap, he would start to move away. Halfway through the lap, I could no longer see him as he came up behind. The last fifty yards, the nightmare began, the faint sound of his bare feet brushing the cinder track bed. Twenty-five yards to go, the sound of his footsteps became louder and louder. Soon it was as if someone was beating a bass drum. *Boom! Boom! Boom!* was the sound as he passed me mere feet from the finish line. No matter how hard I tried, how hard I kicked, the results were always the same, passed in the last second.

Wednesday morning. The entire company filled school buses and was off to the rifle qualification range. The entire battalion was there. The day went well. I still felt a bit queasy from the fever and the drugs, had trouble zeroing in on the 350-yard target, missed six, but still qualified expert.

Eighth Week, Thursday, 0700 Formation

"Well, boys, hope ya had a good breakfast and your bellies are full. Today is the big day. I want ya to make me proud. Yesterday you did real good. Co. C took all honors at the rifle range with Matty coming in second overall. Sergeant Knoweles, Graeve, take these gentlemen over to the proficiency area and let the games begin. I'll meet you there."

"Yes, Sergeant Jones, we're on our way. Platoon, aten-hut. Forward, march."

The test area was only about ten minutes away. The morning melted away with the tests touching all that we had learned in the last seven weeks: knots, bayonet training, weapons, survival, and tactical training.

After lunch, we again boarded school buses and headed for the PT field. Upon arrival, we disembarked the buses, quickly lining up in formation. Sergeant Jones was there along with the others to greet us.

"Do your best men, do your best" was all Sergeant Jones had to say. Sergeant Knoweles came and stood right in front of me, stood for the longest time staring into my eyes and not saying a word.

"Well, Matty," he finally spoke. "Today, it's for all the marbles. Do your best."

"Yes, Sergeant, I will," I replied.

The first event was the low crawl. Nineteen seconds later, it was history. The run, dodge, and jump was next. Seventeen seconds to complete that event. With the adrenaline pumping, I had all but forgotten the fever, chills, and the weakness they brought. The forty-yard one-man carry was next. Twenty-five yards into the event, my strength was gone. I began to stagger, swaying from side to side. "Come on, Matty, you can do it," came a quiet voice in my ear. "You can do it," repeated the voice. It was the voice of my partner whom I was carrying. "Come on, you can make it," came the voice again. Somehow the strength returned to my legs; on I went. Forty,

forty-one, forty-two, the attendant called as I crossed the line. No cigar, but not bad.

The horizontal ladder was next.

"OK, gentlemen. In this event you will transverse the ladder one rung at a time. Your objective is forty-five rungs in sixty seconds. When I tell you to drop, I want you to drop instantly. Any questions? Good. Let us begin."

By the time my turn came, I was feeling the effects of the one-man carry. Arms and legs were aching, felt light-headed, a little disoriented. I was at rung 41 when time ran out. Again, a good showing, but no cigar.

Well, this is it, I thought as I loosened to warm the muscles.

"The last event, the mile run." As the whistle blew, I launched myself along with 190 other comrades in arms. Surprisingly, the first three laps went smoothly. It wasn't until lap 4 that the fun began. With less than one hundred yards to go, the thigh muscles began to burn. The pain accelerated, resulting in cramps in both legs. I instantly slowed to almost a walk. I did, however, cross the finish line at 5:52 with eight seconds to spare. Total PT score 440. Again, close to the 500 club, but no cigar.

Eighth Week, Friday, Morning Formation

"Gentlemen. Today you will graduate. This is your last formation in boot camp. I would like to congratulate each and every one of you on a job well-done. You came eight weeks ago, raw and weak. Today you leave mean green fightin' machines. Private Mattatall, front 'n' center."

Oh no! What now? I thought as I moved to the front to face Sergeant Jones.

"Private, on behalf of the army, it is my pleasure to congratulate you on your achievement and to present you to your fellow trainees as Co. C-3-3's Trainee of the Cycle, Expert Marksman with the M14, M16, .45-cal pistol, and the M60 machine gun. Eighty-nine on the proficiency test and 440 on the PT test. Private Mattatall missed becoming Battalion Trainee of the Cycle by two points at the rifle range. Good job, soldier."

"Thank you, Sergeant."

That afternoon, our company joined the battalion and marched past the parade stand containing the post commander and many of our families. A three-day pass, and it was back to leadership school for two weeks.

DEPARTMENT OF THE ARMY
HEADQUARTERS, 3D BCT BRIGADE
UNITED STATES ARMY TRAINING CENTER
Fort Leonard Wood, Missouri 65473

ALWTC-CO 21 March 1969

SUBJECT: Letter of Commendation

Private William R. Mattatall, US56598501
Company C, 3d Battalion
3d BCT Brigade, USATC
Fort Leonard Wood, Missouri 65473

1. During Basic Combat Training as a member of Company C, 3d Battalion 3d BCT Brigade, you have exhibited the highest degree of proficiency, devotion to duty, and sense of discipline. As a result of your exemplary performance, you have been selected as the outstanding trainee of your company during cycle 1-69.

2. Your desire to excel and your studied application in the adjustment to military life indicate potential future leadership positions with added responsibilities.

3. My congratulations for a job well done. I wish you continued success in your future assignments.

4. A copy of this correspondence will be placed in your field 201 file.

J. CRAWFORD CATON
Colonel, Infantry
Commanding

AIT

After leadership-school graduation Friday afternoon, I snuck out and went home for the weekend.

Sunday Afternoon

I wandered into the barracks at C-1-1, my new home for the next eight weeks.

"Hmmmmm, who are you?" a tall black E-6 queried as I entered the barracks.

"Uhhh, Private Mattatall," I stammered.

"Oh ho, Private, I have heard all about you. Just finished leadership school, right?" asked Sergeant Keeler.

"Yup, that's me."

"Room's at the end of the hall on the right. You're gonna be my new platoon sergeant. Stow your gear, and we'll go over the roster. The gang will be here, I'd say, between four and six. I've got some suggestions for patrol leaders, but it's your call, Sergeant." He handed me the trainee platoon sergeant stripes.

By 7:00 p.m. (1900 hours), everyone was checked in, sixty-one in all.

"OK, Sergeant, your job before bedtime is to create a fire-watch list. Post it and personally make tonight's assignments and have the names of your patrol leaders ready so I can make those assignments in the morning. My room is across the hall from yours. Sometimes I'll be there and sometimes I won't, but rest assured I'll never be too far away if there is a problem."

By 1930, I had randomly completed the fire-watch list. Not being acquainted with anyone, I could not place a name to a face. Minutes after posting the list, eight African Americans approached me while I was still sitting at the check-in table near the front door.

"Hey, man, who do you think you are, puttin' me on fire watch?" screamed the leader of the pack, a big six-foot-eight fellow named Aaron Pollard. "Now get this straight, damn straight. I ain't pull'n' no fire watch."

"You got that right!" snapped one of the others.

"Yeah, we pulled fire watch every other night in basic!" interjected another. "We'd done our share and ain't doin' no more."

"I'm sorry you weren't treated fairly in basic," I replied quietly. "I'll find someone else for tonight. However, there are forty-eight nights of fire-watch times, three men per night. That's 144 divided by 56 of you. I will arrange it so that you will only have to stand watch twice during AIT."

"Do what ya want, man, but I'm tellin' ya right now, we aren't doin' it." With that, all eight stalked out the door.

"Hey, Sarge!" came a voice from a bunk not far from my table. "I was in basic with those guys. They're really a bunch of troublemakers, never want to do anything, always complaining. Name's Underhill, Robert Underhill."

Little did I know, Robert Underhill would become my very best friend in Vietnam.

The next morning, I was awakened by a light tap on my door. It was Platoon Sergeant Keeler.

"May I come in?" he asked quietly. "Wake-up time is 5:45 a.m. I expect you to be up and dressed by then. We are here to set the example. I want it to be you who calls reveille every morning. Can you handle that?"

"You got it, Sarge, no problem."

"You're runnin' the show here," replied Sergeant Keeler. "I'm just here to support you all the way. Got it?"

"Got it."

"Just to let you know, if something comes up that you're not sure of or just don't know, know that I got your back."

The day started with calisthenics followed by breakfast. Our first training session was on bridges, explaining the different types of bridges used by the U.S. Army. The afternoon session covered the assembly of the wooden or timber bridges.

After several days of assembling and disassembling the timber bridge, we moved on. The Bailey bridge was next, an erector-set type of bridge that could be assembled and more or less rolled to drop into place over the stream, gully, etc. We learned of pontoon bridges large enough to carry a tank and small enough for foot soldiers only. The first four weeks passed quickly as we learned about C-4, det cord, how to set and detonate explosives.

Fourth Week, Friday Morning, 2:57 a.m.

Whaaa! Whaaa! Whaaa! screamed the fire alarm, bringing everyone to their feet and out the door.

"Ten-hut!" I shouted, bringing the platoon to attention. "Patrols, report."

"All present and accounted for!" called the patrol leaders completing the platoon.

"Good evening, gentlemen," came a booming voice from the shadows. "I am Lieutenant Frazier, officer of the day!" stated the voice as a young lieutenant moved from the shadows toward the platoon facing front.

"Sergeant, are you in charge here?" he snapped.

"Yes, sir! Sergeant Mattatall reporting, sir!" I replied, saluting.

"Well, Sergeant, it seems we have a problem. This is the third time I have passed through your barracks this evening. At no time, and I repeat, at no time have I found anyone on fire guard. I have only two questions for you. Number 1, have you placed a fire-watch roster where everyone can see it?"

"I have, sir," I replied.

"Number 2, Have you instructed your patrol leaders to inform the guards of their duty on a daily basis?"

"I have," I replied.

"Lieutenant Frazier," called Sergeant Keeler, "here is a copy of the posted roster for the entire eight weeks as well as a copy of the posted daily roster."

"Hmmm," the lieutenant mused while examining the duty rosters. "Would the following men please step forward? Private Alex Irvin, Private Aaron Pollard, and Private Robert Warren! Can you gentlemen tell me why you were not at your posts when I made my rounds?"

Pollard was the first to answer. "Man, we didn't know!"

"Man!_ _ _ Man! I am a commissioned officer in this man's army. Need I remind you that you are a private? You will show proper protocol. You will call me sir! Is that clear?" shouted the lieutenant at the top of his lungs.

"Yes, sir," came back Pollard, saluting.

"Sergeant," the lieutenant called, talking to me, "these men are in line for an Article 15 court-martial. What are your thoughts on the matter?"

"Well, sir," I replied hesitantly, "I think they might have erred in ignorance."

"Are you trying to say they didn't know what they were doing?"

"Exactly."

"What's your opinion, Sergeant Keeler?"

"I completely agree with Sergeant Mattatall."

"Soooo, is it safe to say you both agree they could use a second chance?" We both nodded.

"OK, gentlemen, today's your lucky day. Thanks to your sergeants here, there will be no Article 15. However, the three of you will pull fire watch every Thursday for the remaining four weeks of your AIT course. Understood?"

"Yes, sir," came the reply in unison.

Monday evening of the following week found me in my room trying to pull a nail out of my boot. A pair of pliers and a hammer were working feverishly to complete the task. Suddenly, the door to my room burst open.

"What the hell you think you're doin', man? I told you we ain't pullin' no guard," bellowed Pollard.

My mind began to race. *Those guys are in a terrible rage,* I thought. If push comes to shove, the hammer's the best bet.

"Hey, man, I see ya eye'n' that hammer. That ain't goin' to help ya. We goin' to beat your brains out," yelled Warren.

"Yea, man, we goin' to get you now or later, that's a promise," sneered Pollard.

"Gentlemen, is there a problem here?" chimed Sergeant Keeler.

"Oh no, Platoon Sergeant, we were just talkin' to ole sarge here."

"Very well, it's just about lights-out," replied Sergeant Keeler, giving me a wink.

The next four weeks passed quickly as we learned the ins and outs of being a combat engineer. Lieutenant Frazier was the OD every Thursday, making sure Pollard, Warren, and Irvin lived up to their duty as fireguards. This would not be the last time I would have a run-in with the infamous eight.

Vietnam

5 July 1969, 8:30 a.m.

After a tearful good-bye to my mother, grandfather, and grandmother and a long embrace with my sweetheart, I loaded a plane for Oakland, California, with tears streaming down my face. I left St. Louis where the day was bright and sunny with a warm breeze. I arrived in San Francisco where it was cloudy and cool enough to warrant wearing a jacket. As I flew across the country, looking down at the farms of the Midwest, the beauty of the Rockies, and the vastness of the desert in Nevada, I wondered if I would ever see them again.

After disembarking, I inquired as to the whereabouts of the Oakland Army Base. I learned it was across the Bay about twenty miles away with the only transportation being a limousine ride at the cost of $60. I was really unprepared for this as I only had $20 with me. The limousine driver informed me that I could go together with nine other guys at a cost of $6 each. That was easy enough as the airport was packed with GIs going to Oakland. As we rode to Oakland, we all learned of the fear and trepidation we faced going into an unknown situation.

Upon checking in at Oakland, I was given a schedule or agenda and assigned a bunk number. I entered a room as big as a convention center filled with row upon row upon row of bunk beds. It took quite some time to find my bunk. I stowed my gear and used the little spare time I had to make new acquaintances. I kept seeing two fellows dressed in jungle fatigues and jungle hats. They acted quite strangely and were almost constantly smoking pot. These guys had spent their time and were on their way home.

That evening, we were briefed as to the upcoming events, had a physical recheck, and were given a boarding pass number. That night, I don't believe anyone slept. Guys were all over in small groups, playing cards, talking, writing letters, anything but sleeping.

The next morning, after a quick breakfast, we were assembled according to our boarding pass numbers. There were countless groups of GIs, each group containing about 275 to 280, all assembled in the order that we would leave for the airport. As I sat there on the floor with only a towel, change of underwear, and a shaving kit to my name, waiting for the Grim Reaper to collect me, I heard a familiar voice. It was Underhill. He was assigned to the flight behind mine. I was really glad to see him. He told me that he had almost gone to Canada. It was only through the efforts of his Indonesian girlfriend that he was there at all. The buses would come, load up, and leave for the airport, return to reload and leave again. This was a continuing operation both night and day. There was a buildup of 550,000 GIs in Vietnam with a total of 2 million in the army.

Upon arriving at the airport, we assembled in a wing of the terminal. It was long and narrow with one elevation being all glass facing the runway. I believe it was built especially for this purpose as there were no civilians in this section. There were no chairs, so we all sat on the floor watching the planes coming and going. After about an hour, we were informed that the next plane to land would be the plane that would take us to Vietnam. Soon the plane was in sight. It belonged to Flying Tiger Lines, a contract carrier to the government. The plane bore the same toothed design as the Flying Tiger fighters of World War II.

The plane touched down and began to slow when, to our dismay, a huge shower of sparks erupted from the plane followed by a fireball and a great cloud of smoke. As the plane came to a stop and then taxied away, it seemed no worse for the wear. However, there was a rather large smoking hulk left on the runway. Every GI was on his feet, mouth gaping open. We soon learned from an airline spokesman "Oh, just one of the engines fell out. They'll have it fixed in no time."

Fear and panic shot through the ranks. *That plane is taking us to Vietnam? No way!* I thought.

The two to three hours that were needed to repair the plane lasted into the night and then into the next day. We ended up spending the night and the next morning in that hallway sleeping on the floor. We were each issued a blanket after it was decided the plane would not be repaired that night. Another night without sleep. This time, however, everyone was abuzz about the plane and what we had gotten ourselves into.

By day 2 late afternoon, the plane was fixed and we finally boarded and left. The plane was especially built to carry troops. It was open from the pilot's door to the rear with rows and rows of seats, 280 in all. The first leg of the flight to Anchorage, Alaska, went smoothly, arriving at about 1:00 a.m. I was intrigued, having never been in Alaska. I wandered around the terminal looking at everything. There was a huge stuffed polar bear in a glass case. I had never realized the size they can attain. The plane, refueled and serviced, was off just as the sun was rising. We passed a section of town, the buildings having fire-stop storefronts, the early morning sun rays hitting them gave the appearance of an old Western ghost town. Most of us slept the entire sixteen-hour trip to Japan. We flew over Fujiyama, the peak rising above the cloud bank with nothing, but it was visible. It was light during the entire flight to Japan.

We landed at Osaka U.S. Air Base north of Tokyo, refueled, and left. As the plane was taking off, I noticed the homes were all the same color and were completely made of enameled metal. Each home was a little larger than a two-car garage. As we flew along, I saw a long silver train traveling below us at a tremendous rate of speed. It actually seemed to keep up with the plane for quite a while. We left the airport at 3:00 p.m. according to my watch. Darkness fell quickly.

I awoke as we were flying somewhere over the North China Sea. The landscape, although all water, was dotted with hundreds of very small to medium atolls. We passed little islands the entire day. Some had towns, some didn't. In the early afternoon, we could see a very large landmass in the distance. As we approached the land, the plane made a long banking turn to port, coming parallel to the shoreline of the landmass. As the plane completed its turn, the roar of the engine became a hum as the plane began to slow, settling into its glide pattern. I looked out the window, and I could see great sections of forest, trees broken off leaving jagged stumps. As we moved along the shoreline, there were sections that were completely void of any vegetation. The surface of the land below looked like the surface of the moon. There were craters unbelievably large, appearing to be fifty-or-so feet across and quite deep. The whole landscape was covered with huge pockmarks. The pilot announced over the intercom that we were flying over an area called Chu Lai. It had been overrun by the North Vietnamese some months earlier and that we would be landing at Bein Hoa within the hour.

We flew south along the coastline and passed what looked to be a city of wooden buildings and sandbag bunkers. This was Cam Rahn Bay, we were told, one of the muster-out areas for troops going home. From Cam Rahn to Nha Trang, the landscape was extremely war torn. I learned that bombs being dropped from B-52s had made the craters. There was devastation everywhere.

As we entered our final glide pattern, the landscape had changed from a devastated battlefield to a hustling, bustling city. There were bicycles, motorcycles, and odd-looking motor scooters with big boxes on the back (Lambrettas) packing the highway below. There were guard towers, bunkers, and sandbags everywhere. As the drone of the engines became louder and louder and the plane began its final approach, I kept thinking *When are they going to issue our weapons?* as I was sure we were going to have to fight our way off the plane.

The plane landed safely, and we didn't have to do any fighting. It was early evening, almost dusk. We were immediately taken to the mess hall and fed. What a whole different world! There was nothing that wasn't either completely covered or surrounded with sandbags. BTO and Creedence Clearwater Revival were playing everywhere as if we were in rock-and-roll heaven.

After supper, we were billeted in barracks adjacent to the mess hall. For two days, about fifty GIs were assigned to the mess hall while waiting for orders to come down. I peeled a lot of potatoes and filled a lot more sandbags. On the morning of day 3, as breakfast was winding down, the loudspeakers in the mess hall began barking out names that were to board buses that would take me and about one hundred other guys to the air base where we were to be flown to our units. As I anxiously awaited my name to be called, I was horrified to hear some all-too familiar names; first one and then another until all eight were accounted for. The same eight who had given me so much trouble in AIT and had threatened my very existence. The hair on my neck began to stand. A very sick feeling came over me, starting right in the pit of my stomach. I instantly began to pray, "Please don't call my name, please don't call my name!"

Just as quick, the loudspeaker barked out, "Private first class mattatall." I felt as if a hot large rod was in my tummy. Sweat began to pour off my brow. In a few minutes, these guys will be armed. They threatened—no, promised—they were going to kill me. The names coming across the speaker became a blur as my body went numb. That was until I heard the name Private E-2 Underhill. I then thought, *With him at my side we could take on the world.*

As I left the mess hall, I quickly ducked into the walk-in cooler just outside the back door. Along with my good friends, the potatoes, the cooler was full of apples and oranges. I filled my pockets and my little carry-on bag with the two. I had heard stories of no fresh fruit in the field for months. Underhill was calmly sitting on the bus when I boarded. After a quick embrace and "How ya been?" he began telling me about his flight over from Oakland; a TWA commercial flight that included in-flight movies and a one-day layover in Hawaii. That really made me feel good. The bus ride to the air base was about fifteen minutes long. The morning was cool with a heavy mist hanging over the land. A fog began to gather as we neared the airstrip. The drone of the engines on the C-123 that would take us to Pleiku etched a memory in my brain that can never be erased.

As we dismounted the bus, in the midst of about one hundred other soldiers, there were the infamous eight. Upon seeing me, they quickly regrouped and attached. They gathered around Underhill and me in a New York second, screaming and yelling obscenities. As they came, they began poking and pushing us around like rag dolls. Underhill and I tried to hold our own but to no avail. Just as quickly as they attacked, the MPs gathered around and broke things up. As the MPs escorted our rowdy friends to the plane, they were shouting, "We're going to get you, honkies. Just wait till we're in Pleiku, we're gonna get you."

The plane wasn't large enough to accommodate all of us, so it had to take about half the guys and come back for the rest. Underhill and I were on the second flight. During the hour wait, we stood around and talked, wondering, contemplating what the real war in Pleiku would be like.

As the plane landed at Pleiku Air Base, the sun was shining. It was a warm, beautiful day. Pleiku, a thriving metropolis in the Central Highlands, nestled in the midst of lush jungle-covered mountains about 110 miles west of the South China Sea and probably about 25 to 30 miles from the Cambodian border. The city was completely surrounded on one side by military installations. Camp Holloway, to the east, is a helicopter base and the home of Huey gunships, which is the all-too-familiar multipurpose helicopter used by the army and Cobras, the two-passenger nemeses equipped with twenty-millimeter cannons, automatic grenade launchers, a vast array of rocket launchers, and, if this is not enough, miniguns, a six-barrel automatic Gatling gun capable of firing six thousand rounds per minute, and LOACHs (light observation helicopters), small round-nosed choppers, extremely fast that plagued the VC like a mosquito. There were also a few cranes, a helicopter that looked like a giant dragonfly capable of carrying very large, heavy cargo, and finally the banana-shaped helicopter with a set of blades at each end called a Chinook.

20th Engineers Insignia

The air base was next, followed by the hospital and then Artillery Hill, which was an artillery installation that protected the area. Camp Schmidt was next, an installation that housed mostly journalists and VIP personnel, the tea plantation on the left next to the lake, and, finally, Engineer Hill—my home, the home of the Twentieth Engineer Battalion.

Deuce and a half trucks carried us for the forty-five-minute drive to the 937th Engineer Group on Engineer Hill. The airstrip passed within one-fourth mile of the hill, but the only paved road went through Pleiku by Artillery Hill, past Camp Schmidt, around the Montagnard village and finally to the hill.

The trip through Pleiku was quite interesting. There were hundreds, if not thousands, of people on motorcycles and bicycles crowding the streets. There were also Lambrettas, which were used as taxicabs (holding about six to ten passengers) and delivery trucks. The buildings were mostly left from the thirty years or so of French occupation, made mostly of concrete covered with stucco. None of which were over two stories tall. The telephone poles that paralleled the highway had at least a four-foot-high, eight-foot-wide gob of wires strung on them. When the wire would be cut by the enemy or by hostile fire, there was no attempt to repair the wire. A new wire was strung. As we left, the area was somewhat hilly. There were numerous structures dotting the countryside. As we passed some that were closer to the road, I noticed that some were actually covered with cardboard. Others were covered with Coke cans, tops and bottoms removed, cut down the seam as flattened out to form a four-by-eight-inch shingle. The houses were twelve to fifteen square feet; many had thatched roofs, all with dirt floors and none of the conveniences we were accustomed to, i.e., water, bathroom, and kitchen. After passing Camp Schmidt, we came to a Montagnard village, which was just outside the gate of Engineer Hill. It was totally different than the scattered shacks we had passed earlier. These buildings were all in rows made of wood or thatch with thatched roofs and stood about three to four feet above the ground, being supported by a series of poles. Each house had a plank that led from the ground to the doorway. It looked like the plank we had to our chicken coop when I was a kid. Basically, there were two groups of people in Vietnam: the Vietnamese, a more civilized type who lived in town or in the cardboard shacks, and the Montagnards, which were more like Indians with the women going bare breasted and the men wearing only loincloths.

Upon entering the hill, we were taken straight to group command. To my surprise, there was no one else there. The first planeload had already been assigned to their units and shipped out. I later learned that the Infamous Eight had been assigned to the 299th Engineer Battalion in Bong Son and eventually they all were killed in battle. Bong Song was a hot spot northwest of Pleiku near I Corps and right along the Laotian border.

Underhill and I were assigned to Company B, Twentieth Engineer Battalion. The first GI we met at our new home was one Charles A. Miller. Now specialist 4, Miller was a unique individual. He had been in country for about six or seven months. Miller took Underhill and me over to supply where they issued us clothes, field gear, and a weapon. An M16 was standard issue, but our platoon was short of grenadiers, so we had our choice. When finding out you got a .45-caliber pistol to go along with your M79 grenade launcher, there wasn't much choice. Two weapons are always better than one. After we were issued our M79s, we were told there were no .45 pistols available. Nevertheless, Underhill and I felt pretty cocky with guns that shot bullets ten times bigger than M16 rounds.

I quickly learned what it was that made Miller so unique. "Hey, Mattatall."

"Yeah?"

"You know what?"

"No, what?

"You're all right? Hey, Mattatall."

"Yeah?"

"You know what?"

"No, what?"

"You're all right!"

Now this would go on as long as you would answer, Miller all the while rocking sideways, switching his weight from one foot to the other. We met our patrol leader; he was a specialist 5 with six months in country. His name was Borger.

The barracks, or hooch as they were called, was a twenty-by-thirty-two-foot wooden building with a tin roof. There was a partition wall across the middle of the building, creating two rooms. There were four beds on each side, a walkway down the middle with a door at each end. The first four weatherboards or sidings at the bottom and the last four at the top were tilted out and nailed so as to allow ventilation; screening covered the inside to keep out the bugs.

My patrol consisted of eight men. There was Borger, patrol leader, who slept in the front of the hooch, first bed. Then there was Yogi, a Japanese

American from LA whose mother still lived in Japan. Bomarito, an Italian fellow from Queens, New York. Charles A. Miller from Centerville, Massachusetts. Fair, a cool black guy from the South—Mississippi, I believe. Jones, a fellow with an attitude from Philadelphia. Underhill from San Diego, and me from East St. Louis, Illinois. We had arrived on Friday afternoon, so we were free for the weekend.

Monday morning, our patrol loaded up in the back of a five-ton dump truck and took off to the field. Fifteen miles northwest of Pleiku, our company had built a wooden bridge. Just prior to my arrival in country, the group commander, a full bird colonel, had wanted to drive across the almost-completed bridge before returning to the United States. In order for him to do this, I know not why, but a twelve-inch layer of dirt was put on the bridge deck, making it possible for the colonel to drive across. The dirt was then removed, the first eight to ten inches by the use of a bulldozer and the remaining two to four inches shoveled off by hand, preventing damage to the deck. The day was hot, the work arduous, but finally, the dirt was removed and the deck swept clean. The next morning, the guardrail was installed, thus finishing the structure. The NCOIC (sergeant in charge) had decided to direct the flow of the creek back to its original channel as it had been diverted while the bridge was being constructed. He loaded up the channel with C-4 explosives and set the charge. When the C-4 blew, it shoved rocks and dirt between the layers of the bridge deck as well as blowing the guardrail completely off. Our mission was to police up bridge parts that were scattered across the countryside.

When we arrived, there were Montagnards wandering around trying to salvage whatever they could; no one paid much attention to them. Our patrol went to work immediately, picking up scraps of two-by-four and two-by-six that had once been bridge guardrail. The Montagnard men accompanied us in our work, ready, willing, and able to take any scraps we were willing to part with. The fellow with me was probably about thirty-five though he looked much older due to the hard life he led. He was dressed in only a loincloth, wore no shoes, and carried a machete that was hooked on the end, razor sharp, and called a bush knife. I picked up the bridge scraps and gave them to him; he was very appreciative, quickly handing them to his wife, a bare-breasted woman whose teeth were blackened from chewing beech bark. She too was barefoot, wearing only a skirt fashioned from empty sandbags. The man was very pleased and seemed happy to get the scraps. I noticed some of the other GIs weren't as benevolent as I and refused the scraps to others.

Engineer Hill

Lambretta, Vietnamese Taxi

I reached down to retrieve a rather large piece of two-by-six. As I tugged to remove it from its rest, I saw a silver flash and felt a forceful pressure on my left hand. Quickly the Montagnard shot forward as I fell on my back in despair, his bush knife moving with brute force and lightning speed. The silver flash had been a cobra. The forceful pressure was caused as one of its fangs raked across my thumbnail, leaving a deep scratch. The Montagnard relieved the snake of its head, preventing a second strike. Everyone gathered around to see what the commotion was about. The medics looked at my thumb and related that if the cobra's strike had hit the flesh, the venom would have surely caused certain death before I could have been transported the fifteen miles back to the hospital in Pleiku. That would not be my last encounter with the Montagnard.

The bridge had to be completely disassembled and rebuilt again to remove the rock and debris from between the layers of decking. During the next few weeks we worked diligently, dismantling and reassembling the bridge. We would arrive every morning promptly at 0830 and would leave each evening at 1630. One Monday, we finished up our work for the day a few minutes early as we had poured a concrete apron around one of the abutments. At 1615, we loaded up and headed for the hooch (base camp). As we headed home, with the bridge still in sight, volleys of mortars began to fall. The explosions flat scared the h—out of me. Needless to say, the truck drivers put the pedal to the metal as we all locked and loaded. I was assigned machine gunner, sporting an M60. No one spoke as the trucks sped toward safety. Fear and trepidation were spread throughout the patrol and could be seen on every man's face.

Huey gunships were called to clear the area along with "Puff the Magic Dragon." Now Puff was a World War II C-47 or DC-3 carrying two miniguns (six-barrel electric Gatling guns) capable of unloading six thousand rounds a minute per gun. In about five minutes, these guns could actually shoot the several tons of ammunition the plane carried.

The next morning, being assured the area was clear, we returned along with an escort provided by the Fourteenth Armored Cavalry. As we approached the bridge, we found the bridge was still intact. However, our beloved guardrail was once again spread across the countryside. Again, with the help of the Montagnards, we policed the scraps.

Upstream in a field, a water buffalo had been killed in the skirmish. The weather being hot, the demise of the water buffalo became quite apparent as he grew to two or three times his normal size and various colored liquids spilled out, running down the stream under our bridge. A week passed, the buffalo deflated. That Monday morning, as we were putting the finishing touches to the area around the bridge, three Lambrettas pulled up—two empty and one full of men. The men went to work immediately on the water buffalo. In just a few minutes, they had him all cut up and loaded into the two empty Lambrettas and gone. Boy, were we glad! The whole platoon began to speculate what was to become of the water buffalo. The ARVN interpreter told us that the buffalo would be taken to the market in Pleiku and sold for meat to the general public. No one could believe that repulsive tale. Everyone turned green. Miller and Jones actually dumped their breakfast, making everyone else feel the worse. No one could believe it, so we decided to go into Pleiku. That afternoon at 1500, with just a little left to do the next day, we loaded up our green Cadillacs and headed for Pleiku. As we entered the city, still several blocks from the marketplace, that old familiar odor became pungent in our nostrils. We pulled up to the marketplace and piled out to the dump right in front of the meat market. All eight of us stood there in dismay, disbelief, distraught, and definitely in disgust. Not only was the water buffalo there all piled up with two kids fanning palm leaves to keep the hordes of flies away, but also there were fish, ducks, and chickens hanging without any refrigeration. Some of the fish, and especially the ducks, had turned black from decay. Again, everyone was green. The meat man began to laugh at our dismay. We returned home, heads hanging over the dump-truck sides and out the windows. No one had supper, and breakfast wasn't very well attended.

The next morning, as we arrived, I found a Montagnard woman emptying sandbags that were placed to keep a dirt bank from washing away. I immediately tried to convince her to stop, that I would give her all the empty bags she wanted. Her husband, seeing my pitiful attempt to communicate with his wife, the exact same fellow that had literally saved my life a few days earlier, came over swinging his bush knife, threatening to relieve me of my head. The ARVN interpreter finally came over and explained the situation to the man. He calmed down and began to laugh. I gave him a bundle of sandbags (about fifty). He smiled, bowed, and laid his bush knife on my shoulder. I guess we were friends. Even though we couldn't communicate with our mouths, our eyes said all that needed to be said.

Me and my 50 cal

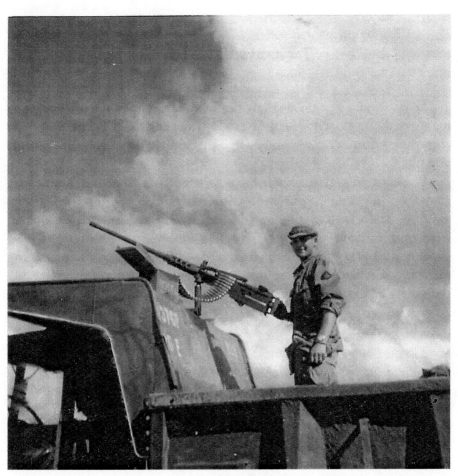

Road Grader

"Hey, guys! Today is our last day at the bridge!" shouted Borger as he entered the hooch. "Grab a bite at the mess hall! Formation is in forty-five minutes, same time, same place. OK! Let's go! Let's go, off and on!"

Breakfast as usual consisted of mouthwatering caramel rolls. The centers heavy with a glazed cinnamon mix loaded with pecans, topped with the sweetest glazed frosting one could imagine followed by a half gallon of fresh milk to wash 'em down. The milk took a little getting used to; a coconut oil-based preservative was mixed with the milk at the processing plant to assure freshness. The preservative gave the milk a taste resembling the smell of a new rubber tire.

0800 Hours

"Ten-hut!" called Sergeant Smith, bringing the Third Platoon to attention.

"Underhill! Matty! I got a little present for you boys!" said Smitty, pressing a specialist 4 patch into each of our hands. "Now don't let this go to your heads," he snickered. "Patrol leaders, you've got your assignments! Platoon! Dismissed!"

The green Cadillac was loaded, and we were on our way. My job on the road was machine-gun security. I had an M60 machine gun that sat atop the transom of the dump truck.

"I'll never get used to this!" cried Underhill above the engine roar of the truck as we bounced and jostled along the gravel and dirt road.

The day passed uneventfully as we graded the approaches and aprons around the bridge. The grader was a standard six wheeler with an eight-foot blade belonging to the 584th.

1600 Hours, +/-

Sergeant Smith pulled up along with Lieutenant Hodgekins, our platoon leader. "Bridge looks great, guys. You're doing a beautiful job," commented the lieutenant.

"Borger, load up the patrol. I want you to escort the grader back to the 584th. You'll have to leave now to get back to the hill before dark." The grader had come out that morning with the daily convoy to Kontum.

"You'll only be able to make ten to twelve miles an hour at top speed. Matty! Look sharp with that M60. That grader is a sitting duck" were Smitty's last words as he drove off in a cloud of dust.

The grader was next, ambling down the road like a big green grasshopper that had lost its wings. The green Cadillac brought up the rear. Soon, Smitty and Lieutenant Hodgekins were out of sight.

Fair drove, Borger rode shotgun. At about two miles out from the bridge, the grader began to slow and finally came to a dead stop. Borger went to investigate. He returned at a dead run, barking orders as he came.

"Grader's got a flat! Fair, come with me. Matty, stay in the truck with the M60. The rest of ya, hit the ditch line, three on one side, three on the other. Keep sharp as we try to figure out what to do!"

Not having a spare, it was decided to remove the right rear tire and wheel, chain the axle arm to the body, leaving the grader traveling on three rear wheels in lieu of the usual four. This worked really well. However, by the time the task was completed, the sun had begun to set, leaving long shadows from the tree line to the road. Our maximum speed now was only five to six miles an hour. The grader bucked violently on the rough road as we attempted to increase our speed. Not a word was said as the tree line and the clear-cut free-fire zone (250 yards from road to jungle) began to blend together. Anticipation and fear hung heavy in the air. *Five more miles and we'll be safe! Just five more miles* kept going through my mind over and over again.

Sooooze, zing-zing, sooooze! called several rounds as they passed close overhead, breaking my train of thought, bringing me back instantly to reality.

"What was that?" yelled Underhill.

"AK-47," stammered Bomarito.

The green telltale streaks of tracer bullets erupted from the tree line. *Clang! Clang! Clang! Clang!* called four rounds smacking the side of the truck bed. Tracers (every fifth round) passed between Yogi and me.

The Infamous Six went instantly into action. Bomarito was the first to answer. A full clip of M16 rounds let go at the muzzle flashes. I wheeled the M60 around and opened up. The next few minutes were a blur of slow motion; rounds smashed into the steel-plate dump bed with red-hot tracers passing much too close like mad hornets in the night. Orange and yellow fireballs erupted at the tree line as Underhill's M79 rounds found their mark. Tracers swarmed the tree line as everyone was at full firepower. Fair was all but pushing the grader down the road. Finally, as we moved out of range, it all stopped as quickly as it began. Again, no one spoke.

"Everybody OK? Anyone take a hit?" questioned Borger, his head sticking over the transom as he crawled out the truck window. With that, everyone spoke at once.

"Man, did you hear those shells hittin' the truck?"

"I can't believe I'm OK. Tracers were passing next to my ear."

"I'm still scared!"

"Am I OK? Am I OK? Somebody check me! Somebody check me! I gotta be hit! I gotta be hit!"

"Did ya hear those bullets goin' by?"

"Man, I was sure we were all goners!"

The rest of the trip to Pleiku was uneventful. Again, dead silence erupted as we began to realize just how close to dead we had been. So went my first battle in the beautiful vacationland of Vietnam.

Saturday, the Next Morning

"Third Platoon, ten-hut!" called Smitty. "Well, Third Patrol! How do ya feel? The grader driver over at the 584th is really grateful for you guys saving his bacon and his grader. I just came from the motor pool, there are no less than sixty-two AK-47 rounds smashed against the plate steel on the side of the dump bed. You all ought to thank Borger for welding that extra plate on the truck. Matty! Here's a gift for ya." Smitty grinned from ear to ear as he threw a bent piece of pipe in my direction. "Pick it up. Go on. What does it look like?"

"Well, Sarge," I replied, "it's an M60 barrel, but it's, ahhh, kinda bent."

"You got that right! That there is the barrel of your M60. In that little skirmish yesterday, you ran no less than two full boxes of ammo, 250-plus rounds through that piece. The barrel got so hot it warped. Now after this here formation, you will go over to supply. They have something for ya that ya can't tear up. Take Underhill with ya. You'll need his help as well as the 3/4."

"Hey, I'm Specialist Mattatall. Sergeant Smith sent me over, said you had something for me to pick up."

"Ohhh, so you're the guy who likes to melt the barrels of my M60s?"

"Yeah, well, I saved the life of one of your road graders. Sounds like a fair trade to me."

"Yeah, I guess you got a point there, pull your 3/4 around back and we'll load your new piece."

"What do ya think he is goin' to give us?"

"I don't know, but he's firing up the forklift."

As we pulled around back, the forklift was waiting. In moments, a large wooden crate was in the back of the 3/4.

"Sign here, and please try not to tear this one up," the supply clerk added as he threw six steel ammo boxes into the 3/4 truck bed.

We hurriedly drove to the motor pool. Upon opening the box, I found a brand-spanking-new .50-caliber machine gun. The gun was so heavy it took Underhill and me both to muscle it up on the transom of the dump. The M60 fired a .308 shell, the same .30-caliber shell used in an M14 rifle. The .50-caliber fired a shell about as big as my thumb and about six inches long.

"Boy, I'll be top dog with this baby!" I said, grinnin' like a possum in the henhouse.

Ben Het

Wheet, wheet!

"Uh-oh, formation! Something's up."

"Outside! Line up. Come on, come on!" yelled Borger as we assembled in the roadway between the hooches.

Captain Robb, First Sergeant Gilbert, and Sergeant Smith, along with the other platoon sergeants, were lined up in front of the CP (command post) at the end of the street.

"Gentlemen," began First Sergeant Gilbert, lowering his whistle, "I know today is Sunday and some of you have just experienced your first taste of combat. I need some special help from a few special soldiers. The 584th, our sister company, is engaged in expanding, maintaining, and rebuilding the MACV compound at Ben Het. Due to the increased enemy presence in the area, the Fourth Infantry Division has deployed several rifle companies to the compound to secure the area. In the past month, the compound has sustained a casualty rate of about 114 percent. Company B has been asked to send ten men to the compound to relieve some of the 584th for two weeks. Let me not deceive you. All who go will certainly be killed or wounded. The CO doesn't feel that an assignment be made sending ten of you to your almost-certain demise. If the whole company were assigned, it would be a different story."

"Gentlemen," interrupted Captain Robb, "I have decided to ask for volunteers rather than make assignments. There are 152 of you in this company. I need ten men to step forward."

The next thirty seconds passed in complete silence. Borger was the first to step forward, then another and another. *What an adventure,* I thought as I stepped forward. Of the 152, 30 stepped forward to include Borger, Miller, Yogi, Johnson, Underhill, Bomarito, Fair, Cummins, and myself.

"Good. Hmmm, good," replied Captain Robb thoughtfully. "I see the entire Third Patrol wants to go. So be it. You from the Second Patrol"—pointing to Johnson—"yeah, you and you from the Fourth Patrol." He pointed to a stubby fellow.

"Company, attention!" growled the first sergeant. "Company, dismissed!"

"The ten of you! As you were!"

I stood with the nine in the middle of the street, feeling somewhat naked as the others dispersed. "Gentlemen, first I would like to commend you for your bravery and sense of duty to your country. You will report to supply. Each of you will be issued a .45-caliber sidearm and as much ammo as you can carry. For those of you who carry M16s, you will be issued ten bandoliers of ammo [one thousand rounds]. Underhill and Mattatall, is it?"

"Yes, First Sergeant."

"You carry an M79, right?"

"Yes, First Sergeant," Underhill and I replied.

"Draw a case each of HE rounds [high explosives]. After you have finished at supply, go back to your hooches and check your weapons first thing. Next, and this is a command from the CO, you will write a letter home. At 1230 hours, you will report to the chopper pad at group command. There you will receive your final briefing and fly out at 1300 hours. This is a hot one, boys. Keep your spirits up and your heads down. WELCOME TO VIETNAM! Dismissed."

At supply, I received ten bandoliers of M79 HE rounds. Each bandolier contained five rounds. I also received a .45-caliber sidearm along with fifty rounds of ammo. I then returned to my hooch, wrote the letter, and spent the next three and a half hours thinking about my childhood adventures and whether or not I would ever again see an autumn sunrise in Illinois.

"OK! Listen up!" yelled Borger over the chop of the Huey's props. "We're goin' to a place called Ben Het. It is just southeast of the Laos-Cambodia-Vietnam border. The Ho Chi Minh Trail passes two miles west of the camp on the ridgeline just across the Laotian border. Our assignment is to relieve some of the troops stationed there. This is definitely a hot one."

"Oh, great. Just what I always wanted to do: die!" grunted Bomarito.

Now Bomarito was a large, kinda bulky fellow—not fat but bulky, an Italian from New York City.

"OK! OK! Calm down," Borger replied as the patrol began to murmur. "This one is going to be tough, but if we keep our heads down and our wits about us, we'll be fine. Six of us in this chopper, the other four in that one. Yogi, you and Johnson take the other bird. You two are the shortest. The brass are flying over to take a look. You'll be safer."

Yogi Yokohama, an American-born Japanese fellow from LA, a short timer (less than ninety days left on his tour).

Johnson, also a short timer, less than thirty days left before his return to the States.

Borger, specialist E-5, patrol leader from somewhere back east—New Jersey, I believe.

Underhill, Robert, PFC, a free spirit from San Diego. We were in the same platoon in AIT. He always pushed the envelope of authority. He and I were the only two GIs who were not African American from our company to be sent to Vietnam.

Charles Miller, specialist 4, was a goofy guy who would "you know what" ya all day long. Also from the east.

Fair, PFC, came into country just after I did. A good-natured black fellow from the Alabama-Mississippi area.

Cummins, specialist 4, a high-strung know-it-all. Been in country about four months.

We all boarded the lead Huey, a U-H1, fully loaded. There were two door gunners, an aircraft commander, the pilot, and the six of us.

Our chopper took the lead with Yogi, Johnson, Bomarito, and the stubby guy from the Fourth Platoon, the group CO and XO bringing up the rear. The twenty-five-minute flight over the Central Highland mountains was spectacular.

"This is Charlie Alpha Romero calling Tango Tango Xray." The pilot's voice cracked in our headphones.

"Hey, Charlie Alpha, you got Ben Het International here. How can we help?" came the reply.

"We're comin' to visit, need some instruction. Over."

"Come in from the north, you'll be comin' in hot, stay high till you're over the runway, then drop like a rock. You will probably receive heavy ground fire from those low-lying hills to the west. We'll lay down a field of fire, maybe it will make 'em keep their heads down long enough for you to land."

"Ten to four. Our ETA is one minute."

"Ten to four. When you see the 105 shells hittin' the hill, drop on in. Good luck. Over."

Seconds later, the hills to our right erupted in puffs of white smoke and great clouds of dust. The air was filled with orange tracers as small arms fire blanketed the area in an effort to ensure our safe landing.

"Here we go," stammered Captain Dulak, a touch of anxiety in his voice. The UH-1 began its descent to the landing strip.

"Charlie Alpha! Charlie Alpha! Abort! Abort! We've got incoming on the runway."

Captain Dulak quickly pulled up and circled for another try. *Zing! Zing!* came the sound of two bullets passing through the Plexiglas nose bubble of the aircraft.

"We got machine-gun fire about two o'clock, halfway up the rise of that hill," barked Captain Dulak.

Tunk, tunk, tunk, tunk. Four more rounds hit the side of the chopper.

"I got 'em!" came a voice over the headphones.

The colonel's ride broke off from our rear and headed straight toward the bursts of machine-gun fire. Two streaks of red flame erupted from the left side of the aircraft, then two more from the right. Four white smoke trails headed straight to the machine gunners. Seconds later, the hillside erupted as the four rockets from the CO's bird found their mark.

"AH!" came the voice over the headphones. "Colonel Kratz 1, VC. Zip!"

"OK, boys, here we go again! Open up the doors when I hit the ground. You guys get off and get off quick 'cause I ain't hangin' around!"

The CO's chopper found more targets, this time a mortar battery. More rockets launched, and the shells coming into camp ceased momentarily. Down we went.

"What do ya think they'll do if we just stay on the chopper?" Underhill asked, grinning.

"Five years at the Hilton in Long Binh," came the reply over the headphones. With that, the chopper landed with a thud. Everyone jumped off and scrambled for the nearest bunker. Captain Dulak made no bones about his retreat. He was out of sight in seconds.

"Howdy, boys. I'm Captain Walker, CO of this unit. I would like to start by thankin' ya'll for coming and relievin' some of my men. I know ya'll ain't grunts, so you won't be goin' out on patrols, but we do need our runway repaired, and most of our bunkers could use a little tidying up as the VC like to kiss us every day at noon with 112 sixty-millimeter mortar shells. They also like to take your snapshot with an AK-47 every chance they get. So keep your pots and your flak jackets on at all times. The standing rule of this camp is to shoot anyone in camp without a pot on his head. We have had VC in camp before, collecting information. Just to let you know, we have a celebrity here in camp. Her act starts at 1200 hours and runs till first light. Thank you, and I hope ya'll make it back home OK."

"OK, OK, OK! Listen up. I'm Sergeant Carter. Follow me, I will show ya the ropes. This here's your home for the next couple a weeks. Half of ya in this bunker, the other half in that one yonder. That building over there with the sandbags all over the road, the long one, is the mess hall. You might get somethin' to eat there, and you might not. Just depends on what kinda mood Charlie is in that day. There are, however, plenty of C-rats in each bunker. The motor pool and supply are over there." Sergeant Carter pointed. "You'll be able to get whatever you need to complete your assignment. If they ain't got it, consider the assignment done. Gentlemen, the way to survive here is to keep your head on straight. The time now is 1527 hours. Set your watches. Supper is at 1700 hours. It goes until everyone has eaten, if it goes at all. There's to never be more than twenty-five in the mess hall at one time, so eat fast so the next guy can get in. The showers and latrines are located in the center of the bunker complex. Lunch is at 1300 hours or as soon as the dust clears. At 1157 hours, you will be in your bunkers until the honeybees have departed unless you hear the siren. This will alert you to the fact that there is a ground attack and gooks are in the wire. You are then to take up your defensive positions around the wire. Your position is the perimeter wire closest to your bunker. Lastly, breakfast starts at 0600 hours. Any questions? Take the rest of the day to get settled. See ya in the morning."

The bunker was about twelve-by-fourteen-feet with two bunks end to end on one side with two more bunks arranged in the same manner on the other side, leaving about a six-inch-wide, fourteen-inch-long common area between the bunks. The inside of the bunker was lined with solid landing mats (twenty-four-by-ninety-six-foot steel panels that interlocked to form a portable runway). The roof consisted of six-by-six timbers laid across the short distance followed by more landing mats. The walls of the bunker were six sandbags, thick, about six inches. The roof was also six bags high, about four feet thick. The interior was illuminated by one sixty-watt pull-chain light fixture. That is, if the generator wasn't suffering shrapnel wounds from our daily barrage.

"Well, what do ya think?" asked Borger in his usual soft-spoken manner.

"Don't look too good," Bomarito answered, shaking his head.

"Yeah, ya know, they've really got us pinned down here," came back Johnson.

"There's sniper fire comin' at us all the time. Where's Puff? Where's the napalm?" whimpered Cummins.

"I don't think we're goin' to make it outta here. Me and Fair and Mattatall, we ain't been here a month yet," stated Underhill rather dejectedly.

"Hey, Borger, you know what?" called Miller.

"No, what, Miller?" Borger came back.

"You're all right," replied Miller.

"Hey, Borger, you know what?"

"No, what, Miller?"

"You're all right!"

"Borger, quit eggin' him on. You know he'll do that all night," objected Johnson.

"Hey, Matty, what do you think about this whole mess? You haven't said a word."

"To be perfectly honest, Underhill, I'm too scared to talk."

As night fell, the camp at Ben Het was as peaceful as a midsummer's eve in Hometown, USA. Sleep did not come easy. Everyone in our bunker tossed and turned, not knowing whether or not they would see the light of day.

"Guys, guys! Come look! Come look at this. The ridgeline is all lit up!" cried Fair. "I was going to the latrine when I saw it."

We all clambered outside to see the ridgeline illuminated by what looked like rows and rows of floodlights.

"What's all the commotion about out here?" came a voice from one of the other bunkers.

"What's all the lights on the ridgeline?" we replied.

"Oh, that? It's just the Ho Chi Minh Trail. Those are the headlights of trucks carrying supplies to the VC and NVA. You'll see that steady stream of headlights from dusk till dawn, day in and day out. You had better get some sleep. Hanna goes on at midnight."

"Hanna? Midnight? Who the hell's Hanna?" bellowed Bomarito.

"Just wait, you'll see," came the voice from the bunker.

"If that's the Vietcong, why don't we shell 'em or bomb 'em or napalm 'em? Something besides just watching?" cried Cummins, his voice laced with fear and trepidation.

"Well, ya see," came back Borger, his voice laid-back, "that whole ridgeline is in Laos, and Laos is a neutral country. We can't touch 'em."

"How can we win this war," stammered Cummins, "if we can't shoot into tea and coffee plantations? If we can't shoot at trucks carrying supplies to the enemy?"

"Lot of politics," replied Borger.

The cool mountain air finally caused sleep to overcome our little group.

"Hey, you GIs in Camp Ben Het. It's time to wake up! Have I got a program for you today!" came a sexy voice over a loudspeaker.

"Oh man, what time is it?" came a voice from within the bunker.

"I don't know," came another. "But it is still zero dark thirty."

"Oh shit! It's only midnight!" came the husky voice of Bomarito as the loudspeaker continued to blare.

"I'd like to dedicate this first song to those brave young men who came in this afternoon on the two Hueys. I think you'll enjoy it. Here it is, 'At the Zoo' by Simon and Garfunkel."

"What the hell is going on?" groaned Underhill.

"That's just Hanoi Hanna," Borger replied, pulling his flak vest up over his head.

"What do you mean Hanoi Hanna?" yelled Cummins, on the verge of hysterics.

"Calm down, Cummins, calm down," said Borger, sitting up in his cot. "Hanoi Hanna is a name given to that girl on the loudspeaker. It is a propaganda ploy to harass us. A girl, usually educated in the States, will get on a PA system and broadcast all night, play your favorite music, tell ya about all the current events back home with commercial breaks telling you how poorly we're doing at the war or how many GIs have been captured even to the point of name and rank."

Borger was right; hearing things that had meaning to us coming over a loudspeaker from the enemy was certainly unnerving and definitely not a boost to your morale. The night went on with "LA Woman" from the Doors, BTO, Creedence Clearwater Revival, and others. Fatigue finally overcame the noise, and sleep again crept in.

"It's 0545, time to rise and shine, boys. Mess hall in fifteen minutes," came the voice of Sergeant Carter at the bunker door.

Breakfast seemed to come and go in a daze. Our first assignment was to repair mortar damage to the bunkers. Sandbag after sandbag was filled. By 1100 hours, we had filled and set over five hundred sandbags. The bags were actually filled with the red volcanic soil that was prevalent in the Central Highlands. By 1145 hours, all tools had been put away and we were back in the bunker.

For 1200 hours straight up came the report, then another and another. The sixty-millimeter shells exploded with kind of a dull thud. Soon there were so many it sounded like raindrops falling on a tin roof. Thirty minutes later, it was all over.

"So that's it?" asked Fair.

"I don't know. Let's take a look," I replied. Very cautiously, Fair and I peeked out from the bunker entrance. A thick haze of gray smoke hung over the camp like a mortician's wreath. Just below the layer of smoke, a red dust cloud hung ominously in the air. There were pockmarks everywhere, the signature of a mortar shell. Sandbags lay in shambles everywhere, our morning's work devastated. The front loader that had been assigned to Cummins had two flat tires. The all clear was sounded. We quickly went into action. Fair and Underhill helped Cummins get the tires off the front loader as it would be needed to fill more sandbags.

"Matty, Yogi, Johnson, Bomarito, Miller. Come with me. A C-130 is going to do a touch-and-go. He'll come in as if to land. Just as the wheels touch down, he'll power up as they're shovin' the cargo out the back. Our job is to get the crates off the field as fast as possible. Any questions?" asked Borger.

Minutes later, the drone of a C-130 was heard.

"Boy, he's awfully high to try to land."

"Yeah, now watch this," replied Borger.

The C-130 dropped almost straight down to the runway like a hawk dropping out of the sky on an unsuspecting mouse. The C-130 screeched with a large blue puff of smoke as the wheels hit the runway. Four large boxes came tumbling out of the plane as the engines revved, and the plane was again airborne, climbing out of sight.

Bomarito was ready and waiting. His forklift nimbly picked up each crate and set it on the back of a deuce and a half. Yogi drove one and Johnson the other. The two trucks quickly scooted into the supply area. Just as gently, Bomarito set the crates on the ground. Borger, me, Miller, and the others opened the crates, revealing their contents. The first was a pallet of C rations. The second and third contained various supply items to include much-needed medical supplies. The fourth box, to our surprise, contained five thousand sandbags.

"Hmmm," murmured Johnson. "Why couldn't they have sent these already filled?" Everyone just looked at him and laughed.

The afternoon was spent filling shell divots around the runway left by the day's mortar attack. Sixty-millimeter mortars are rather small and had no real effect on the landing-mat runway. The balance of the day was spent filling more sandbags. Sporadic gunfire was heard throughout the day as sentinels in the guard towers fired at muzzle flashes coming from the tree line.

As evening approached, the sun set behind the mountains overlooking the ridgeline, causing darkness to fall up there a little before it settled on our camp. As the darkness thickened, the headlights on the ridgeline became more prevalent and numerous. As I sat there on top of the bunker watching the parade go by, I counted just over fifty sets of headlights in an hour. *Hmmm,* I thought. *That's like 1,200 trucks every twenty-four hours. That's crazy. How can we allow this to happen?*

I found myself dozing off as the events of the past two days caught up. I retired to the bunker's interior, this time having no trouble going to sleep. Again at 1200 hours, Hanna was right on cue. This time, however, she didn't keep us awake as she did the night before. After several days, one could almost sleep completely through one of her broadcasts.

Almost all the GIs assigned to Ben Het were members of the Fourth Infantry Division. Patrols were sent out daily in an attempt to seek out and destroy the mortar units. Their success was marginal as the VC and NVA units would retreat over the Cambodian or Laotian borders to the safety of the neutral countries.

One afternoon found us at our daily task of filling and stacking sandbags. This time, we were working on the communications bunker at HQ.

"Tango, tango, x-ray, come in." The radio crackled. "This is foxtrot one. Come in."

"Tango, tango, x-ray here," answered the operator at our end.

"We're about two clicks up the Phen Zen Road [Route 512]. We've got a definite problem," came the voice over the radio. "We are currently pinned down. I repeat, pinned down. It appears to be a tank. I repeat, a tank. We need an air strike pronto! Ten to four."

"Two clicks up Phen Zen Road. Ten-four. Did I hear you right, a tank has your unit pinned down?"

"Affirmative, affirmative. We are on the north side of the road. The tank is to our west. Ten to four."

"Bird is in the air."

Minutes later, two U.S.-flown Skyraiders streaked over our heads toward the ridgeline. Two clicks, that's about one and a half miles. We could see the two planes climbing and banking, preparing for the attack. They then swooped like two angry wasps. Fireballs could be seen erupting above the trees as the payloads found their targets. The radio crackled again. "Sky hawks one, tank zilch, nada."

The camp siren began to wail. Sergeant Carter came running up.

"Get the loader and forklift ready. We'll also need a ten-ton flatbed! Bring all the ammo ya got. Five minutes. Supply yard!"

"You heard the man!' snapped Borger. "Get your spare ammo, now! Move! Move! Move!"

The next few minutes were chaos as we ran to the bunker for our extra ammo. As we gathered at the supply yard, we found Company C also assembling. The troops were mounting deuce and a halves, four jeeps with 105-millimiter recoilless rifles aboard, and one oh-so-sweet APC with a quad 40 ack-ack gun mounted on top.

"Borger, are your men ready?" queried Sergeant Carter.

"We are," replied Borger.

"Good. Take your position behind the first four deuce and a halves. Loader, first forklift next, then the flatbed. We're going after that tank."

The convoy left camp without haste. The APC with the quad 40 was in the lead. Two jeeps with recoilless rifles were next, followed by four deuce and a halves. We were next with four more deuce and a halves and the remaining two jeeps bringing up the rear. We moved steadily up the road. The patrol that had been pinned down by the tank was acting as our forward observer, ready to alert us of additional enemy activity.

The trip took all of three minutes. The tank laid at the side of the road a hulk, still smoldering from the recent Skyraider attack. Bomarito and Cummins went instantly into action, taking the front loader and the forklift and pushing the bombed-out tank toward the middle of the road. Company C dismounted the deuce and a half, taking up a defensive perimeter around the work site. All the vehicles were turned in the opposite direction for their return trip. The flatbed pulled up alongside the tank skeleton. Bomarito was on one side, and Cummins was on the other, gently lifting the tank. Yogi then guided the truck bed beneath the uplifted tank. Bomarito and Cummins then lowered the tank onto the bed.

"Ahhh, smooth as Kentucky bourbon," replied Sergeant Carter. "OK, let's get this show outta here."

Five minutes later, we were back in camp. The whole operation had taken less than thirty minutes from start to finish. We discussed the events of the day in the mess hall over our supper consisting of mystery meat, mashed potatoes, and gravy with applesauce on the side.

"Hey, Borger, what do ya think that tank was up to when our patrol came across it?" asked Miller.

"I don't know. But as close to the camp as it was, it was probably goin' to drop in and say hello. Cummins, Bomarito, you guys sure did a nifty job loading that thing on the truck."

The rest of the evening was cool and quiet. We were later told that the tank was Russian made, a much-smaller vehicle than our own M60. We also were told that it was the first time the enemy had brought a tank to the war. (Additional information at a later date proved that to be inaccurate.)

The days came and went. The endless task of filling and stacking sandbags began to wear on our morale. Ten days had passed, only four more if we were to leave as originally planned. Hanoi Hanna went on night after night along with the honeybees at noon. We had grown so accustomed to her she barely scratched the subconscious as we slept. However, this night would be a little different.

"Hey, boys down at Ben Het. How ya doin'?" came Hanna's voice as she signed on. "I've got some special news for a special soldier tonight. That's right, this news goes to Spec. 4 Dwight Cummins, Company B, Twentieth Engineers."

With that, everyone in the bunker sat straight up in bed.

"How the hell does she know me? That I'm in Company B of the Twentieth? Oh hell, this is serious," spurted Cummins.

"Dwight, the news I have for you is from your wife, Tracy. Dwight, honey, I'm sorry I have to tell you this, but Tracy is three months pregnant. She couldn't tell you herself, so she asked us if we would. And you know we are here to serve."

"Oh shit, shit, shit! What does she mean my wife's pregnant?"

"Is your wife's name Tracy?" asked Bomarito.

"Yes! Yes! Yes! I just got a letter from her four days ago. She said everything was fine!" sobbed Cummins. "What'll I do now? What will I do now?" screamed Cummins as he began running around the bunker, pulling at his ears as if he were trying to pull them off.

"Quick, grab him before he hurts himself."

Fair was the first to grab Cummins. He ended up being slammed against the wall like a puppet. It took all five of us to subdue him. Others came from the other bunkers to help. He continued to yell and scream and thrash about. We finally got him calmed down with the help of the medics. The CO had us take him over to the communication bunker at HQ. There they called the Mars station at Pleiku Air Base. The Mars station called the

States via shortwave radio. The Mars station in Phoenix, Arizona, received the call from the Pleiku station. They called Cummin's wife, Tracy, via land telephone, thus allowing Cummins to talk directly with his wife. She assured him that everything was fine.

The next day, an investigation was launched to figure out how Charlie had gotten the information about Cummins. It was learned that our trash dump site was outside the wire, and the letter received by Cummins four days earlier was found by someone going through the trash and forwarding it to Hanna. This incident led to more stringent regulations concerning destroying all forms of communication.

The sniping from the tree line around the perimeter became more prevalent as the days went on. First, Skyraiders were brought in to clear the snipers out, to no avail. F-4 Phantoms were next. Their napalm burned the trees and scorched the jungle, but not the snipers. Finally, B-52s were brought in, dropping their five-hundred-pound bombs three hundred yards off our perimeter.

"This bunker feels like the inside of a rocking boat!" yelled Johnson as explosion after explosion decimated the jungle just outside our perimeter.

"Yeah, look out the doorway, there's rocks and dirt, tree branches, even leaves, falling all around us!" I bellowed above the roar.

"I hope this thing doesn't fall in on us!" yelled Underhill as the metal ceiling groaned and creaked.

Then it was all over—the bombing, the honeybees, Hanoi Hanna, and Ben Het—as a chopper came in under the cover of darkness and extracted us like a thief in the night.

Hooches at Ben Het

Central Highlands near Ben Het

QL-14 Mine Sweep

The road from Pleiku to Kontum wandered through the mountains in a northwesterly direction. After passing Artillery Hill, QL-14 turned from an oily and chip-paved road to dirt. Our assignment for the next thirty days was to clear the road of land mines, allowing traffic to pass in safety. The twenty-five-mile stretch was broken down into five five-mile sectors. Companies A, B, and C of the Twentieth were assigned the first fifteen miles. Two companies from the Kontum area were assigned the northern two sectors. All five sectors were swept at the same time, so the entire road would be more or less open from the south and from the north at the same time.

"Borger, your patrol has QL-14 sector 1 for the next thirty days. Can ya handle it? Oh, and here's a new guy just in country."

"Yeah, yeah, we can handle it. Smitty, when have we ever let you down?"

"OK, OK. Point well-taken."

"Murphy, huh?"

"Yeah."

"You look a little scared. You OK?"

"Yeah, just a little nervous."

"Well, ya oughtta be, there's a war going on here. Just hang with Mattatall, you'll be fine."

"Hey, Matty, take care a' this guy, will ya?"

"Yea, sure. Got your weapon yet?"

"No. Just came in from Leng Bien an hour ago."

"Wow, that was an early flight. Come on, let's go get ya something to shoot with."

Murphy was issued several pairs of jungle fatigues, socks, shorts, etc., five bandoliers of ammo, and a brand-new M16. Thirty minutes later, we were loaded in the green Caddy dump truck heading for the outskirts of Pleiku, me in my usual position, standing behind the transom, brandishing my .50-caliber.

"This is it, boys," Borger called as the truck came to a stop. "Two sweepers. Bomarito, Cummins, take the lead. The other five of us will pull security. Fair will drive the truck today. We'll alternate around every day. We have to be at the end of our sector by 1030 hours. That's five miles in two and a half hours. Guys, let's get hoppin'. A mile up the road, we'll pass the Fourteenth Armored Calvary, an ARVN unit, an M60 tank will join us there and move along the free-fire zone for additional security."

The morning passed without incident. The tank joined us at the appointed place, the five miles passed quickly as we laughed and joked along the way. No mines, all's clear. The first week went without a hitch.

Second Week, Tuesday Morning

Underhill and I were working the sweepers. We were about one mile past the Fourteenth's position. Our AVRN tank was lumbering along. *Crack! Crack! Crack! Crack!* came the report from the tree line on the opposite side of the road from the tank. Bullets danced across the road, leaving red puffs of dust as we scrambled to the ditch line, seeking cover. We expected the tank to turn and fire at the muzzle flashes, but instead, the tank shifted into high and was heading down the road.

"You SOB!" I screamed, grabbing Murphy's M16, firing a full clip at the tank. Everyone else jumped up at my lead and began firing as if M16 rounds could hurt a tank, the sniper all but forgotten.

At the three-mile marker, we passed several Vietnamese hooches. One morning, as we passed, two small girls and a boy stood by the roadside watching us. Without thinking, I reached into my pocket and pulled out three Jolly Ranchers as I always had candy. The children hesitantly took them and quickly retreated. The next morning, there were five kids there, this time with their hands out. Day 3 yielded twenty-five-plus kids, and day 4, there were thirty-five-plus kids standing along the roadside, all wanting a little piece of heaven.

Every day I would go to the PX for more candy. A bag of candy was fifty cents. I finally bought three or four bags at a time to ensure an ample supply. As I placed a piece of candy in the hand of each child, one of the older ones replied, "*Boo coo* number one." After that, every child would say "*Boo coo* number one" as they received their daily allotment. I could never figure out where all those kids came from as there were only three hooches there by the roadside.

The .50-caliber was so heavy and bulky it was almost impossible to maintain on the truck transom. One free afternoon, I took the truck over to the ASP yard and cut an eight-inch-long piece of a two-inch pipe and welded it to the top of the truck's transom. The mounting pin of the .50-caliber slipped right into the pipe, stabilizing the weapon so it could be turned and fired in any direction. It was the last week of our sweeping assignment. Bomarito had traded some prized possessions for a Thompson submachine gun. He showed up Monday morning, grinning from ear to ear.

"What's that?" Murphy made the mistake of asking.

"You don't know what this is?" snapped Bomarito. "Oh, silly boy, where you been? This here's a bona fide .45-caliber Thompson fully automatic submachine gun."

"Why ya carrying it?" came back Murphy.

"More knockdown power, my boy. Won't jam," replied Bomarito.

"Listen up," replied Borger. "I need you guys to be really on top of it. Last week, A Company lost five sweepers. They all gathered up for a smoke at the end of the sweep. A small boy rode up on a bike. It was packed with C-4, command detonated, killing all five GIs and the small boy."

Company A had sector 2. They had a lot of casualties due to command-detonated mines being exploded before the sweepers got to them. Things were so bad in sector 2 a remote-control jeep was built with five sweeping units attached to a bar running across the front of the jeep, spanning the entire roadway. The crossbar had balloon tire training wheels on each end. The jeep lasted two days before being blown to smithereens.

Tuesday Morning

Two weeks had passed since our only incident with the sniper. Fair and Miller were on the sweepers, the rest of us pulling security. As we arrived at the exact spot of the prior incident, *Crack! Crack! Crack! Crack!* came the report as bullets danced across the roadway. Instantly Underhill, I, and others went to the ditch line. That is, all except Fair and Bomarito. Fair stood in the middle of the road as if he had turned to salt.

"Fair, get the hell outta the road!" I yelled. No response.

"Fair!" bellowed Borger and Underhill. No response.

The next thing I knew, Underhill and I were heading back to the middle of the road for Fair, bullets still dancing across the road from the sniper's AK-47.

"Fair, come on! We gotta get outta the road!"

Fair just stared forward with the sweeper still in his hands. His eyes had a kind of glaze over them.

Underhill and I pulled on him, trying to get him to move. His body was as stiff as a concrete statue.

"We'll have to carry him. Take his feet." As we tried to pick Fair up, not a muscle in his body moved. He was as rigid as could be. Underhill and I managed to pick him up, sweeper and all, and carry him to the ditch line. Upon reaching the ditch a mere fifteen feet away, we were both exhausted. We literally threw rigor mortis Fair into the ditch. As Fair collided with the bottom of the ditch, his whole body turned to mush.

He began sobbing uncontrollably, "Let 'em kill me. Let 'em kill me," he kept saying over and over again.

In the meantime, Bomarito had disappeared.

"Where's Bomarito?" questioned Borger.

"There he is, running across the free-fire zone firing his Thompson!"

"Oh, shit!" stammered Borger. "Let's go. That idiot. Who knows what's out there."

All of us, including Fair, began to run after Bomarito. His crazy antics must have scared the sniper as he left his perch, jumped to the ground, and ran into the jungle with Bomarito in hot pursuit. Twenty yards into the jungle, the sniper ran into a large hooch. Without hesitation, Bomarito followed.

"What do we do now?" I questioned.

"I don't know!" was Borger's reply. "There could be a tunnel system in there. Who knows, even full of VC."

Borger's sentence was cut short by the sound of gunfire. The bamboo hooch seemed to dance as rounds pierced its sides, sending us instantly for cover. Tense seconds passed. The door of the hooch flew open; a cloud of gunpowder smoke erupted followed by Bomarito, both hands up in the air, his machine gun in one, a clenched fist in the other.

"Bomarito one, VC. Zip!" yelled Bomarito.

"You idiot, you freakin' idiot!" shouted Borger, his voice trembling.

That afternoon, the incident was reported to Sergeant Smith. It was decided by Sergeant Smith and the patrol that the incident wouldn't be reported to the CO or group command as Bomarito would probably be facing a court-martial for his actions of putting his patrol in imminent danger.

The last five days of our minesweeping assignment went without an incident. However, on the last day of the sweep, we were needed in

Kontum to install some drain culverts. Upon completing the sweep, we loaded up and proceeded to Kontum. Halfway through sector 4, the tree line came alive with small arms fire. *Zing, zing, zing,* the sound of bullets passing close overhead. *Bam, bam, bam,* more bullets hitting the side of the truck. I instantly turned and began to fire the .50-caliber. There's no mistaking the sound of a .50-caliber. I could see the rounds tearing at the jungle-infested tree line.

"Ohhh, am I dead?" I asked, opening my eyes. I felt a searing hot weight on my chest. I couldn't move. Fair had the truck moving at a high rate of speed. As my eyes focused and I could look around, I noticed I was lying in the bed of the dump. Further investigation revealed the .50-caliber lying on my chest. The recoil of the weapon had torn the half-inch steel plate of the transom loose around the outside at the weld that held my eight-inch-long two-inch pipe in place, causing the weapon to recoil right on top of me, flattening me in the bed of the truck. Now there was a perfectly round hole in the transom to hold the mounting pin of the .50-caliber.

"Matty, got a question for ya."

"Yeah, Murphy, what is it?"

"I was just wonderin' why all the jeeps have that rod welded to the bumpers sticking straight up in the air?"

"Charlie is pretty smart. They know how fast we like to drive even though the speed limit is only twenty-five miles per hour. Charlie's been stringing piano wire across the road about four feet above the road bed. We'd come zooming along, hit the wire about throat high. A lot of GIs were garroted, several were even decapitated. So we welded fence pickets on all the jeeps. You see how the top of the picket is bent forward?" Murphy nodded. "The wire would catch in that curve and break. Sounded like a guitar string breakin'. We used to love to hear that sound, knowing we had gotten over on Charlie. But Charlie, he ain't no dummy. You see, he knew that one of our own grenades would fit perfectly, spoon and all, in a C-rats peach can, so he would nail a peach can to a post or a stick on each side of the road, insert one grenade each can, pull the piano wire between the two, and leave. We come along thinking we'd snap the wire. To our surprise, the wire didn't snap but pulled the grenades out of the cans allowing the spoons to fly. Now we had two live grenades in the backseat of the jeep. Now we keep the 250-yard free-fire zone on both sides of the road much cleaner. The zone is sprayed with Agent Orange about once a month."

QL-14 Mine Sweep

"Wooly Bully"

"Heyyyyy, Matty! Whatcha got there? Looks like a PX in your footlocker."

"Hey, Borg. Yeah, I'm just stockin' up, you know me, king of the junk food junkies."

"You must have fifteen cans of Cheetos along with Jolly Ranchers, M&Ms. Mmmmmm, let's see, peanuts, Poppycock. You really got it!"

"Yeah, ya know, I never know when we might have to go out in the field. I just want to be prepared."

"Well, I hope you're ready, tomorrow's the day."

"Oh yeah! What's up?"

"Hey, Matty! Got a minute?" said Smitty, entering the hooch.

"Sure, Smitty, what do ya need?"

"We're movin' out in the morning, place called Wooly Bully."

"Wooly Bully! You mean like the song?"

"Yep, the place is so rugged they named it after the song. We're going to build some hooches in the compound. The real operation is an asphalt plant. Last month, sappers came through the wire with no one seeing them. Took out the asphalt plant. Satchel charged two bunkers on their way out, taking out six GIs. The ARVN unit next to the compound was pulling most of the security. They're moving two rifle companies in from the Fourth at Camp Enari to watch over the new plant. I know how resourceful you can be. Been watching you barter with the others with hot PX items. You're a regular Mexican Jew. We have everything we need for the operation except sixteen-penny nails. I need you to get me five to six fifty-pound boxes. Can ya handle it?"

"I think I can, Sarge. What have we got to trade?"

"Anything our supply or ASP yard has that might be of interest."

"OK! Give me a requisition chit to supply."

"What do you want?"

"Five jungle hats." Smitty hastily scribbled out the chit for the hats.

Forty-five minutes later, Underhill and I pulled up in the 3/4.

"Well, any luck?" questioned Smitty.

"Hey, Smitty, you said it yourself. I'm a pro. Feast your eyes on these babies," I gloated while leading Smitty to the rear of the 3/4. There in the back were ten, not five, fifty-pound boxes of nails.

"You are a Mexican Jew! I looked everywhere for these nails. Where did you get 'em?"

"Sarge," I said, "ask me no questions and I'll tell you no lies. You just got to know your market." I didn't have the heart to tell Smitty the nails only cost us three fatigue hats, leaving one each for Underhill and myself for our trouble.

The next morning, Third Platoon B Company Twentieth Engineers were on their way. Our convoy consisted of eight dump trucks loaded with cement blocks, sand, and cement; five five-ton flatbeds carrying two-by-ten and two-by-four wood siding; one-by-twelve flooring planks; corrugated metal roof decking; a ten-ton flatbed with a D9 Cat, another with a front loader; and the 3/4 was loaded to the hilt with nails, screen wire, trim wood, and hinges.

Patrols 1, 2, and 4 drove and rode in the various trucks. Third Patrol, our patrol, rode in Fair's dump. We were armed to the teeth. We had cases of grenades, cases of M79 rounds, cases of M16 rounds, six ammo boxes of .50-caliber rounds, and six ammo boxes of M60 rounds. Fair was driving with Borger up front. I stood behind the transom with my trusty .50-caliber at the ready. Bomarito and Cummins perched on one side, Miller and Murphy on the other. Underhill was driving the 3/4 with Smitty riding shotgun. Wooly Bully was about six miles south of Kontum on QL-14. The twenty-mile trip would take just short of an hour. As we passed the three hooches on the minesweep route, Fair slowed so I could throw handfuls of candy to my kids.

As we approached our infamous bridge, the events with the road grader passed through my mind, almost a roaring nightmare, the tracers whizzing overhead, the clang of the bullets hitting the side of the truck.

"Aaay, Matty!" bellowed Bomarito over the din of the trucks' exhaust. "Remember this place?"

"How could I forget?" I shot back. As I looked around, I could see the fear and anxiety in the faces of my comrades, each with his weapon at the ready for the first sign of trouble.

Clump, clump, clump, clump called the tires of the dump as we passed over the wooden timbers of the bridge. Five more miles and we were there.

The perimeter wire of the compound sat within ten feet of the road. The entrance to the camp sat some fifty feet from the road and had a ranchlike facade. There was a column rising about twelve feet high on each side of the road with a wide cross member bridging the two columns. In the center of the bridge sat a rather large full-color plywood Tasmanian devil. As we entered the gateway, the familiar lyrics met us at full volume: "Hattie told Mattie about a thing she saw, had two big horns and a wooly jaw."

"Yup, this is it, 'Wooly Bully,'" snickered Miller.

"We're here!" called Borger with his head protruding above the dump bed.

"Here's your new home." The Caddy came to a stop next to a long row of wall tents each sitting on its own wooden platform. There were eight beds per tent. The heads faced the four points of the compass. Naturally, Underhill and I bunked next to each other. The heads of our beds faced north.

At 0600 hours the next morning, we were awakened abruptly by gunfire.

"Everybody up!" yelled Borger. "Sounds like a firefight."

"Yeah, and it's close, real close!" moaned Underhill, shoving a shell into his 79.

"Oh! Oh!" gasped Murphy as he threw open the rear flaps of the tent.

To our surprise, two feet behind the tent sat a barbed wire fence four single strands high (about four and a half feet tall). Just beyond the wire at the front of the compound sat a large French-era stucco and stone building. There on the back porch were five or six ARVN soldiers taking target practice, the hot lead passing along the side of our tents toward targets located near the rear of the compound.

"Aaaaah, I hope these guys aim good. We're almost in the line of fire!"

"Yeah, yeah, and look at that! What is that? The Hotel California? They got that? They got that? And we got tents?" stammered Underhill, pointing to the stone building.

The whole north side of the compound was guarded only by the four strands of barbed wire and an ARVN CQ (MP) outpost.

After breakfast, the first hooch started goin' up. Crews from the 584th, 102nd, and our own Company B of the 20th all worked on the first building. By the end of the day, the building was ready to receive its metal roof. On day 2, we were on our own. The 584th started the foundation of the next building while the 102nd had other assignments.

"Matty," called Borger, "HQ didn't send any 8d nails for the roof. How about checking supply, see if they've got anything we can use."

"Ten to four, on my way." After a thorough search of supply, I found one box of very rusty 8d nails.

"Sorry, boss, this is all there is," I said, dropping the box at Borger's feet.

"I guess it'll have to do till we get more." Borger sighed.

Underhill and I started on the first sheet. *Bang, bang.* "Yeow!" I yelled as the nail I was driving snapped, allowing the hammer to flatten my thumb. Underhill and Borger yelled almost simultaneously as they experienced the same problem. Nail after nail snapped.

"How's your thumb?" Borger queried as we finished the roof right at quitting time.

"Not good, not good. The whole bottom is torn loose at the first joint. I think you can see the bone."

"Yeah, my thumb's pretty bad too."

"Wow! What did you do to your thumb?" exclaimed Cummins. "Is that all bandage? Your thumb is ten times bigger than the other one."

"Yeah, I had to wrap it up like that to keep the hammer from doin' any more damage. Nails were so rusty, every other one snapped."

The heat of the day kept us out of the wall tents until after the sunset. As evening approached, a cool mountain breeze greeted our new Central Highland home. By morning, a light blanket was needed. However, sleep did not come easy as my thumb continued to throb most of the night. Sleep finally came just before dawn only to be awakened by the pungent odor of burning mahogany.

"Ugh! What is that smell?" complained Murphy.

"Aww, it's just the Montagnards across the road cooking with mahogany," replied Cummins.

The following day saw another hooch go up. The convoy from Pleiku came through at about 1000 hours, stopping long enough to drop off a couple of boxes of 8d galvanized nails.

"Thank you! Thank you! Thank you!" we all moaned, kneeling and bowing at the truck driver's feet.

"You guys must really be sufferin' from the heat," he replied, shaking his head and walking away. "All that for a couple of boxes of nails. Wonder what they would have done if I brought them a girl?"

I can tell you one thing; the thumb on my left hand really appreciated the new nails as he wouldn't have to be kissed by the hammer with every other nail.

"Well, boss, how we doin'? Today's Friday, we got five hooches up in five days."

"Doin' good, Matty, doin' good," replied Borger. "HQ figured one hooch every two days. So we're way ahead of schedule."

"Yeah, well, I'm glad it's Friday. Got two whole days to heal up. My thumb is still in bad shape."

"Hey, look who it is." Underhill laughed as Sergeant Smith sauntered up to our tent.

"Hey, guys, how ya doin'? Got any hooches up?" called Smitty as he approached.

"Yep, yep, yep. Got five up," Borger came back. "What are you doin' way up here anyway?"

"Well, I am your platoon sergeant. Thought I'd catch the afternoon convoy, see how you're doin' if you needed anything, AND there is a show here tonight."

"Oh yeah, what kinda show?"

"It's a Korean band. They have a floor show, the whole nine yards, and you know the shows in the field are much more interesting than the ones at base camp."

"You mean they actually have bands performing here?"

"Oh yeah," came back Miller. "Have one probably every other month or so."

"You were up in Ben Het when they had one in Pleiku," snorted Smitty.

"What's the difference between a show in base camp and a show in the field?" I asked.

"You'll see, you'll see." Bomarito smiled. "Um on! Um on!" stammered Bomarito, half choking after wolfing down half a plate of mashed potatoes.

"Let's go! Let's go! Let's go! I want to get a front-row seat! This show is going to be a hot one!"

"Go on, go on, just save us a seat," Borger quietly replied. Out the door Bomarito went, practically throwing his tray at the KP attendant.

After finishing supper, the rest of the patrol, including Smitty, wandered over to the stage, which consisted of four flatbed trailers parked side by side, creating a thirty-two-by-forty-foot stage. A large crowd had already gathered.

"Over here, over here," called Bomarito, waving frantically. "Over here!"

We made our way to the front of the crowd to find Mad Dog Bomarito viciously guarding nine front-row spaces.

As the shadows lengthened and the sun set, the crowd continued to grow. Deuce and a halves filled with GIs arrived from Kontum, Dak To, and the surrounding camps.

"Hellllo! Vietnam!" came a voice over the PA system. "Are ya ready for the best damn show of your life?"

The crowd erupted.

"OK! OK! Good! Let the show begin!"

"Born to Be Wild" by Steppenwolf blared over the speakers. The crowd went wild as a makeshift curtain at the rear of the stage began to rise, revealing a Korean band playing the gig. "Born to Be Wild" was followed by "Proud Mary" by Creedence Clearwater Revival at which time everyone that had 'em lit up. Next up was "White Room" by Cream. By now, the smoke from the MJ hung low in the cool night air, giving almost everyone a contact high. "Hello, I Love You" by the Doors was next.

As the band began to play, six very pretty, very curvy girls came out and began to dance. The crowd went bonkers. At the beginning of the second chorus, the girls threw the audience a kiss along with their tops. The crowd exploded, pushing toward the front, pinning our group against the trailer stage. The show lasted about an hour, leaving GIs high, drunk, or exhausted in its wake.

"Well, Underdog, Matty, what do ya think about our shows out in the field?" asked Miller, grinning sheepishly.

"I'm not sure," I replied, still in shock with my head pounding from all the smoke.

Morning came much too early. I was awakened by a *crack, crack, crack*. Each crack pierced the center of my brain. "What, what is that?" I groaned, sitting up.

"Oh, that's just the ARVNs and their morning target practice," replied Cummins. "Not used to the party life, huh?"

"Not really," I moaned. "I think it was all that MJ smoke floating around." By midmorning, my head had cleared and work was moving forward as usual.

Wednesday, Day 8 on the Job

"Well, Borg, looks like we're doin' real good. This one'll be done in an hour."

"Yeah, its lunchtime, but I would really like to get this one done before we get chow."

"Yeah, the rest of the guys have already gone to lunch."

"I'm just going to sit here and take five and enjoy the sunshine," replied Borger.

The next few minutes, Borger and I just lay on the metal roof, soaking up the sunshine.

Borger noticed him first.

"Look over there, the fence at the asphalt plant," he whispered. A local Vietnamese fellow had backed up to the fence surrounding the asphalt plant. He then paced the distance from that fence to the four-strand fence adjacent to the ARVN camp. He paced it not once, but twice.

"Where's your weapon?" Borger whispered.

"Hangin' at the rear edge on the back side," I replied. Slowly we crawled to the back side of the roof, out of the fellow's sight line.

"I'll go down and get the drop on him. You cover me. If anything goes wrong, you plunk him with your 79," whispered Borger as he climbed down.

I crawled back to the ridge and peeked over my M79 at the ready. *Wow,* I thought. *This guy is pacing the distance for a third time.*

"Hands up! Down on the ground!" yelled Borger.

His M16 leveled on the guy. The guy turned, saw Borger's 16 leveled at his head. The color on his face drained. He quickly threw up his hands and fell facedown in the dirt. He began to sob and plead in Vietnamese. The Vietnamese CQs (MPs) hauled him off still sobbing and babbling in Vietnamese. The day went on without any further interruptions.

As the day closed and we were getting ready to settle in for the evening, a chunky PFC came to our tent.

"I'm looking for Specialists Borger and Mattatall."

"Yeah, that's us!" came back Borger.

"The CO, Major Moore, wants to see you two at HQ pronto."

I wonder what he wants, I thought as we trotted over to HQ.

"CO's office is in that hooch. Go right on in, he's expectin' ya," panted the PFC, totally out of breath. Borger and I came to attention as we entered the CO's office.

"Specialists Borger and Mattatall, reporting as ordered," snapped Borger, the both of us saluting.

"Wellllll . . .," sighed the major. "Looks like we got ourselves a couple of bona fide heroes. The fellow you popped this morning turned out to be an NVA operative, explosive expert. The plan was to take out the asphalt plant at the next new moon. I just wanted to thank you guys personally for a job well-done, not to mention the fantastic job you are doing on the hooches."

"Thank you, sir," we replied, saluting.

"That'll be all." the major grinned, returning our salute.

"Hey, Matty, hey, Borg, ya know what?" came the all-too-familiar voice.

"No, Miller, what?" we replied simultaneously.

"You're all right."

"What are you doing way out here?" came back Borger, trying to shut Miller up.

"Ahhh, just bored, too hot! Supper didn't agree with me too well."

"Hah!" I gasped. "Charlie, you ate everything but the table. I mean, six baked potatoes, half a roast, and a gallon of gravy. No wonder you feel funny."

"Awww, come on, I didn't eat that much."

"Well, ya sure didn't miss it by a lot," snickered Borger.

Sleep came easily as the cool evening breeze wafted through the tent. The days were long and hot. The work was hard. At 0418 hours, the camp siren began to blow, calling the camp to full alert. Flares shot up from every tower, illuminating the whole camp. Everyone scampered into their clothes, grabbed their weapons, and were out the door. Our area of responsibility was the section of four string wires right behind our tent.

"OK, guys," called Borger. "Keep your heads, stay together. Keep quiet, just wait for instructions."

Time crawled on. The silence, the anticipation were all but unbearable, just waiting for the other shoe to fall. Ever so slowly, daylight began to break. Soon, the sun peered over the jungle canopy. Still no word, and an hour later, the all clear sounded.

Three miles to our north, the river bridge just south of Kontum had been hit. Sappers took out supports, dropping the center section into the river. At 0837 hours, a deuce and a half pulled into the compound and came to a halt just across from our hooch project. Soon, a crowd gathered around the rear of the truck.

"What do ya think is going on over there?"

"I'm goin' to go see," snorted Miller.

After pushing his way to the front of the crowd, Miller came running back almost immediately.

Framing Hooch at Wooly Bully

Completed Hooches at Wooly Bully

"Ya gotta go see! Ya got go see!" panted Miller breathlessly. "They got dead gooks in the truck! One of 'em got his head caved in. Got a 79 round right in the forehead!"

"OK, OK, let's go look. We'll never get anything done until we do," Borger replied, rather disgusted. As we approached, the crowd had started to thin.

The rear of the truck revealed seven dead VC, one having taken an M79 round right in the center of his forehead. The round hadn't traveled the needed ninety feet to arm itself before hitting its target, so instead of detonating upon impact, blowing the fellow's head apart, the round simply left a two-inch-diameter dimple about one and a half inches deep. Nevertheless, the results were still the same, one less Vietcong trying to kill us. Members of the Fourth Infantry Division and the 102nd Engineers engaged these unfortunate fellows just after they had blown the Kontum bridge. The engagement was short with the demise of that VC patrol.

The next ten days passed quickly with a building a day going up.

"Well, boss, looks like this is it. Hooch number 15 bitin' the dust."

"Yep, today will be it." Walker grinned. "Tomorrow I be sleepin' in my own bed."

"Awwww, damn," came back Cummins. "I was just getting used to that hot tent. Oh well, duty calls."

The next morning, we waved with a tear in our eye as the green Cadillac pulled through the gate and left Wooly Bully in the dust, never to return. As we pulled into the motor pool at B Company Twentieth, Sergeant Smith was waiting along with our CO. As the truck came to a halt, the patrol quickly exited, lining up, facing the CO.

"At ease, men. Just here to congratulate you on a job well-done and for your exemplary conduct as representatives of Co. B. I'd give you all a three-day pass, but there's no place for you to go. So next three days, NO DUTY at all. Dismissed!"

Firebase Julie

"Everybody up! Off and on! We're going out."

"Where to now?" moaned Miller.

"Let's go!" barked Smitty.

We hurriedly dressed, ran through the mess hall, and were heading north by 0830 hours.

"I hate this place, either the dust is a foot deep or we're up to our necks in mud, wet all the time," grumbled Bomarito.

We soon caught up with the minesweep team that had taken over our five-mile sector, that same old tank escorting them.

"Hey, there's our buddy, that SOB. Where's my M79?" stammered Underhill as we passed our infamous tank.

I was in the second truck along with Fair, Underhill, Bomarito, Borger, and the rest of the patrol. We were on our way north to a firebase located just northeast of Dak To. About six miles north of the city of Kontum, QL-14 is intersected by Route 512 at the village of Tan Canh, also known as Kon Hojan. Route 512 runs west through the CIDG camps of Dak To and Ben Het, then continues toward the tricounty border.

The firebase lay on a large flattop hill near the base of Dak To Mountain. The Dak To airstrip in the valley below made quite a majestic view. Dak To is ten miles northeast of the infamous Ben Het, ten miles northwest of Kontum and thirty-five miles northwest of Pleiku. As we approached, there was a small river crossing the road right near the entrance. A concrete bridge had been constructed across the river; however, the road had never been built to the bridge. A temporary steel bridge called a Bailey bridge had been erected while the new bridge was being built. By the looks of things, both bridges had been there for some years. There was a MACV platoon permanently camped on the bridge as security. The platoon consisted of one American Special Forces sergeant and thirty-two Vietnamese soldiers.

As we pulled into the compound, I noticed several large light-gray odd-looking tanks.

"Hey, Borger, those sure are funny-looking tanks."

"Ahhh, they're not tanks, just 155 motorized guns. They don't have any armor, just gray sheet metal," replied Smitty.

"Even though they look like tanks, the bodies are made of sheet metal rather than armored steel. Our first mission is to check into Hotel Julie. Borger, you check with the first sergeant, and I'll report to the CO. Get the guys a place to stay," instructed Smitty.

"Smoke 'em if ya got 'em!" yelled Borger as he went off looking for the first sergeant.

Ten minutes later, he was back.

"Grab your gear, I got you all the best rooms in the house, follow me." Borger led us to a row of low-rise bunkers.

"How the heck are we supposed to fit in them things, they ain't but three feet tall, I ain't never goin' to fit in one of them." Miller just kept going on and on and on. The rooms were constructed thusly: They started with an army cot. Sandbags were piled up along the two sides of the cot and across one end to the height of the cot. Half sections of steel culvert were then placed on the sandbags, forming a Quonset hut-type ceiling. Five layers of sandbags were then placed on top, forming a snug personal bunker. The ceiling height from the top of the bunk was thirty-six inches. If you were to rise up quickly in the night, you would most assuredly be kissed on the forehead by the steel ceiling.

1205 Hours, First Night

Kaboom! went gun number 1, then 2, and 3. As 4 went off, I finally awoke. My first thought was incoming. I rose up, and sure enough, *kabong!* went my head, stars flying and ears ringing. It took me a whole week to keep from sitting straight up in bed every time one of those big guns went off. I had to live down my new name, Lumpy, from all the knots on my head.

The bunkers were in rows with the open ends facing one another. A four-foot-tall sandbag revetment wall ran between the facing open ends. There were thirty-six inches between the open end of our bunker and the wall. It would take virtually a direct hit for any shrapnel to get to us. My bunker was at the end of the row, so I had an extra forty-eight-inch-tall wall down the open side.

The firebase was in the early stages of construction. The guns had been placed a little prematurely as to give fire support to the Ben Het area, Dak To, and to the firebase itself. As I said, the firebase was located on a flattop hill. To the north and the east, the hill dropped off in an almost clifflike decline into a vast, very deep valley. To the south, the terrain dropped abruptly to the road, the river, and into Dak To valley. To the west, the terrain rose quite rapidly up Dak To Mountain. The standard seven strands of concertina wire along with tanglefoot protected this elevation. At the outer edge of the wire, a ten-inch dirt berm had been built for additional protection. The east and south also were protected by a seven-strand system. The Fourteenth Armored Cavalry, however, manned the north elevation (our old friends with the tank). They were also there for security. Their section of the perimeter was secured by four strands of barbed wire, not the standard seven rows of three-strand concertina, just a four-strand cattle fence.

Tanglefoot is a term used for the wire that is placed between the three rows of concertina wire. A single strand of barbed wire staked six inches above the ground in a checkerboard pattern, with each square being about eighteen inches by eighteen inches.

Our mission was to erect guard towers around the perimeter. The 584th Engineer Company sent up a twenty-ton wheeled crane and a pile driver to set the poles, ten-inch-diameter telephone poles about twenty feet long. The crew had stopped in Kontum on their way up and was soused by the time they arrived at the site.

"Matty, you see those guys? They're so drunk they can barely walk. What are they going to do?"

"I don't know, but if the CO sees them, it will be an Article 15 for sure," I replied.

The twenty-ton crane was soon in place, and the first pole began to sink into the earth.

"Borger, look at that pole, it's at least a foot out of plumb," I suggested. As the driver continued to sink the pole, the angle of the degree became more severe. *Kachunk*, *kachunk*, and *kachunk!* The steam-driven driver continued.

"Stop! stop! stop!" shouted Borger, trying to scream above the noise of the driver.

"Whadya yaaa want?" asked one of the driver operators, wavering at the controls.

"You're settin' the pole cockeyed."

"Ahhhh, yaw don't know what the hell ya talking about. That pole's as straight as an arrow. You guys from the Twentieth ain't shit."

"I'm telling ya, the pole is cockeyed, ya gotta set it over."

"We ain't doin' nothing of the kind. These poles are goin' in, so get out of the way."

They set the six poles for the first tower and left. They ended up setting the rest of the poles to match the first. They were all leaning forward. Borger went to Sergeant Smith for direction. He had me cut the pole tops off and level the tower platform. When it was completed, the tower looked as if it were leaning forward. Colonel Kratz, 937th CO, flew out to check our progress. When he saw the tower, his first response was "What is this, the Tower of Pisa? Who built this thing?"

Underhill and I confessed. He then went on threatening to court-martial the both of us. Smitty came to our defense.

"Colonel Kratz, sir, calm down. The crew from the 584th was drunk when they arrived and set all the poles out of plumb. The guys tried to stop them, but the operators continued on."

Colonel Kratz apologized and told us to continue. The next day, a new pile-driving crew arrived and set the rest of the poles, and they were all perfect.

The day was Sunday, a beautiful fall day in Illinois, just another day in Vietnam, although not too hot. Sunday was the only day we didn't have to work. Miller, a few others, and I were sitting at a picnic table we had built, just lounging around. Several of the guys were getting haircuts. Every Sunday, a barber from one of the villages would come onto the compound and cut hair for one hundred piastres per head.

A piastre was a Vietnamese dollar. One hundred eighteen piastres equaled one dollar MPC (Military Payment Certificate). MPC, as it was called, was the type of currency that was used in Vietnam. American greenbacks were totally outlawed as the VC could use it on an international market to buy arms. MPC came in twenty-, ten-, five-, and one-dollar denominations. Anyone caught passing greenbacks to a local national was subject to imprisonment. The rules were to even exchange MPC to piastres for any exchanges with local nationals. However, one could always get a much-better deal using MPC. The hooch girls were always paid in MPC. They would just do a better job. Hooch girls were the housekeepers, cleaned the hooch, washed our clothes, but nothing else. They were definitely not ladies of the night. Sin City was reserved for that activity.

"Hey, Bomarito, you know what?"

"No, what, Miller?"

"You're all right," replied Miller.

"Hey, Bomarito, you know what?"

"Get the hell away from me, Miller, I told you before about that stupid stuff. Do it again, and I'll kill you an inch at a time, GOT ME?"

"Heyyyyyy, I was just tryin' to make conversation, man."

"Well, go make it somewhere else."

Holy—! An armored personal carrier ran right over our picnic table. Guys jumped for their lives.

"Ugggghh, what happened?" I asked, crawling out from a pile of scrap wood. "Is everyone OK?"

"What the hell was that?" groaned Underhill.

"APC," moaned Borger from under a nearby hooch.

"Them SOBs, them SOBs, them SOBs. I'm gonna kill 'em, kill all of 'em right now. I'm gonna kill 'em!" Bomarito screamed as he ran toward his bunker.

Moments later, he came back with his flak jacket, grenades, Thompson .45, flares, twenty bandoliers of ammo. "I'm gonna KILL 'EM!" he shouted as he ran past our group toward the Fourteenth Armored Cavalry area.

"We'd better stop him, there are too many of them. Come on, let's get him!" I shouted.

The four of us barely caught him as he neared the Fourteenth's area. Borger dropped him with a flying tackle.

"Lemme go! Lemme go! I'm gonna kill those sorry sacks of shit."

All four of us piled on, trying to hold Bomarito down. The ARVNs (what that means I don't know, maybe the Vietnamese word for *chicken*, who knows) at first were amused at the antics of these GIs, but at some point, they realized Bomarito was serious; probably when the interpreter told them. Instantly, they locked and loaded their M14s.

"Let's get him out of here, NOW!" shouted Borger.

Bomarito had since broken down and was crying like a baby. This was not the first time the Fourteenth had gone astray and driven all over the compound. The next morning, we installed a single row of concertina wire down each side of the road, hoping it would keep the pecan-tan boys from the west on the road.

Two days later, 0800 hours, I just finished guard duty, was heading back to the bunker, dead tired, had to change clothes and go to tower building. *Boom! Boom, boom, boom!* Incoming. Four shells hit the Fourteenth's area. I increased my pace toward the bunker. *Clankaty clank, clankaty clank.* Here came an APC hell-bent for election right down the road. (Probably the same one that ran over us.) Just as he passed me, his left track hooked the concertina. The wire began to stretch like a rubber band.

"OHHHHH NOOOOOOO!" was all I could get out of my mouth. The wire came loose and began to retreat. I didn't even have a chance to move a muscle. The retreating wire hit me like a freight train. As it recoiled, I was turned end over end, finally coming to a stop, my feet straight over my head, arms extended, totally encased in an eight-foot-tall ball of wire. Underhill was the first on the scene.

"Oh, man, are you dead?"

"DO I LOOK DEAD?" I bellowed at the top of my lungs.

The whole compound came out and had a good laugh, finding out that I wasn't seriously injured. Two and a half hours later, I was a free man again. The medic gave me a clean bill of health. Only four puncture wounds, one in each arm and two in one leg.

"Listen up. Listen up. There will be a crane coming in this morning. It will drop two diaphragms, five hundred gallons each, one diesel fuel, one gasoline. The drop will be just outside the wire on the southwest corner of the base. I want, and I repeat, I want no one near that area. When the crane comes in, it will blow dust, gravel, and rock everywhere any of which could cause serious injury or even death."

A crane is a helicopter looking a lot like a giant spider. It has a short nose, a very long narrow fuselage, with the wheel gear protruding from the sides of the aircraft at the end of very long arms. The crane had the capacity to carry extremely heavy loads, two deuce and a half trucks at the same time. One instance, a Chinook helicopter and a deuce and a half at the same time.

"Matty, why don't you and I go up on the new platform and watch that thing come in? We will be high enough not to be killed by the flying debris."

"I don't know, Underhill. You know what Smitty said."

"Yeah, but you know we could get some really neat pictures."

"Yeah, you might have a point there, Underhill. I have never seen a crane up close and personal."

1005 Hours

The drone of the crane could be heard as it cleared the tree line. Underhill and I were up on that platform like two raccoons. As the crane approached, we were greeted by a hundred-mile-an-hour wind. The wash of twenty-five-foot propellers created a sandstorm so dense you couldn't see your hand in front of you.

"Are you OK?" Underhill yelled.

"Yeah, but I'm being sandblasted and can barely hang on!" I screamed back.

The wind was so strong it was virtually blowing us off the platform. We were both hanging on by the tips of our fingers, feet straight out behind us blowing like flags at full mast. The crane finally dropped the diaphragms and was on its way. As the chopper flew off, we could see the crewmen laughing and pointing at us.

Underhill looked as if he had been dunked in a lobster pot. He was beet red on every part of his body that wasn't covered. My back had a very severe burning sensation.

"Well, I guess you two will always have to learn the hard way," replied Smitty, looking at us in disgust. "Mattatall, you don't look too bad, but you're half black anyway. Underhill! You had better go and hide. If the CO sees you, it will be an Article 15." (An Article 15 is a form of court-martial, usually two weeks confinement to base, but could be much more severe, loss of a grade and a severe fine.)

Smitty just walked away, shaking his head. The next few days were pure hell as the sand had rubbed away the top layers of skin. The burning continued night and day, keeping us awake at night, and the sun tortured our tender skin unmercifully during the day.

The next few days passed rather uneventfully. The heat of the day became more intense as each day passed. The towers, one by one, were completed. The place finally was starting to look like an army base. As the weekend approached, we were all thinking about Sunday and how we could just take it easy. Saturday evening came, and the workweek was over. Everyone collapsed in a heap. The days were at their hottest as it was just before monsoon season. The temperature was hitting the very high nineties. Borger and I had constructed a makeshift shower: four poles, two half tents, a five-gallon bucket, and a rope. Worked great. He and I could have become millionaires if we could have only charged two dollars per head. The line to the shower was long, and the MPs had to keep the crowds at bay. Everyone had finished their showers as dusk was settling. The sun had gone down as a huge apricot ball, coloring the sky with hues of orange, pink, and purple. The rain forest was truly a beautiful place.

2333 Hours

Woosh, woosh, woosh! The sound of flares going up seemed to wake everyone. *Kaboom!* Gun number 1 went off. This time it seemed excessively loud. The base siren began to wail; at first, it seemed like a low moan, then turned into a high-pitched shrill.

"This is it. Everybody, up. Get dressed. Go to your stations. Gooks in the wire." Smitty's voice seemed rather calm for what was going on.

Seconds later, our patrol and platoon were positioned behind the low berm, fifty feet behind the first row of concertina.

"Underdog! Look at that! What did that? There is a twenty-foot hole in the main berm. Look at the jungle out past the wire. All the trees are knocked down."

"I don't know, Matty, must have been something big."

"Beehive round, came out of the 155. See this arrow in my hat? Shell has five thousand of 'em in it. It is used only for close combat."

Bomarito showed us a small metal arrow that looked like a hat pin. It had an arrowhead and feathers. The whole thing was an inch long, all metal.

"The head and feathers make it fly straight," Bomarito continued.

Ten to twenty flares went airborne, revealing men in the wire. They were between the sixth and seventh rows of concertina. Some were dressed in uniforms to include pith helmets. Some were dressed in loincloths only.

"VC and NVA regulars both," called Smitty in a low voice. "Open fire at will. Matty, you and Underdog lay those M79s right on top of 'em. Borger, Fair, Miller, take the left side. Bomarito, Cummings, Murphy, take the right side."

About then, all hell broke loose. Everyone just started firing. I was so scared; I don't think I could hit the side of a barn. Bullets whizzed over our heads. The high-pitched sound reminded me of mad hornets. Air support was called in. First, Huey gunships from Kontum arrived, spraying the enemy with M60 machine guns and rocket fire. As the rockets exploded, the illumination revealed many, many more soldiers behind the wire. One Huey took a direct hit, causing it to leave for home immediately, smoking violently from the engine compartment. The fight went on for what seemed like hours. The big guns were useless at this close range. The beehive rounds would just destroy the wire.

As quick as they came, the Hueys were gone.

"Fall back, fall back to your bunkers!" came the shrill command of our platoon leader, a young lieutenant that had arrived that morning. He hadn't even been introduced to us.

"Fall back, fall back. Do as Lieutenant Grimes says," Smitty snapped.

"You don't have to tell us twice, Sarge. We're outta here."

As we backed our way toward the bunkers, we could hear the drone of an airplane engine coming up quickly.

"Borger, what is that?"

"Puff, Puff the Magic Dragon," Borger said softly.

"Quickly, quickly, everyone in their bunkers! Don't come out till I give the signal!" For the first time, Smitty seemed to be excited.

As the plane approached, I could hear the whirl of the twin miniguns mounted in the cargo area of a WWII-era C-47 cargo plane. The tracer rounds left a steady red glow on the revetment wall at the end of my bunker. Within minutes, it was all over. Puff had annihilated and scattered the enemy.

"All clear, come on out," called Smitty. "Form up by patrols. Patrol leaders, report."

When it was all said and done, not one member of our platoon had been killed. Several had minor wounds but were treated and released. Everyone was put on guard duty for the rest of the night. Three of the 155s were moved to the north end of the camp. They positioned themselves between the ARVNs and us. Several Huey gunships patrolled the wire, making sure no one removed the dead during the night.

First Light

The west side of the camp truly looked like a battlefield. The ground was still smoking from the spent rounds. There were bodies hanging in the wire. There were huge sections of wire blown away, either by our rockets or bandolier torpedoes used by the enemy.

The next job was to remove the bodies and repair the wire. The local nationals were used to collect the bodies, bringing them to the command center where they were checked for any covert information they might have had in their possession. They were then flown back to Pleiku. GIs were assigned to supervise the work, making sure the local nationals removed nothing from the bodies.

The bodies removed and the wire repaired, we settled back for the rest of Sunday afternoon.

"Anyone in the mood for a haircut or a shave? How about a shampoo?" snickered Smitty.

"That sounds good to me."

"Miller, you ain't had a shampoo in ten years."

"Have too, Bomarito. I get a shave, haircut, and a shampoo every two weeks, and today's my day."

"Well, Miller, my boy, you just follow me. Have I got a special treat for you." Smitty could barely contain himself. "The rest of you guys might as well come along too, you'll enjoy this."

Smitty marched us right up to the row of the dead. "Meet your barber."

Smitty grinned as he unzipped the body bag, revealing the face of our barber who every Sunday came and gave us haircuts. By day he was our friend; someone we trusted, even confided in. By night he was our enemy, a Vietcong trying to kill us. This was the war in which we were engaged.

The rest of Sunday and Monday went uneventfully. I had guard duty Monday night. My shift was from 2000 till 1200. Everyone was still quite jittery. At 1200, my shift was over. I was on my way back to the bunker, reflecting on the events of the past few days. As I walked along next to one of the strands of concertina protecting the camp from the road, I bounced my hand along the top of it.

"What the—? Where am I?" Everything looked groggy. Slowly my eyes began to clear. I noticed I was at the bottom of some kind of hole. It wasn't very deep. I could see over the top. I was lying on my back with my feet kinda sticking out. I tried to get up. "Ahhhhh! My leg, my leg!" There was a very sharp pain going through my right leg just below my knee. As I touched the area, the pain increased. I could feel something sticking out the side of my leg. It was a piece of that rotten concertina. *Would I ever learn to stay away from that stuff?* I thought. Not being able to right myself, I started yelling. "Help me, help me!" Soon there were guys all around. They picked me up and carried me to the medic's tent.

"Oh no, not you again. Been playing with the concertina again? Oh shit, you got a big piece stickin' out of your leg, boy. We goin' to have to operate, and there ain't no facilities here for that."

"Pull the thing out, Sarge, it's killing me."

"Nah, you ain't goin' to die, boy. You sure you want me to pull it out? Might cause some permanent damage."

"Pull it out. I can't move my leg with it in there."

"What do you think, Smitty?"

"Don't look that bad to me. Give him a local and pull it out."

Two shots and minutes later, the wire was gone. Felt a lot better. The wire had gone into the muscle of my leg just below the kneecap.

"Matty, what happened?"

"I don't know. I was walking along the wire coming back from guard duty. The next thing I knew I was in that rocket hole."

"There is a big hole in the wire, looks like that incoming shell hit right close to you."

"What shell, Sarge? I didn't hear any incoming."

"Yep, musta been it. Hit so close to you, you became part of the explosion. It might even have hit you. That's why you aren't dead."

"I don't think he is going to be able to walk, Smitty."

"Well, let's see. Try to stand up. Good, now try to take a step or two. He'll be OK, put a Band-Aid on the hole and let's go."

Tuesday Afternoon

The day was hot; the towers were almost finished. Smitty and Borger were already talking about our next job twenty-five miles east of Pleiku, at the Oasis airstrip near Ple-Me. Shortly, two Skyraiders flew over. Down into the canyon on the west side they went, releasing two cylinder-shaped objects. *Boom! Boom!*

"Oh no, here we go again."

"Nah, not to worry."

"What makes you say that, Bomarito?"

"You see how high they were when they released the bombs? They're ARVN pilots. They never get close to the action."

Thirty minutes later, the same two planes flew over again, dropping this time eight bombs in the valley below. A short time later they were back, six bombs apiece this time.

Fellows, this is getting serious, I thought. The camp siren began to wail, alerting the camp to don helmets and flak jackets. (This was the standing rule during an alert: anyone without a helmet was the enemy and should be shot on sight.)

Two F-4 Phantoms flew over so close the afterburners singed the hair on our arms. Down into the valley they went, flying out of sight below the treetops. As they pulled up, two long canisters were released. They seemed to tumble through the air. As the cylinders hit the ground, a path of flame erupted above the treetops as least two hundred feet long.

"Unbelievable," said Underhill with his mouth open.

"Napalm, jellied gasoline. Must be a lot of them down there." Borger was reserved when he explained napalm to us, almost as if he were in a trance.

All afternoon, the F-4s napalmed the valley with heavy smoke hovering over the camp like a cloud. The heat and the stench belched up out of the valley, making me want to run for cover.

"That smell, what is it?"

"Human flesh," replied Borger.

Our friends of a few nights before had regrouped and were coming to finish the job. An alert bird dog spotter plane saw them and called in the big dogs. By 1700 hours, only a scarred landscape remained in the valley below.

Wednesday Morning, First Light

The *chop, chop* of Hueys could be heard along with some now famous music: *na na na, na-naaaa, na na na-na naaa, na na na na naa, na na naaaa.* This was the call sign of the *big red one*, the First Infantry Division. The lead Hueys had huge speakers attached to the skid bars and would play Richard Wagner's "Ride of the Valkyries" at full volume. This seemed to do a very good job of breaking the enemy's spirit. The Hueys dropped load after load of GIs into the valley below. The whole day was spent on a search-and-destroy mission. Chinooks came in, taking out the dead. The operation CO reported to our CO, telling him that a battalion of NVA regulars had been amassing for another assault on our firebase. (NVA—North Vietnamese Army—regulars were highly trained, highly skilled troops from the north, unlike the Vietcong who were more or less ragtag militia.)

That afternoon, a 937th jeep came into the compound, pulled right up to our platoon, and stopped.

"Ahh, what now?" murmured Fair. "Ain't we been through enough?"

"Hey, I'm Specialist Brown. I am looking for Specialist 4 Mattatall."

"Ahhhh, here I am, what do you want?"

"I have been sent to replace you. Your carriage awaits."

"What are you talking about, my carriage awaits?"

"You are hereby summoned to report to group command immediately."

"Well, guys, it's been nice. See ya when the sun shines." With that, I was in the jeep and on my way to group command.

The Leaning Tower at Fire Base Julie

Napalm in the valley below

Sergeant Major Elkey

The seventy-five-minute drive back to the hill took us through the city of Kontum. The city was heavily influenced by the French occupation. Most of the buildings were of the cement and stucco architecture. A large Catholic church lies on the western edge of the city. The church housed an orphanage. A stone wall encompassed the compound. The top of the wall was covered with broken glass, inserted into the wet cement when the wall was built, keeping intruders out. Twenty to thirty neatly dressed children waved as we passed.

The Dak Bla River flowed along the southern edge of the city limits. A large bridge ferried QL-19 traffic across with the river winding through the valley about one hundred feet below. GIs were busily engaged in washing their trucks as we passed. The city of Kontum was clean and peaceful. Kontum is a much smaller city and lacked the hustle and bustle sported by Pleiku. The city lay nestled in the mountains of the Central Highlands surrounded mostly by Montagnard villages and coffee and tea plantations. Several miles east of the city, QL-14 again crossed the river. This bridge, however, was much smaller than the first.

As the jeep moved through the countryside, my mind reflected on the events of the past few weeks. "See the clerk," the driver explained as the jeep came to a halt at group command. As I entered HQ, there on the counter lay a sparkling new uniform including a spit-shined pair of boots.

"Specialist 4 Mattatall, reporting as ordered."

"Yeah, that uniform belongs to you. You'll need to change quickly. You are up for Soldier of the Month. You'll need to be at the mess hall at the 584th in forty-five minutes. You can change in Colonel Cole's office as he is away for the day." The clerk was a pleasant young man, very helpful.

"Soldier of the Month?" I inquired. "What is this all about?"

"You have been selected as Soldier of the Month representing Company B. If you make that, you will then go to group battalion and then on to brigade."

What have I gotten myself into now? I thought as I changed my clothes. My new uniform even had a new name tag sewn on.

The four-to-five-block walk over to the 584th Engineer Company seemed long as my mind rehearsed scenario after scenario as to what would happen. Upon entering the mess hall, there were GIs representing every company in the area sitting in a carded-off area with more arriving by the minute.

As the competition (for lack of a better word) began, we were broken down by groups. The members of each group were interviewed by a panel with a victor being selected.

"Specialist 4 Mattatall, you have been selected to represent the 937th Engineer Group. You will move to that area and await another interview." One of the panel members pointed to an area on the other side of the mess hall.

The group had diminished from eighty GIs to four. The interview, though less in numbers, became more intense. It was here at the battalion level that I came in second. Although a little rejected, I felt pretty good that I had made it as far as battalion.

Specialist 4 Pierce was waiting as I entered HQ. "Well, congratulations. You made it to battalion. Quite an honor."

"Thanks. How do I get back to my unit?"

"Not so fast. Sergeant Major wants to speak at ya. His office is down the hall, second on the right."

"Sergeant Major, you wanted to see me?" I questioned as I entered the sergeant major's office.

"Yes, have a seat," replied the sergeant major, a graying man somewhere in his midfifties. "Specialist! Do you know who I am?"

"Well, yes. You are Sergeant Major Robert W. Elkey," I stammered, somewhat taken aback as his name tag was right there on his desk in front of me.

"No. I mean, do you really know who I am?" he came back.

"I guess not," I replied feeling somewhat distraught.

"I was your brigade sergeant major at C-1-1. I have been in this man's army for almost twenty-eight years. You are, by far, the most diligent and determined recruit I have ever encountered, 96 out of 96 on the induction center testing, 89 out of 100 on the basic training performance test, 440 out of 500 on the five-event basic physical training test, Basic Trainee of the Cycle, 500 club advanced individual physical training, Trainee Leader of the Cycle, AIT, 98 percent proficient leadership school, and finally, 96 percent AIT proficiency test.

"The only two questions you missed on that test were one, how many pieces does an M60 break down to and two, how to tie a bowline knot."

"Beggin' your pardon, Sergeant Major, the instructor had me tie the bowline left-handed. The knot was right. It was just facing the opposite direction, so he discounted it. And as to the first question, I know frontward and backwards. An M60 breaks down into six major components. Why I wrote five, I will never know."

"Did it not seem strange to you that you and that troublemaker, Underhill, were the only Caucasians in your whole company of 205 men that were sent here to Vietnam?"

Indeed! Indeed! I thought as he continued.

"Did it not seem strange that after applying for helicopter school and almost maxing the test that your orders to go never came down?" His voice escalated. "You, my son, are in Vietnam because I convinced the CO to deep six your orders to Fort Rutker, Alabama, and to cut orders, sending you here with me!"

I could feel my face begin to flush. My blood pressure was rising as I sat there quietly, listening to my certain death warrant.

"First, I would like to congratulate you on making it to Battalion Soldier of the Month. Secondly, I have called you here into my office to offer you a wonderful opportunity that will take you out of that hellhole north of Kontum. As you know, Colonel Kratz is the CO of the 937th Engineer Group. He is in need of a jeep driver, chauffer if you will. I am here to offer you that job. A warm bed every night, three hot meals a day, hot showers, an opportunity to be part of the command on Engineer Hill. Sooooo what do ya think?"

A long moment I said nothing as I tried to digest the sergeant major's statements. *He had the gall to tell me he brought me here with him!* In that split second, rage overcame me. I quickly reconsidered and calmed down, not saying a word.

"Well, Sergeant Major," I replied, "if you feel this is in my own best interest I will be glad to accept your offer." *Wow!* I thought. *Why did I say that?* Still reeling inwardly from the sergeant major's confession.

"Good. Good. Your room is in the building across the lot, first room on the left. Any questions?"

"No, Sergeant Major."

"Get settled in. Your first assignment will be to the motor pool in the morning. There you will be issued your jeep. Spec. 4 Pierce will show you the ropes as to radio protocol. Familiarize yourself with routes to Camp Holloway, Camp Enari at Dragon Mountain, home of the Fourth Division with whom we are attached to, also the helipad and the Officers' Club."

The next morning came and went. I, in a brand-new jeep, went first all around Engineer Hill learning the location of every company.

Lunchtime

The 937th ate in the A Company mess hall. Not yet knowing anyone, I found an empty table and began my lunch.

"Hey, I see you decided to stay," came the familiar voice of Specialist 4 Pierce. "Here is the next week's lists of your call signs along with the call signs of the CO, XO, and the two choppers at the pad. I'll be glad to further explain them or answer any questions."

"I think I'll be OK," I answered. "Seems simple enough to me."

"What are ya doin' this afternoon?"

"The sergeant major told me I need to know the way to Camp Enari, Camp Hallowacs [CTA yard], and Camp Holloway. The others are on the way and should be easy enough."

"I have the afternoon off, I would be glad to show you the way if ya don't mind stoppin' in Pleiku for a few minutes," replied Pierce, kinda grinnin'.

"Sounds good to me," I replied with the last mouthful of mashed potatoes going down. Soon, Specialist Pierce and I were through the main gate and on our way.

The Montagnard village was next. It sat just outside the main gate about one hundred yards left of the road. A mile and a half down the road, we passed a small cone-shaped lake surrounded on three sides by a hillside taking on a striking resemblance to a volcano. The west and south portions of the hillside were covered with strange-looking trees almost as if it were an orchard.

"The lake is where all our water comes from. That small building to the left is the water purification plant," offered Pierce.

"What are all the trees on the hillside?"

"Tea plantation owned by a local national. Big, big business in Vietnam along with coffee and rubber plantations."

Camp Schmidt came next, a quarter mile past the lake and almost directly across the road from the tea plantation. Artillery Hill was next at the southwest corner of QL-14 and our access road. As the access road terminated at QL-14, I made a left, and we were on our way to Pleiku. Four miles farther was the hospital followed by the air base. The metropolis of Pleiku followed. As we entered the city, an older man worked diligently, mixing sand and cement, which he would then pour into wooden box-type molds, forming concrete blocks. A vast array of small shops and businesses followed, the largest of which was an open-air market.

"Pull over to that building. The one on the corner around that little square," instructed Pierce. "Just be a couple a minutes."

Pierce slipped out of the jeep and into a shop filled with Chinese lanterns as the jeep came to a stop at the curb. Instantly, we were surrounded by young boys. All had their hand out, ready to accept anything I would be willing to give to them. I had brought a towel as well as my camera. When the boys saw that I had nothing in which to pay homage with, they became rowdy. A streak of lightning shot across the seat, then quickly retreated with the towel, with the camera close behind only to stop as the strap around my wrist became taut. Realizing the situation was becoming serious, I started the jeep and moved away from the curb, dragging two boys along with me as they were trying to dislodge and abscond with my five-gallon spare-gas can mounted on the rear of the jeep. The jeep wobbled violently as I moved along.

Oh boy, what now? I thought, pulling back to the curb several blocks away. To my dismay, I discovered the spare-gas can had been completely disconnected from the rear of the vehicle. The full can evidently was too heavy for the boys to lift from its cradle.

The violent wobbling was caused by the loosening of all five of the lug bolts on the passenger rear wheel. I imagine their plan was to remove the five lug nuts and wait until I pulled away, causing the tire to come off, allowing them to leave with it while we were occupied with a three-wheeled jeep. Needless to say, my future trips to Pleiku were much more guarded.

The next month passed. I felt as if I might have died and gone to heaven. I had my own room, slept in my own bed every night. Food was the best.

"Specialist Mattatall!"

"Yes, sir!"

"I am Lieutenant Colonel Cole, the XO [executive officer] here at the 937th. I have a sick daughter at home. I would like you to take me to the air base tonight. I want to leave at 1200 hours. Line up another troop to go along as additional security."

"Yes, sir. We'll be ready," I replied. *This guy must be nuts,* I thought, *wanting to go through hostile territory as well as Pleiku in the middle of the night.*

During the next several weeks, trip after trip was made in the middle of the night to the air base in order for Colonel Cole to call home on AVES shortwave radio as this was the only means to call the United States at the time.

"Aaa, Matty, I am going flying Sunday morning. Would you like to go?"

"Yes, sir, I would," I replied, trying to withhold the excitement.

"OK! Meet me at the helipad at 0600 Sunday morning. Deal?"

"Deal, sir. I'll be there for sure."

Sunday, 0600 Hours

I could hear the whirl of a chopper being started as I approached. Here sat Colonel Cole in a 52 model, the plastic bubble helicopter resembling the ones seen on the TV show *MASH*.

"Where we goin'?" I asked, entering the right side of the chopper.

"Hunting," replied Colonel Cole.

"Hunting?" I asked. "I think we are a little underarmed to go after the VC."

"Noooo," laughed Colonel Cole. "We're going after big game. A wild boar, I hope. If we see one, we'll shoot him with the M60 mounted on the right strut. Buckle up, we're off."

Colonel Cole handled the bird like a pro. A few minutes later, we were after the catch of the day. The prop wash had startled a large one. The M60 made short work of him as he darted up a hillside. A few minutes later, the boar was filled, dressed, and latched to the chopper strut.

"Would you like to drive home?" queried Colonel Cole.

"You bet," I came back, not being able to contain my enthusiasm.

"OK, in the left side. This switch controls the fuel pump. Engage."

"Check," I replied.

"This one, the ignition switch. Engage."

"Check." Slowly, the props began to turn.

"OK, good, now increase the fuel. The top of the joystick controls the fuel flow. Turn it. Watch the tack, bring 'er up to 2,500 rpms. Good.

Good. Ease the stick forward just a little. Now slowly, very slowly, raise the collector while lightly, very lightly, give 'er a little left rudder."

As I raised the collector handle with my left hand, the craft began to rise and became airborne. As I pressed the rudder pedal, the aircraft began to spin to the left.

"Less rudder! Less rudder!" gasped Colonel Cole as the aircraft made its first complete circle.

Instantly I moved my foot from the pedal. The craft halted its circular motion and slowly began to circle in the other direction.

"OK! OK! Now just a little rudder!" called Colonel Cole, his face flushing, the hair on his arms bristling.

Ever so gingerly, I again took control of the rudder pedal. The craft slowly came to a halt as I applied pressure to the pedal. The craft sat motionless two feet above the ground.

"Good job. Now ease the joystick forward just a little more."

The nose of the aircraft began to tilt toward the ground as I moved the joystick.

"OK! OK!" shouted Colonel Cole. "Good! Good! You're doin' great. Move up on the collector." As I slowly rose the handle up, up went the aircraft.

Soon, the altimeter read 1,200 feet.

"Now back off on the collector till we can hold at 1,200 feet."

My body felt stiff. The spinning had scared me, and trying to do things gradually and in small increments was very difficult.

"Now I want you go get used to holding the stick. Ease it to the right."

As I did, the aircraft tilted kind of sideways to the right.

"Now, to the left."

Same effect to the left.

"Now to the rear."

The nose rose as I pulled back the stick. The craft would literally lean in any direction I would point the stick.

"OK, let's go home."

I mashed the gas and away we went. "Eeeeho!" I shouted, the adrenaline coursing, pulsating through my body.

"OK, bring 'er up to 2,500 feet, about three hundred feet a minute is a good rate of ascent. Good," exclaimed Colonel Cole as the craft leveled off at 2,500 feet. "Try to stay as far from the mountains as possible. Many are higher then 2,500, and if you get too close, you're a lot better target for Charlie to practice on."

We arrived back at the helipad just after 0730 hours. Several cooks from the mess hall were there waiting. Our prize was loaded into the back of a 3/4. Soon we were behind the mess hall. The pig was threaded on a spit, and the barbecue was under way. What a feast!

Every Sunday morning, Colonel Cole and I would go hunting. Sometimes the prize would be a pig, and others it would be a deer, or so I thought. The animals were larger than our whitetail or mule deer. The hair making up their coat was long and very shaggy. They resembled our elk but were only about half the size. Still they were about all the chopper could carry.

"Hey, Matty! The CO wants to see you in his office!" Pierce chirped cheerfully as I entered the HQ.

"You wanted to see me, sir?"

"Yes, Matty, I do. Stand at ease, we're family here."

"Sir," I replied, relaxing a bit.

"At 1700 hours, I will need you to be at the helipad. Major General Dillard is coming in. You need to look sharp. You'll need the two star plaques on the jeep as well as the red flags. We are having a reception for him at the Officers' Club. I'll need you to drop him off there. Go back to HQ and await my call. It will probably be around 2030 to 2300. You will then take him to the VIP quarters. You will need to have him at the mess hall at 0700 hours. After breakfast, it's back to the helipad. Any questions?"

"No, sir."

"Very well. Dismissed."

I've been the CO's driver for about a month now, I thought as I walked to the motor pool, *and already I feel I have known Colonel Kratz my whole life.* He was a kinda tall fellow in his early fifties, had graying hair and a prominent jawline. He possessed the quiet, absolute authority needed for command. However, he also possessed a genuine good nature and was always concerned about the welfare and well-being of those under his command. As he said, "We are family here."

"Hey, Matty!"

My train of thought was broken by the shrill voice of the motor pool sergeant.

"This vehicle will need to be spit shined by 1700 hours!"

"I know. I know, Colonel Kratz has already briefed me."

Man! Some guys just got to show their authority no matter how little they have, I thought as I climbed into my jeep. The afternoon was spent washing, waxing, and polishing. By 1630 hours, that baby looked better than new.

1700 Hours

The UH-1 carrying General Dillard and his aide arrived.

"Specialist 4 Mattatall, reporting. Colonel Kratz sends his regards. I am to escort you to the Officers' Club, sir," I replied, saluting.

"Carry on," replied the general, returning my salute.

The evening seemed unusually quiet as we drove to our destination. It was early November, a nice fall day for the jungle. The daytime highs were in the low eighties with the temperature dropping a few degrees as the sun went down.

I noticed the general eyeing my name tag as we drove along. Finally, after what seemed like several minutes, "Sir, is there something wrong?" I queried.

"No no, your name tag just brings back old memories. Where are you from, soldier?"

"East St. Louis, Illinois, sir, born and raised."

"Hmmmm, do you know a Bill Mattatall?" the general asked.

"Sir, I am Bill Mattatall," I came back.

"No, what I mean," said the general, laughing. "I knew a Bill Mattatall a long time ago. He owned a plumbing supply business. I worked there when I was a young man."

"In East St. Louis?"

"Yeah."

"That was my grandfather."

"Is he still alive?"

"Oh yes," I replied, "and doing very well."

"What a small world we live in."

"Here we are, sir." The jeep came to a stop.

"It was nice to meet you, son, tell your grandfather hello for me."

"Will do, sir."

The evening came and went. The next morning, it was off to the mess hall and then to the helipad. Off General Dillard flew. That was the one and only time I would see him.

Sunday morning as usual, 0600 hours, I'm at the helipad. No Colonel Cole. At 0603 hours, up came the colonel.

"Sir, what's the matter? You look subjected, rejected, and neglected."

"Ohhhh, just got a call from brigade command, General Dillard's aide. Call came in at 0545 hours. Seems the general heard about our Sunday-morning adventure. The general feels we're putting U.S. Army property in imminent danger. He feels that with the recent increase in enemy activity in the area, we are sure to be shot down or captured when we land to claim our prize. Soooo, the orders are no more chopper hunting till further notice."

"Ahhh, that takes the fun out of life."

"Yeah, I know, but really he's right. What we were doing is just a little crazy."

"Yeah, I guess you're right. Well, I guess it's back to the hooch."

"Yep, but I need you to take me to the air base tonight."

"OK, I'll be ready, see ya then."

Our midnight run to the air base to call home went without a hitch.

Some days later, "Specialist Mattatall!" came a voice from the doorway. "I hate to interrupt your English class, but I have an assignment of the utmost importance."

"No problem, sir" I replied, rising from my seat, heading for the door. Colonel Cole's face was slightly drawn with concern.

"There is a VIP here that you will have to take to the air base. I can't tell you who he is, so don't ask. I have to tell you the VC would love to either grab or kill this guy. Your orders are to have him at the air base by 2330 hours. You are not to speak to him unless spoken to. You will need one additional troop for security. I want you to have the canopy on the jeep so no one can see in, and I want you to go like hell. You drive like the wind! Any questions?"

"No, sir!"

"You leave in fifteen minutes. It is now 2230 hours."

"Yes, sir," I replied, running for the door.

The only person I could find available at that late hour was Charles E. Miller (Miller number 2). He had been transferred to the 937th from Company B. He wasn't able to adjust to life in Vietnam and was awaiting orders to be transferred to a noncombatant area.

In seven minutes, the jeep canopy was on and we were ready to go. I really wasn't comfortable taking Miller, knowing his previous antics in Company B. On several occasions he was found, flashlight in hand, his M16 locked and loaded, searching for VC under his hooch. *He'll have to do,* I thought. *There was no time to get someone else out of bed and ready.*

I picked up our guest at the VIP hooch with three minutes to spare, a stout gentleman in his late forties, early fifties. He quickly left the hooch and entered the jeep. He was dressed in OD jungle fatigues and a field jacket; a floppy jungle hat graced his head. He had no name tag and no insignia whatsoever on his uniform.

"Evening . . ."

"Good evening, sir," I replied.

"Been in country long?"

"Five months, sir."

"Made this run at night before?"

"Many times."

"How safe is it?"

"It's not. Tea plantation is always teeming with VC."

"How long's it take?"

"Forty to forty-five minutes."

"Can you make it in thirty?"

"Yep."

"Let's do it."

The drive to the main gate was the usual 15 miles per hour, max. As we cleared the main gate, it was full speed ahead. As we passed the Montagnard village just northwest of the gate, we were already hitting 60. As we approached the water tank (lake), the speedometer read 80 miles per hour. As we approached the tea plantation, the jeep was flat out at 102 miles per hour.

Uh-oh, my mind soared as a single muzzle flash appeared to the left side of the jeep across the road from the plantation. Simultaneously I heard a *plop, plop* sound with a slight rustle in the canopy. I instantly looked in the rearview mirror to see Miller with his mouth open, eyes as big as saucers. Time dragged on with the jeep motor screaming. Soon, Artillery Hill faded in the rearview mirror as we shot through Pleiku. Next stop, the air base.

"Thirty-one minutes," our guest replied, checking his watch as we dropped him off at HQ. "Good job, Specialist, good job." He smiled as he opened the door to the HQ.

"Yeowww! What a trip!" I groaned, looking back at Miller. He spoke not a word; his eyes were still bulging, grunting sounds came from his mouth as he tried to speak. Slowly, his voice returned.

"Look! Look!" he exclaimed. "Behind your head, look at the window."

Eight inches behind my seat, the round from the single muzzle flash had pierced the plastic window of the canopy, leaving a one-inch hole in its wake. A matching hole was also found in the passenger side of the canopy.

"Wow, are we lucky or what?" shouted Miller, his voice in full force. "That bullet passed right between you and me. I saw it, I saw it. It was green!" he shouted excitedly.

The bullet, a tracer, had passed through the jeep between the front and the rear seats, narrowly missing all three of us.

"Wellllll, how we gonna get back?" groaned Miller.

"Same way we came." I grimaced, and we were off.

This place is going to be my undoing, I thought as we once again passed the infamous tea plantation.

The Next Morning, 0700 Hours

"Matty, CO's office, ten minutes," chimed Gibbons as he passed the doorway to my room.

I instantly headed for the door. As I crossed the lot between my hooch and the HQ building, Captain Black, a young helicopter pilot, and Sergeant Major Elkey passed each other as they too crossed the lot from opposite directions. When Sergeant Major Elkey continued walking after passing the captain, Captain Black called to him, "Sergeant Major!"

Sergeant Major Elkey stopped, turned, and returned to the captain's position.

"Sergeant Major, I know I'm only a captain and only a kid, but you will salute me when we pass."

"Yes, sir," replied Sergeant Major Elkey, coming to attention and saluting. Captain Black returned the sergeant major's salute, and they continued on their way.

I followed Sergeant Major Elkey into HQ. He was cursing under his breath every step of the way. He continued into the CO's office just ahead of me.

"Morning, Matty. We need to know how things went last night. Did our friend get to the air base in one piece?" asked Colonel Cole.

"Oh yes, sir, just one small casualty."

"Oh, and what was that?" questioned Colonel Kratz sternly.

"Well, the jeep canopy took a hit, an AK-47 round went through both sides. As we passed the tea plantation at a hundred-plus miles an hour, a sniper fired one shot, a tracer that passed between the front and the back seats."

"What about Miller?" asked Colonel Kratz.

"Really shook him up, but he was OK."

"We need to get him out of here posthaste," replied Colonel Cole. "Sergeant Major, see that orders are cut right away. Send him anywhere away from combat. We don't want him getting out of control or having a breakdown. It's not beyond him to shoot first and then ask questions." Charles E. Miller was not seen or heard from again.

"Sir! Sir!" cried Pierce as he ran into the CO's office out of breath.

"Calm down, Pierce, calm down. What's wrong?"

"It's Captain Black. He took off a few minutes ago in a LOH [Loch]. He's gone down just north of Camp Enari."

"OOOOK. Fred, call General Walker [Major General Glenn D. Walker, commanding] at Enari. Tell him of the situation. The jungle in that area is so dense there is no way we can airlift him out. We'll have to go in on foot."

"I'll head up the mission myself," Colonel Cole said disgustedly. "Matty, I want you to go along to cover my back."

"No problem, sir."

Within an hour, Colonel Cole, me, and eight, eleven Bravos from Enari were in the jungle searching for Black. A spotter plane had located the LOH about four clicks due north of Camp Enari. As the spotter circled, he picked up heavy ground fire. Artillery Hill was notified. A blanket of artillery shells were laid around the LOH's coordinates. After about two hours of hacking and chopping, we came upon the smoldering hulk that was Black's ride. The LOH lay upside down on its rotors, landing struts sticking straight up.

"Look at that," snickered Colonel Cole. "Looks like a big dead cockroach."

"Yeah, it sure does." I laughed.

Just on the other side of the LOH sat Captain Black, puffin' on a Pall Mall. "I was beginning to wonder if anyone was coming to rescue me."

"Soldier, I hope you've got an explanation for all this!" snapped Colonel Cole. "Mind telling me just what happened that caused you to destroy a $350,000 piece of equipment?"

"Well, sir" Captain Black replied sheepishly, "the hydraulics went out, and ah, I couldn't control the aircraft. Down she went."

"Well, just so you know, soldier, just so you know, there will be a full inquiry. And if I find you at fault any way, you will pay for that bird! Understood?"

"Yes, sir!"

Lady Luck shone down on us. The trip back to Enari went without a hitch. I did, however, read in the *Stars & Stripes* about a week later that a patrol out of Camp Enari had encountered a bit of an adventure. The patrol had gone out at night. One of the patrol members heard a rustling in the nearby bush. Upon investigating, he poked his shotgun in the area of the disturbance. A Bengal tiger leaped from the brush, catching the GI by the leg and proceeded to drag him away. The other members of the patrol heard the cries of the less-fortunate fella and came to his rescue. After somewhat of a tug-of-war, the tiger relinquished his prey and retreated into the canopy. A week or so later, the same patrol was in the same section, this time bivouacked for the night (manning an LP, listening post). Again a tiger was involved. This time he picked up a sleeping GI, bag and all, and proceeded to leave camp with the GI in his mouth. Again, his mates came to the rescue, this time yelling and hitting at the animal with their weapons, fearing a shot might hit their comrade. Again, the tiger became frustrated, dropped its prey, and bound off into the jungle. In both scenarios, the victims received multiple bite wounds, none being life threatening.

Same patrol, same area sometime later, a twenty-six-foot python dropped out of the canopy and began to constrict around the point man. Again, his patrolmates to the rescue. The snake was killed. The soldier this time suffered several broken ribs and a broken arm. The area between Camp Enari and Camp Hallowacs was always a wild and dangerous place. The wild animals and VC seemed to live in harmony there.

"Alpha Tango Bravo, come in," the radio in my jeep crackled.

"Alpha Tango Bravo here," I replied.

"Got guests that need a ride, you available? Over."

"Ten-four," I came back. "What's their twenty? Over."

"HQ over."

"Be there in two. Alpha Tango Bravo out."

Moments later, I pulled up in front of the headquarters building to find the CO, Colonel Cole, Lieutenant Sands, and Sergeant Major Elkey waiting.

"Morning, sir," I replied, saluting as Colonel Kratz and the others climbed aboard.

"To the helipad," stressed Colonel Kratz over the clatter of the jeep engine. "We're off to Ben Het, would you like to go along?" asked the colonel as we pulled up to the helipad.

Fred's Chopper

Mr. Adams, a W-3, sat in the pilot's seat, a jovial fellow in his early thirties who'd been in country about a month. Captain Dulak sat on the AC (aircraft commander's) side, also a fun-loving guy in his late twenties, in country a long time, eight to nine months, maybe longer. The chopper, a UH-1, was soon at full rotor speed, and we were off. We followed QL-14 north to Kontum, then turned west, bypassing Dak To. As we circled the compound at Ben Het just prior to landing, the events of just a few months past flooded the memory banks.

"You OK, Matty?" asked Lieutenant Sands.

"Yeah, yeah, why do you ask?"

"Well, you looked like you were kinda in a fog."

"Lieutenant Sands," chimed Colonel Kratz, "he and I, along with Fred, had quite an adventure right here several months ago."

The Huey thudded softly as it landed. I wandered around camp for about an hour, reminiscing while the CO and the others tended to their business.

"Well, Specialist, things are sure different from the last time we were here, aren't they?" Captain Dulak smiled as I approached the chopper.

"Yep, sure are, sir," I replied as he commenced to fill Mr. Adams on the details of our visit to the compound back in early August: the ground fire, the mortars all over the runway, B-40s streaking toward the aircraft.

Soon we were in the air again. Barely five minutes out, the starboard door gun began to chatter. At first, the bursts were short and then became steadier. Soon, both door gunners were at full report.

"Ground fire at the base of that knoll," the radio crackled.

Instantly, the door next to Sergeant Major Elkey flew open.

"What are you doing?" I shouted above the prop wash through the headphones.

"Well, ya see," came back Sergeant Major Elkey calmly, "I have gone down four times in helicopters. I'll jump out of this bird rather than crash again."

The Huey jerked and then kinda skidded sideways. *Whoosh, whoosh.* Two of the chopper's children were on their way from the portside launchers. Two more left the starboard launchers almost simultaneously.

Boom, boom, boom, boom! the mountainside reported. The ground fire ceased. Not a word was spoken as we headed back to group command. As we disembarked the chopper, everyone appeared somewhat pale. While driving back to the HQ, I finally broke the silence.

"Would you have really jumped?"

"You bet."

"Sergeant Major, we had to be about four thousand feet."

"Well, I would have waited till we were a little lower." He smiled.

Whenever we flew, Sergeant Major would always sit next to the starboard side door just behind the jump seat.

Engineer Hill: The Quarry

The bluff at the rock quarry, 5,400 yards to the northwest, was a constant source of harassment to Engineer Hill. The long-abandoned quarry sat on a large hill several hundred feet above our location. The Vietcong would regularly use the quarry as a launching site. Their target was usually the Pleiku Air Force Base. However, Engineer Hill was in the path of any missiles launched at the air base. At times the missile would fall short, resulting in a direct hit on Engineer Hill. Other times an all-out attack would be launched at the hill. A battery of 4.2 mortar launches was maintained in the northwest quadrant of the compound. This battery would respond almost immediately at the first sign of an attack from the quarry.

The evening was warm. The surrounding area from Camp Holloway back to the hill was quiet, actually too quiet. The fireworks began with a single stream of sparks leaving the quarry. Within seconds, the rocket was directly over the hill. The burning solid fuel left a long trail of sparks resembling the tail of a large comet. The missile fell short of the air base, landing harmlessly in a quarter mile of no man's land between the air base and the hill.

The 4.2s went instantly into action. *Pook! Pook! Pook! Pook!* were their reports as the mortars left the launching tubes. By this time, the sky was alive with fire trails. The B-22 rocket left a long white flowing trail of sparks. The eighty-millimeter mortars left a much smaller trail of red sparks. At the sight of the red fire tails, we knew we had problems as the eighty-millimeters didn't have the range to reach the air base.

Immediately, the hill went to full alert as the rounds began falling in the perimeter wire, taking out large sections of wire, weakening the camp's defensive ability. Additional troops were sent to those areas in case a ground assault followed the mortar attacks. The enemy began walking the mortar rounds into the camp, resulting in one of our 4.2 tubes being taken out. The rounds quickly moved past the mortar battery and began falling in an area occupied by the 167th Signal Corps.

The shells fell with such ferocity we were unable to move. Cobra gunships were dispatched from Holloway. The heavy armament of the Cobras quickly dispersed the enemy. Soon, tranquility and peacefulness returned to the area. The gaping hole in the perimeter wire and several damaged bunkers were the only signs that such an attack had taken place.

As morning came, the results of the attack were much more prevalent. The sandbag retaining wall that surrounded the mortar battery was destroyed. The 4.2 was but a memory. The service road around the perimeter that accessed the guard towers lay in waste, pockmarked by large mortar craters. Several small storage buildings in the 167th lay in ruin. A wisp of smoke could be seen here and there. All in all, the camp had sustained minimal damage with casualties only to the one mortar crew and no loss of life.

By early afternoon, the engineer crews had sealed the breach in the perimeter wire. The retaining wall was rebuilt with a new 4.2 mortar tube taking center stage. The road was regraded as if nothing had ever happened.

"Hey, Matty, the CO wants to see you in his office, PRONTO!" came the smiling voice of Specialist 4 Gibbons as he stuck his head through the door of my room. I quickly made myself presentable and scampered over to the CO's office. As I entered the office after knocking, there sat Sergeant Major Elkey, Lieutenant Colonel Cole, Colonel Kratz, Major Turny, and Lieutenant Colonel Simmons, the group chaplain.

"Specialist 4 Mattatall, reporting," I replied, standing at attention.

"At ease, Matty," replied Colonel Kratz, returning my salute. "I have a mission for you and Colonel Simmons. During last night's attack, one of our mortar shells fell short of the quarry, hitting the Montagnard village south of the quarry, killing one of the tribesmen. The chief of the village has been instrumental, informing us of the movements of the enemy in the area around camp. I feel it imperative that we replace the loss of that man. Colonel Simmons, you will take my sincerest apologies to the chief for our part in the loss of his man. Matty, you are to go to supply and secure the items I have listed as well as to the mess supply. Understood?" Colonel Kratz handed me a sheet of paper containing his list.

"Yes, sir!" I replied.

Sarge Matty

Montangard Chief's Home

"Colonel Simmons, I want you to give these things to the chief as a token of the loss of his man and as a partial replacement to the contribution the fallen man would have made to the tribe. The chief will want you to contribute to certain ceremonies. I want you to fully cooperate with his wishes."

"Yes, sir," replied Colonel Simmons.

By 1600 hours, the jeep was fully loaded with the supplies requested by Colonel Kratz. The rear seat was filled almost to the top of the canopy, extending into the cockpit area between the two front seats, leaving just enough room for Colonel Simmons and myself.

The drive from the camp to the village was much shorter than I had imagined. Upon leaving the front gate of Engineer Hill, we proceeded down the blacktop about a quarter of a mile. We then turned north on a dirt road for another half mile. The village was located on the west side of the road at the base of the mountain. All the huts were of standard Montagnard style, basically ten-by-twelve-feet with some being a bit larger at twelve-by-twenty-feet. Each hut was built on stilts or poles with the floor level about four to five feet above the ground. The village consisted of two rows of huts, the first row sitting about fifty feet from the road with the chief's hut sitting in the center forefront at about twenty-five feet from the road. His home was a little larger than the others. It consisted of the standard twelve-by-twenty with an additional room attached to the rear. Entrance to the home was gained via a plank runway extending from the front doorway to the ground.

As we arrived, the chief and two women stood at the roadside in front of his residence. They eagerly greeted the chaplain and myself and escorted us into their home. The floor of the hut was rough-sewn planks roughly eight inches wide, spaced about a half inch apart, allowing the daylight from below to be seen. The walls as well as the roof were thatched. The only furniture in the room were three very crudely made chairs along with several rolled-up sleeping mats in one corner. The attached room was actually a separate hut connected to the main building via a plank runway. The smaller structure appeared to be a preparation room or kitchen. The chief had Colonel Simmons and I sit down. One of the tribesmen entered and acted as an interpreter.

"Please extend to the chief our sincere regret and apology for the most unfortunate incident that took one of your kinsmen from you. My chief, Colonel Kratz, has asked that I and Specialist Mattatall come at this time of sadness. We bring a small token to replace the loss of the productivity of your fellowman. We hope that you will accept these items. All that is in the jeep is yours."

After a brief conversation with the chief, the interpreter replied, "The chief is most grateful for the gifts you have sent. They are much needed as you can see we are a simple people. Tell your chief, Colonel Kratz, that we are most grateful and appreciative of the things you do to help us and the protection you give us, keeping the VC from taking our young men. He asks that you share in a feast of mourning. Will you join us?"

"We would be glad to," replied Colonel Simmons.

The chief nodded and smiled. He barked several commands to the women in the adjoining hut. With a bustle and a clatter, the whole village seemed to come alive. Men could be seen removing the items from the jeep as there was no front door on the hut. Others built a fire in the front yard. Young women brought in quart-size jars filled with clear liquid and set them down very ceremoniously at the side of our chairs. As there were only three chairs, the interpreter had to squat in a ducklike position at the right hand of the chief. The young women brought in four long plastic tubes, which I recognized immediately as hospital surgical tubing used in administering IV drips. The women inserted one end of the tubes into the jars of the clear liquid, then handed the other end to each one of us.

"The chief would like you to join him," interjected the interpreter. "First we drink the jar of rice wine. This clears our minds and bodies of the memory of the awful tragedy that has befallen us."

The chief then smiled and nodded again, putting the free end of the tube in his mouth and began to suck the liquid from the jar.

My mind began to race. *Man! I can't believe this,* I thought. *This tube could have all kinds of diseases inside of it.* I knew just as sure as I was sitting there that those tubes had been rescued from the dump. Every time we had taken a load to the dump, there would be hordes of people there sifting through the trash, gleaning even the smallest item that might be usable. Cardboard was regularly used as siding in the construction of many Vietnamese homes along with soda cans being used as roof shingles or wall covering. The top and bottom of the cans were cut out, and the remaining cylinder was then cut lengthwise, the can flattened, forming a five-to-six-inch square. These were nailed to the side or roof of the home in an overlapping pattern.

My mind continued to race. Fear and trepidation overcame me. What disease would I be putting into my mouth? The words of Colonel Kratz came into mind: “Do whatever the chief asks.” I closed my eyes, put the tube in my mouth, and began to suck.

The liquid hit my throat like a forty-pound porcupine. I dropped the tube, grabbing at my throat with both hands, choking, coughing, and spitting all at the same time. The chief and the interpreter smiled and chuckled, never missing a lick on their own tubes.

“It will get better,” murmured the interpreter around the tube in his mouth. “You got to drink the whole thing.” Again I closed my eyes and began to suck. This time, the porcupine only weighed twenty pounds.

A great clamor erupted in the village. Several of the tribesmen were chasing something in and around the village. Upon catching it, the animal began to yelp and snarl. Through the open doorway, I could see the men carrying a medium-size dog across the front yard of the chief’s home. To my horror, the dog was thrown into the fire. He instantly tried to escape. The men blocked his retreat using long poles. The stench of burning fur filled my nostrils. With my eyes wide open, I began to suck on the tube more violently, almost with a passion. Soon, the dog ceased to struggle. The men using the poles began to rub the remaining fur and skin from the animal.

By now, the jar of rice wine was all but gone. There was no feeling at all in my throat or in my feet or hands. The young women again returned, this time bearing large wooden plates each containing a portion of the less-fortunate animal that moments before had been thrust into the fire. The plate was also garnished with breadfruit and an avocado-like fruit. Again the chief smiled and nodded as he began to eat. There were no knives, forks, or spoons. The wolfing down of the food became a blur as the jar of rice wine was finished. The chief again thanked us for our generosity, and we were on our way back to the hill.

“Ohhhhhh, where am I?” I groaned, sunlight piercing my eyelids like two hot daggers. “What’s on my head, I can’t lift it.”

“Take it easy, Matty. You will be fine. Just let things come naturally.”

“Wow! Who are you? You are beautiful!”

“Yeah, right, and I’ll bet you got land in Florida you’d like to sell me to. I’m Nurse Riggons. You and Lieutenant Colonel Simmons are here at Pleiku Hospital for observation. It seems you and the colonel had way too much rice wine to drink. Last night, the MPs apprehended you and the colonel. Apparently, you were driving your jeep on both sides of the road to include the shoulders. When they finally stopped you, the jeep was driving around in circles in the field just outside the main gate. The MPs were afraid you were going to run into one of the Montagnard huts in the village that lies to the south of the road. Lieutenant Colonel Simmons and you were laughing uncontrollably. Colonel Kratz was called immediately as one of his field grade officers was arrested for drunken disorderly conduct and is the chaplain on top of it. Colonel Kratz had you sent over here as you were under his direct orders."

Mid-December, the hill went yet again on full alert. The camp was on a blackout. I was assigned along with Charles Miller to roving patrol. We were to drive around the perimeter road as an extra measure of security, making sure there was no activity or attempt to breach the perimeter wire between the towers. Sapper activity was on the increase in some of the other camps.

Sappers were highly trained individuals, sometimes Vietcong but usually North Vietnamese regulars. The duty of the sapper was to penetrate the perimeter defenses undetected. The perimeter defense was commonly known as a seven-strand system. These are seven strands or rows of concertina wire. Concertina was barbed wire made in a circular fashion. When the roll was extended, it formed a tube. The strand or row was formed by placing two rolls of concertina fully extended side by side. Each roll was attached to U-shaped or D-shaped fence pickets driven into the ground between the two rolls. The pickets were about eight feet apart. The height of the pickets was about 7 feet. A third roll of wire was then placed over the pickets resting on the saddle or center of the two lower rolls, the top roll also being attached to the pickets. Three single strands of barbed wire were then laced through the top row of concertina also attached to the pickets. When completed, the strand or row was a 7-foot-tall barbed wire barrier, very difficult to penetrate. The strands or rows were placed at 50-foot intervals with a total of 350 feet from the outside edge of the wire to the exterior boundary at the camp. Tanglefoot was installed in the 50-foot spaces between the strands (concertina walls). Tanglefoot consisted of single-strand barbed wire attached to stakes driven into the ground six inches above ground level. The wire was strung in a diagonal pattern with the second row being strung diagonally in the opposite direction, forming a square pattern with each square being eighteen-by-eighteen-inches, making it very difficult for an individual to run in these areas.

Sappers dressed only in loincloths could breach the entire system in less than six minutes. They would pull the bottoms of the concertina together and attach one circle of the wire to another by using S hooks, forming a pathway though the wall. They would then go through the tanglefoot at full speed on hands and knees.

"Boy, it sure is dark out here," I said, trying to navigate the jeep along the narrow gravel road that ran along the perimeter of the camp, with only the blackout lights on.

"Yeah, really dark. Even the moon is hiding," Miller replied.

The sapper activity, in many cases, was to harass and demoralize the U.S. troops. They would regularly come through the wire and turn our claymore mines around prior to a ground attack. Claymores and foo gas were our last means of defense when the wire was being breached. A claymore looked exactly like an older Polaroid camera in its folded-up mode. The mine contained two pounds of C-4 plastic explosive along with two hundred ball bearings. It was detonated by one of the guards in the tower and was only to be used when the enemy was between the first and second strands of concertina. The practice of turning the claymores around became so prevalent that we secured all our claymores in concrete.

The night passed drudgingly slow as the jeep felt its way around the compound again and again.

"What was that?" queried Miller in his loudest whisper.

"What was what?"

"There, at the base of the wire. Did you see that?"

"Miller, it is so dark I can't even see you."

"Something shiny by the wire! There, stop the jeep, I'll check it out." I quickly raised my M79 to the ready as Miller crept toward the wire.

"Flare! Shoot a flare!" Miller yelled, the darkness shattered by the muzzle blasts of his M16.

Instantly, flares went up from the two adjoining towers, revealing several individuals scampering through the last strand of wire. M60s, M16s, and my M79 instantly erupted. The black night turned to noonday as flares cluttered the sky, being shot from every tower of the compound.

The OD's jeep pulled up behind me. It was Lieutenant Gaines.

"What's up?" he asked, a slight tremble in his voice.

"Sappers in the wire," I replied. "Miller spotted them. They were in the compound."

Soon the air was filled with the sound of choppers as Huey gunships and Cobra assault choppers scoured the countryside. The fiery tail of a B-40 pierced the night sky as it left its launcher and headed toward a Huey gunship. The gunship maneuvered, avoiding the strike of the rocket. It righted itself and, just as quickly, sent six of its own children in reply to the rocket's launcher.

The hillside and the jungle echoed menacingly as the six rockets streaked home. The night sky filled with tracers as the hillside erupted with small arms fire. The fiery tails from B-40s were seen all across that section of jungle. One of the gunships sprouted a smoke trail as flames poured from the engine's exhaust. It retreated toward Camp Holloway. The Hueys and Cobras pounded the hillside and adjoining valley. The hillside pounded back. Artillery Hill got involved. Some 105 and 155 shells slammed into the hillside to no avail. The small arms and rocket fire just increased. Mortar strikes began in the wire and slowly walked toward the compound.

The battle continued on savagely for some time. The mortar strikes stopped as the gunships found their targets. The signal was given in the compound for everyone to hunker down. ("Get into the bunkers, and don't show your face.") Miller and I took off for the nearest bunker. We had traveled all of a hundred feet when it happened.

The front of the jeep disappeared as the road melted away. The jeep jerked violently, instantly throwing Miller out of sight. I too was ejected; however, as I had a hold of the steering wheel, my body was propelled vertically, extending my feet to full height above my head as I would not relinquish my grip on the wheel. I was then snapped back into the jeep like the crack of a whip, landing in a heap atop the steering wheel.

"Miller," I groaned, trying to reinflate my lungs after colliding with the wheel and jeep seat. "You OK? Where are ya? Miller? Miller?" I called.

"Yeah, I'm here." A hand emerged over the side of the jeep.

Slowly, Miller's face appeared. "Ohhhhh! What happened?"

"I don't know!" I groaned. "Something musta hit the jeep."

"See if it will move, this is getting bad!" shouted Miller, grimacing and rubbing his back.

I started the jeep and tried to move forward. The vehicle groaned in response. The rear wheels began to spin, but the jeep moved not an inch.

"Something's holding us up. Check it out!"

Miller slowly crawled from the jeep, his face glowering in pain.

"Front wheel's in a ditch," came the reply. "Try to back it up."

I slammed the jeep in reverse, back we went.

"Ditch! Ditch!" I screamed, hostile fire still heavily erupting from the hillside.

The camp siren began to wail, awakening everyone to again get out of the open area. Miller and I scrambled toward the nearest bunker. The guard towers emptied with the troops seeking the shelter of the bunkers below. The drone of an approaching aircraft could be heard.

"Puff," whispered Miller.

A red line streaked toward the hillside as the minigun began to stir. The line divided into several as the gun recorded top speed. The second gun began its journey as Puff made its first pass. The small arms tracers from the hillside were now only spermatic.

"Wow! Look at that!" I thought as puff banked and began his second run with both miniguns firing at full speed. The sky actually looked as if red rain was literally falling on the hillside. As Puff completed his second pass, all became quiet. All that could be heard was the drone of the C-47 fading off into the night.

The enemy had been defeated at least for this night. Not another shot was fired from the hillside. The all clear was given. Miller and I went to retrieve the jeep.

"What kinda hole did we fall into? Musta been a mortar or rocket crater." I was puzzled.

"Naaa, it's a ditch," replied Miller. "A ditch all the way across the road."

"Miller, we been driving along this road all night long. How can there be a ditch across the road?" I sputtered, getting out and looking for myself.

Sure enough, a two-foot-wide-by-two-foot-deep trench had been dug across the road toward the four-inch mortar battery. It was later surmised that the enemy had planned to take control of the battery, turning the monitors against us. It was also summarized that the trench would have been used to ferry supplies to the monitor battery.

It was unusual that Miller and I would be pulling guard duty together as we were now in different units. I did not know it at the time that this would be our last adventure together as Miller would go home just prior to my returning to the Twentieth.

The rest of December passed quietly. As Christmas approached, a temporary cease-fire had been called at the peace talks in Paris.

Christmas Eve

Guard duty again. My assignment was a guard tower located on the south side of the compound. The view of the surrounding area was astounding. The air base lay almost directly to the front, Camp Holloway to the left with the evac hospital. Camp Schmidt and the Montagnard village were to the right and sprawling Pleiku to the rear.

The evening passed quietly. The night was cool enough to warrant a field jacket; nothing like the winter blasts that were being experienced at home. At midnight, I just happened to be in the tower pulling my two-hour shift when, almost simultaneously, the entire area erupted as every guard tower in all camps shot up red, white, and green flares, truly illuminating the entire valley in the colors of Christmas. What a sight! From this point forward, the war seemed to de-escalate in our part of the vineyard.

Back to the Twentieth

"Matty, CO wants to see ya in his office," called Gibbons as I entered the HQ.

"Sir, you need to see me?" I asked as I entered Colonel Kratz's office.

"Yes, yes I do. I need to go down to Fourth Corps for several days to a briefing. While I'm gone, I would like you to help Specialist Pierce box up some of my personal items. Fred will tell you just what goes where. I know that you're unaware, but in two weeks, I will PCS back to the States. A BG [brigadier general] position is open at the Pentagon, and I have been requested to fill it."

"Does that mean you will be promoted to general?"

"Well, yes, but probably not right away."

"Congratulations, sir. You deserve it."

"Well! I'm not so sure about that, but thank you."

Colonel Cole, Pierce, and I spent the next few days sorting through and packing up Colonel Kratz's personal effects.

"Pierce, who are these girls? Are they the CO's daughters?" I asked, picking up two pictures that were lying on the CO's desk in his trailer.

"Oh no," replied Pierce, smiling. "Those are Colonel Cole's girls. The oldest one is about thirteen or fourteen, and I think the younger one is eight or nine."

Colonel Cole had never shared with me the names of his girls even though he and I had made numerous trips to the air base to call home, the oldest having been sick.

"I think that about does it. You fellas did a nice job. The CO will be back tomorrow. In two days, he will start the clearing process. I'm sure he will spend his remaining time here speaking to each of us, getting his farewells in order," Colonel Cole replied, deep in thought.

"Matty."

"Morning, Pierce, what ya doing?" I asked as I entered the clerk's area at HQ.

"Awww, nothin', just printing my orders back home."

"Oh, is it time?"

"Yep, tomorrow's my last day. I start clearing Saturday morning."

"Humph, I didn't even know you were short."

"Yeah, just trying to keep my head down. Low profile, ya know."

"Hey, ain't you from LA?"

"Yeah, yeah I am," answered Pierce.

"Well, how come these orders give your home as Oahu, Hawaii?"

"Well, I, ah, kinda met this girl there while on R & R, and I wanted to go back and see her. If I clear at Oakland, I can go for $65, military discount. Round trip out of LA would cost me $300 plus."

"Well, how ya going to get home afterwards?"

"Oh, I just happen to have orders PCS-ing me from the naval base at Oahu back to LA. Fifty-seven dollars military discount."

"Oh, Matty, can I see you in my office?"

"Morning, sir. Yes, sir," I replied, following Colonel Kratz back to his office.

"Have a seat."

"Thank you, sir," I said, sitting down.

"I'm sure you know by now I will be leaving Pleiku and the 937th for what I hope will be forever."

"Yes, sir, I do."

"I just wanted to thank you personally for all those little things you have done in my behalf that were above and beyond the call of duty."

"Thank you, sir. You and Pierce will be leaving together?"

"Well, no, not exactly. Pierce starts his clearing process Saturday. I go to Long Binh for three to four days of debriefing before I start to clear."

"Who will be taking your place if I may ask, sir?"

"Certainly, a brigadier general, General Carroll Adams, just about to pin the star on. From what I have heard, he is a lot drier and military than I am."

"Sir, I would like permission to return to my old outfit. I would like to be an E-5, and as you know, beggin' your pardon, sir, but as the CO's jeep driver, I can't advance above spec 4."

"Ahh, you're getting bored here, huh? Missing the thrill and the excitement of being in the field, are ya?"

"Well, sir, I guess so. I've always wanted to be a patrol leader."

"And a good one you'll be, you have those leadership traits. Pack up your gear, son, I have a letter of commendation for your 201 file, not quite finished. Pick it up in the morning on the way out. Pierce will have it ready for you. Just promise me one thing, that is you'll go back to school when you leave this man's army."

"I will, sir," I promised, saluting. That was the last time I saw Colonel Kratz.

That afternoon was spent packing my duffel for the return to Company B. As I packed, I mulled over and over in my mind. Am I making the right decision? My current job was much safer than the return to the Twentieth would be.

The next morning, I picked up my letter, told everyone good-bye, and was off to Company B of the Twentieth. Third Platoon had moved from the patrol-size hooches to a barracks large enough to house the whole platoon. The walk was still only about ten minutes from my old home.

"Hey, look who it is!" cawed Underhill as I approached. "Are ya lost? Your mansion on the hill is that way!"

"Nahh, I'm back."

"Oh, ya missed us, huh?"

"Yeah, I did. Guess just too many days with not enough to do. I'm a soldier, not a driver."

"Well, welcome home, buddy. Smitty will be glad to see ya. Borger's gettin' short, ya know. He'll be glad to see ya."

"Yeah, to tell the truth I really missed everyone too."

"Ya know that Miller went home?"

"Ya mean 'You're all right' Miller went home?"

"He sure did, just a few days ago. Ya just missed 'im. How'd ya find us here in our new home?"

"Well, First Sergeant told me where to come. There's a bunk here somewhere in this barn?" I queried. The barracks was an open building, twenty feet wide and about eighty feet long.

"Ahhh, you'll have to go down to supply and pick one up. You can bunk right here with Holman and me."

"Sounds good."

"Yeah, just like old times."

"Who's Holman anyway?"

"Ahh, kind of a new guy. Been here about a month or so. Good Southern boy from Georgia. He's the rations driver when we're in base camp. You'll like 'im."

"Borger still here?"

"Yeah, him and Smitty are out lookin' at tomorrow's job. They should be back soon, been gone all morning."

Minutes later, the 3/4 came to a rumbling stop just outside our barracks.

"Hey!" I called. "Any short timers in this wreck?"

"Ho, Matty!" shouted Borger, jumping from the truck and throwing an arm around me, nearly knocking me to the ground.

"How ya been?" said Smitty, taking my hand, his head nodding in approval along with his typical Cheshire cat grin. "First Sarge said you'd be comin' soon."

"Well, here I am."

"Yeah, and I got plenty a work for ya." Smitty grinned. "Got a place to lay your head yet?"

"I do, Underdog and I went to supply, grabbed a bunk. I'll be in there with him and Holman."

"Good 'cause Monday I want you and Underhill to build rooms in the barracks. There is just no privacy with that open billeting."

The afternoon melted away making new acquaintances and renewing old ones. That evening, I finally met Private First Class Holman, an average-looking fellow about nineteen, five feet seven, 160 pounds, brown hair and maybe hazel eyes, and a little Southern drawl when he spoke.

Sunday Afternoon

"Looky what I found," Holman chirped, throwing a cardboard box at Underhill's and my feet. "Steaks! A whole case of 'em."

"Are you kiddin' me?" I came back, tearing the top of the box open, revealing fifty T-bone steaks. "Whoo-wee! We gonna party tonight!"

Within minutes, we had commandeered a skillet, salt, pepper, butter, and a camping stove from the mess hall. Soon I was frying steaks like a big dog. With everyone in the platoon fed, we still had eleven steaks left. Underhill, Holman, Smitty, Borger, and I finished off these eleven in the blink of an eye. The whole barracks smelled like a Bonanza Steakhouse.

The next morning, the platoon was off clearing the free-fire zone somewhere along QL-19, leaving Underhill and me alone to our work.

"Hmmm, this is the last of it." Underhill grinned, driving in the final nail.

"Not bad, not bad. Twenty rooms in five days," said Smitty in approval.

The barracks now sported a four-foot hall running the length of the building with ten rooms on each side. Each room measured about eight-by-eight-feet with the exception of our room, which measured eight-by-sixteen-feet; we were the only threesome in the platoon.

The next Monday found Underhill and me along with the rest of the platoon west of Pleiku clearing the free-fire zone between the road and the jungle.

"Matty, I want you to run the guys on this side of the road. I'll be on the side if yer need me," Borger stated. My crew consisted of Underhill, Holmes, and four other fellows who were relatively new in country.

Midmorning

A Lambretta pulled up. Six nice-looking young ladies disembarked followed by a somewhat older lady yet still attractive and shapely.

"Hey, Sarge, you number 1 here?" she asked as she approached.

"Yeah, I guess I am, but I'm not a sergeant, I'm just a spec 4."

"I mama-san. You let GIs have girls. I give you girl for free."

"How much for a girl?" Underhill interrupted, his eyes glowing.

"For you, GI, only five dollar. Five dollar MPC."

"No! No! Can't do it," Underhill came back. "I give you five hundred P."

"No! No! No! My girls *boo coo* number 1. You pay MPC."

"Mama-san," I interrupted, "I can't let my men pay you with MPC. It's against the law. The army would put me in the Long Binh Hilton."

"OK! OK! OK! But six hundred P, NO LESS!"

I looked at Underhill, shook my head, and left. Soon my whole crew was in the bushes, leaving me alone to my work.

"Hey, Sarge. Hey, Sarge!" called the mama-san. "Which girl you want? I tell you she free. My word good."

I just looked at her and smiled.

"What matter with you, Sarge? You gay? You no like girls?"

With this I almost went hysterical. I guess I should have been offended being called gay, but for some reason, it just struck me as being funny.

"Mama-san, I'm not gay. Far from it. I just have a girl at home. I belong to her."

"Sarge, you sure different. Most GIs boom-boom everything. Sarge, you really different. Most sergeants won't let GIs go with girls, why you different?"

"Well, Mama-san, I told you earlier I'm not a sergeant. I am just the crew leader. If these guys want girls, I have nothing to say about it."

"Hmmph, you number one. What name?"

"Matty, my name's Matty."

"You never want girl? You sure you no gay?"

"No no, I just don't believe that way."

"You OK, you no run me off. You OK. We come back tomorrow?"

"No, no. Too soon. Have work to finish. Come back next week."

"OK, OK, be here next week." Soon the Lambretta was gone, and it was back to work as usual. By the end of the week our project was finished, and we were off to greener pastures.

The following Monday found the 3/4 and the green Cadillac rumbling along the same stretch of QL-19. As we passed the prior week's project, I began to wonder. *Just where are we going today?*

Soon we came upon two bridges that had been blown. The abutment had been taken out of the first, and the center pier had been blown in the second, dropping the spans into the river. Culverts had been placed in the river on the downstream side. Fill had been added along with blacktop diverting the road around the downed bridges. The road (QL-19) turned north three or four miles and then back to the east, weaving its way through the mountains on its trek to Qui Nhon and the South China Sea.

As the miles passed, the road became more dirt than blacktop. The lead trucks in the convoy were throwing up thick clouds of dust. Combined with the heat of the day, the gritty dust stuck to us like glue. Every breath coated the inside of my mouth. It was as if I were eating a Ritz cracker made of sand.

Just before lunch, the 3/4 followed by the green Cadillac left the convoy, pulling into a small compound containing the usual seven-strand concertina perimeter, two guard towers, and the usual array of sandbag bunkers. However, within this compound, there were two very large artillery pieces. Soon the 3/4 came to a stop.

"Well, guys," called Borger, emerging from the dump. "This'll be your new home for the next week or two."

Smitty and Underhill had brought the 3/4 filled with the necessary supplies needed to complete the project. First we unloaded the 3/4, then there was lunch. Again, the usual C rations. Again, the new guys jockeying for their favorites with the veterans just taking a box and moving on.

"What ya get, Matty?" asked Snyder, with a mouthful of turkey loaf.

"Hmmph, I don't know," I replied. "Let's see. Can says beef and potatoes."

"Ya mean ya can't tell the difference?" Snyder came back, dismay all over his face.

"Naaah, you eat 'em long enough, they all taste the same."

"Man, you really are hard-core!" said Snyder, shaking his head in disgust.

After lunch, Smitty and the 3/4 were gone catching the afternoon convoy back to Pleiku.

"Yo!" called Borger. "Let's go see what we gotta do." He led the way to the first of the two artillery pieces.

As we approached, we were met by a rather portly middle-aged E-6. "Good afternoon, gentlemen. Welcome to An Khe. I am Sergeant Barneko. This emplacement is my responsibility, and am I glad to see you. As you can see, the platform beneath the cannon is disintegrating. We desperately need you to rebuild it. I have to apologize to you, the wall tents that were to be your billeting were kinda disintegrated in a mortar attack the other night, and their replacements haven't made it yet. So for the next few days you'll be billeted here in the powder and shell magazines. The safest place in camp as long as you don't smoke," replied the sergeant laughingly.

The guns were 175 howitzers with a barrel length of about 21 feet. The range of the weapon was 37.5 miles. Firing to the east, the shell could reach within 8 miles of the sea. Firing to the southwest, it could almost reach Pleiku, just short of Kontum to the northwest, and to the north, the A Shau Valley could easily be reached. The only problem the 175 had was the projectile could be up to a grid square off target (a grid is 400 yards, that's 1,200 feet, almost 1/4 of a mile). But I guess 1,200 feet in 37.5 miles is not that bad.

Each howitzer sat on a circular platform allowing the gun to be turned or maneuvered in any direction. The platforms were approximately thirty-six inches tall with the top six inches being above grade. The platforms were constructed very similarly to the wooden, timber bridge. The platform consisted of several layers of different-size timbers. The first layer, eighteen-by-eighteen-inch timber, were cut and laid abreast, forming a thirty-foot circle eighteen inches tall. Layers two and three consisted of six-by-twelve-inch timber cut and laid abreast with the joints perpendicular to the joints below. Layers four and five were three-by-twelve-inch timber cut and laid, again with the joints perpendicular to the joints below. Only the two layers of three-by-twelve-inches were nailed together, allowing the lower timbers to move as the piece was fired. If the upper deck (two rows, three-by-twelve-inches) were attached to the lower members, the firing of the weapon would cause the whole platform to tilt as the rear end was driven into the ground by the weapon's recoil.

Days 1, 2, and 3 went smoothly as the platform of the first piece was disassembled then reassembled using new timber.

"Hey, Underdog," complained Holman at lunchtime. "How ya been sleepin'? The wooden floor in that projectile magazine is just killin' me."

The powder and projectile magazines were built around the gun emplacements. Each magazine was about ten feet wide and eighty feet long built in a semicircle. The two buildings completely encircled the artillery piece and the platform. At the east and west ends, there was a twenty-foot space separating the two buildings, creating an entrance and an exit, allowing the artillery piece to be moved in and out. Each building was constructed using vertical two-by-sixes spaced six inches on center. The exterior had no siding or sheeting, leaving a one-inch space between the studs for ventilation. A sandbag retaining wall surrounded the outside of the buildings with a twelve-inch airspace between the exterior walls and the sandbag walls. The roofs were reinforced timbers covered with corrugated metal sheeting followed by three layers of sandbags. The inside of the buildings were open, allowing easy access. Each building followed the curve of the platform with about fifteen feet between magazine and platform.

"Hmmmp." Underhill rubbed his grizzled chin thoughtfully. "We been sleepin' like babies over in the powder magazine. Those bags of gunpowder pellets make beautiful mattresses."

"Are ya nuts, sleepin' on those things?"

"Nope, ya oughtta try it. Tell 'em, Borg, tell 'em, Matty."

"Yep, best I slept since I been here."

"You got that right, Borg. I'm sleepin' on a stack about five feet tall, just like sleepin' on my grandma's feather bed."

That evening, Holman moved over to the powder magazine with Bomarito, Borger, Underhill, and me, leaving Fair and the two new guys (Snyder and Monroe) to the hardwood floor of the projectile magazine.

Monsoon on the Hill

0217 Hours

Kawhamm! came the report, not only awakening me from a sound sleep but throwing me from my bed onto the hard floor below.

"Ohhhhh!" groaned Bomarito. "My head, my head!"

Both hands covered his ears. My ears too were ringing loudly. I could barely hear the cries and groans of the others. The 175 next door had received a fire mission. The gun crews, not realizing we were so close, fired the weapon without warning. Two full days passed before the ringing in my ears subsided. From that day forward, we all wore earplugs both day and night. However, the damage had already been done.

The next five days saw the completion of both platforms. When the 175 fired, if one stood to the rear of the gun at a safe distance, of course, you could actually see the projectile leaving the barrel.

It was back to the hooch to await our next assignment.

Free Fire Zone, QL-14

The Bridges of Highway 19

February 1970

Just east of Pleiku on the road to An Khe, two bridges about a mile apart had been destroyed by the enemy. The first consisted of a single span with a total length of forty feet with the southern abutment taken out, dropping the span into the creek.

"Third Patrol! Third Patrol, gather around! Come on, let's go!" shouted Borger. "Tomorrow's a new day, and boy, do I have an assignment for you. The two bridges just past Camp Holloway that we have been going around for months are to be rebuilt. Our mission is to demolish what's left, rebuild the abutment, and set a new span."

The next morning Borger, Snyder, Underhill, Fair, Bomarito, Holman, Jennings, and myself loaded into a 3/4-ton pickup along with Sergeant Smith and were on our way. The balance of the Third Platoon Company B followed in five-ton dump trucks, along with a D9 Caterpillar high lift. When we arrived at the bridge site, Smitty began barking out orders.

"First Patrol, spread out! Infiltrate! Take the north side of the creek. Second Patrol, you take the south side! Keep your eyes open! There is a lot of VC activity in this area, and you know they don't want this bridge rebuilt. Fourth Patrol, the trucks and dozer are yours! Third Patrol, you know your assignment!"

"Fair, Bomarito, Jennings, Holman, I need a series of holes drilled in the bridge deck four feet from the edge and four feet on center," commanded Borger. "Underhill, you and Matty grab the C-4, det cord, get things ready. Snyder, you pull security around the trucks."

The holes took all morning to drill. The work was accomplished using a pneumatic drill powered by an Ingersoll Rand diesel-driven air compressor. Upon completion, there were three rows of holes running the length of the span. Each hole was one inch in diameter and eight inches in depth with a total depth of the deck being about twelve inches thick. By lunchtime, Fourth Patrol had all the loose debris cleaned up.

"Wooo-oo," called Snyder, "lunchtime" as he emerged from the 3/4, carrying a case of C rations. A quick scurry made short work of the box as everyone had their favorite.

"Well, what did you get?" I queried as Underhill began opening his box.

"Hmmmm, looks like spaghetti and meatballs" was his reply. "Gimme some C-4, I'm going to warm this stuff up." His P38 went into action, opening first the can of spaghetti and then the can containing the biscuit (some called it a cracker). He discarded the biscuit, which had been baked in 1949 as our present C rations were leftovers from the Korean War. The biscuit was about two inches in diameter and about one and one-fourth inches thick, resembling a bagel without the hole. The biscuit was so hard it could not be eaten even after a long soaking. The local kids, who would eat anyth0069ng you gave them, would invariably object to receiving the biscuit to the point of returning it in a most harmful manner.

After punching a few holes in the biscuit tin, Underhill was ready.

"What the hell are you doing?" yelled Jennings as Underhill lit the ball of C-4 with his lighter. "You're going to blow us all up, you idiot!"

"Calm down, take it easy," Borger replied softly. "You can burn C-4 all day and not hurt a thing. Just don't drop it or stomp on it while on fire."

A look of relief came over Jennings's face; however, he removed himself to the far end of the bridge to eat his lunch.

Underhill, using the biscuit tin as an oven containing the burning C-4, placed the can of spaghetti on the level top of the inverted tin.

"There, in a minute I'll have a hot lunch." As the can warmed, the surface of the spaghetti began to bubble, making many of us envious of Underhill's resourcefulness.

"Just a few more seconds and I'll be in tall cotton!" snickered Underhill, reaching for the can.

Kaboom! The report sent everyone diving for cover. Underhill and I, being closest to the explosion, were thrown flat on our backs by the concussion.

As I plummeted rearward, I could see a missile, almost looking like a rocket, heading skyward at a high rate of speed.

"I knew it! I knew it!" screamed Jennings, literally in tears. "We don't have to worry about the VC, you two idiots are going to do the job for them."

Borger, Bomarito, Underhill, and I were laughing uncontrollably with Underhill and me still on our backs. "Underdog," I said, laughing so hard I was choking, "next time you cook spaghetti, make sure you stir it up in the can first."

The spaghetti and one meatball had formed a very solid gelatin-like mass in the can. As the can warmed, the spaghetti in the bottom of the can began to boil. The forming gases pushed the mass of spaghetti out of the can in the same manner as a bullet is ejected from a shell casing by the burning powder. Underhill's spaghetti was never seen or heard of again.

By 3:00 p.m., the charges were set, each hole firmly packed with C-4, primer inserted, followed by a cone-shaped TNT block sitting atop each hole. The charges were interconnected by means of a det cord (detonation cord). Det cord looked much like a plastic clothesline but highly explosive, burning at the rate of about six hundred feet per second, causing the charges to detonate simultaneously. Upon the ready signal from Borger, Patrols 1, 2, and 4 were loaded into the trucks along with Snyder, Bomarito, Fair, Jennings, and Holman and moved about a quarter of a mile from the site, leaving Sergeant Smith, Borger, Underhill, and myself to the dirty work.

"Well, Borger," said Smitty in his sheepish smiling manner, "this will be your last assignment, would you like the honors?"

"I certainly would," replied Borger, grinning from ear to ear.

The spool of wire leading from the first charge to the detonator was about 250 feet long. A new roll consisted of about 500 feet, but as it was used, several feet would be lost due to the explosion of each detonation.

"Think we've got enough wire?" queried Borger as we hunkered beneath the 3/4 to protect us from falling debris.

"All will be fine, nothin' to worry about, there's plenty" was Smitty's reply.

"Well, are we ready? Final check!" called Smitty. "Troops at a safe distance?"

"Check," I replied.

"Road blocked off to a safe distance?"

"Check."

"Area cleared of unauthorized personnel?"

"Wait! Wait! Wait! There's a couple of kids coming down the creek. Looks like they got fishin' poles."

"This is Alpha Bravo Tango," barked Smitty into the field phone. "Come in, Sierra November Zebra."

"This is Sierra November Zebra," crackled the radio.

"There's two kids coming down the creek on the south side. Get the QCs to clear them out of there!" shouted Smitty rather sternly.

"Sorry, no QCs available, and if we leave our position, the roadblock will be breached" came back the reply.

"Oh, shit! Been here for three tours. Nothin' has ever changed! Nothin' is ever gonna change. Those damn ARVNs are never where they are supposed to be," stammered Smitty. "Ten-four. We'll take care of it. Alpha Bravo Tango, out. Matty, get those kids out of there. We can't hold the traffic much longer."

"Hey, you kids, *di di mouw boo coo* boom boom!" I shouted as I ran along the creek toward the boys.

The boys just looked at me and kind of smiled.

"*Di di boo coo* VC. *Di di.*"

With that, a look of terror came over them. They quickly turned and returned up the creek and out of sight. I quickly scurried back under the truck.

"OK! OK!" clamored Smitty. "Final check. Area clear?"

"Check."

"OK, Borger, hook up the wires."

"Check," replied Borger, carefully connecting the wires to the hand detonator.

"Are we ready?"

"Ready," came our reply.

"Fire in the hole! Fire in the hole! Fire in the hole!" Borger shouted in his loudest voice as he squeezed the plunger on the detonator. The charges erupted in a roar of thunder, sending a great ball of fire and smoke high into the air, carrying thousands of bridge fragments with it. The explosion shook the earth mightily, raising a dust cloud 125 feet in diameter around the blast site.

After several seconds, the small deck debris began falling back to the earth, causing a hailstorm of gravel. As the minutes passed, the dust settled, the air began to clear, revealing the bridge deck broken and shattered in the creek bottom. Our mission had been successful, resulting in basketball-size pieces of concrete left to clean up.

"Good job! Good job!" beamed Smitty as the all clear was given. "Call the guys back. Let's get the temporary cleaned up so we can get traffic moving again."

The temporary was a roadway that had been constructed around the downed bridge using a culvert six feet in diameter covered with earth, thus allowing traffic to pass. The Fourth Patrol made short work of cleaning the roadway of debris. Soon motorcycles, Lambrettas, and a few cars were jockeying for their position in a congested folly.

The day had been a long hot one. A sigh of relief came over our little group as Engineer Hill came into view. The cool of the evening brought sleep on early. The next morning came quickly. There was much to do.

"Hey, Underhill, you and Matty go over to the ASP yard. Got a lot of steel for you to bend. Say good-bye to Borger, he clears today," Smitty replied, almost teary eyed.

I found Borger sitting on the porch of our hooch with a blank look on his face, just more or less staring into space. "Hey, Borger. You OK?"

"Yeah, just sittin' here, thinking about home. What it's going to be like. I'm sure a lot of things have changed. I'm a little scared. I've been here for a year. Four more days, and I'll be there, almost made it," came Borger's reply, hands shaking and tears streaming down his face.

"I had to come find you, tell ya good-bye, good luck, and thanks. You've taught me so much, oh great mentor!"

"Shut up!" came his reply, a grin overcoming the gloominess.

With that I left, never seeing Borger again. His memory will be forever etched in my mind as if it were yesterday.

As the next two weeks passed, Underhill and I bent steel both day and night. The ASP yard was the storehouse of all our supplies. It was located two blocks south of our platoon. Underhill and I would start about 7:30 a.m., breaking only for lunch and supper and would work till dark. At the end of the two-week period, a total of twenty-one tons of steel had been cut and bent to be the reinforcing for the two new bridges. The steel used was number 4 rebar (half-inch diameter reinforcing rod) and number 6 rebar (three-fourth-inch diameter reinforcing rod).

The next step in the process was to pour a series of concrete slabs. The first series consisted of ten slabs each measuring eight-by-eleven-feet, eight inches thick. Prior to pouring, a twelve-inch-long piece of four-inch angle iron was set in each corner of the form (a box being eight feet long and eleven feet wide built out of two-by-ten lumber rip-sawn to a height of eight inches) with an additional piece of twelve-inch angle being set along the sides of the form at the midpoint. A mat of three-fourth-inch rebar went into the form next. The bars were placed in the form eight inches on center with the first and last bars set two inches from the sides of the form. Thirteen bars ten feet and eight inches long formed the first row. Seventeen bars seven feet and eight inches long formed the second row. The bars were tied together at each intersection using tie wire (baling wire). This formed the first mat. It was suspended off the bottom of the form two inches by using chairs (one-half-pint milk cartons filled with hardened concrete). A second identical mat was placed in the form in the same manner. The form was then filled with concrete. Number 4 rebar loops were inserted in each corner of the slab into the wet cement. The time line to complete the slabs was six days.

With the completion of the slabs, Underhill and I went back to bending steel.

"Matty," came the stiff command from Smitty. "Tomorrow you go before the board. Are you ready to be an E-5?"

"Yes, Sergeant," I replied. That afternoon, three new sergeants came to our platoon: Larry Ditto, E-6, a tall Texan from Port Aranses, Texas; Claud Lemrise, E-5; and Felty, also an E-5. These three young men had spent eight weeks in basic training, eight to ten weeks in AIT (advanced individual training), and about ten to twelve weeks at NCO school (noncommissioned officer). They were then shipped to our unit. All were made patrol leaders upon their arrival with Lemrise being assigned to our patrol, taking Borger's place.

When it was learned that these fellows had no combat experience, it became a concern to the other platoon members.

"Sergeant Smith, sir! Sergeant Smith, sir!" called Aaron, a specialist 5 in Second Patrol.

"Aaron, what is the matter with you?" yelled Smitty. "I work for a living. You don't call me sir. What's a matter with you, boy?"

"How come these shake and bakes are runnin' the show? They ain't been in country but a week?"

"This is what the CO wants, so be it," snapped Sergeant Smith. "You all will just have to watch out for 'em and teach 'em, OK?"

"Yes, Sergeant!" came the reply from the whole platoon. Sergeant Smith was loved by all. He was a good leader, always concerned about his platoon members.

The next day came with a lot of trepidation. I have never felt comfortable being grilled and judged by others. Nevertheless, I passed and became a sergeant E-5 at thirteen months in the army.

Life continued on as the slabs took seven days minimum to cure and become strong enough to be transported. Underhill and I continued to bend steel for bridge number 2. Ditto was put in charge of sitting and securing the forty-foot-long, thirty-six-inch tall I beam girders that would span the creek abutment to abutment, forming the main support (superstructure) for the bridge deck.

On the morning of the eighth day, after the slabs were poured, a twenty-ton crane arrived at the ASP yard along with five five-ton flatbed semis. The crane belonged to the 584th; the trucks were ours. Cables were hooked to the loops in each corner of each slab. The slab was then lifted and set on the flatbed. Each truck could carry two slabs; approximate weight of each slab was nine thousand pounds. The slabs were then transported to the bridge site. The slabs were then set atop the I beam girders, two wide and five long, forming the bridge deck twenty-two-feet-wide-by-forty-feet-long. The slabs were then welded directly to the girders by means of the angle irons that were placed at the bottom of the slabs. The loops in the slab corners were then cut off, leaving a more or less smooth bridge deck. The 584th then came in, covered the deck with six inches of asphalt paving. They also installed the handrail as well as the approach aprons. In all, the bridge was completed from demolition to finish in five weeks.

6:00 a.m. the Following Day

"OK! OK! OK! Off and on!" came the bark of Sergeant Smith. "No formation this morning. Get dressed! Hit the mess hall. Formation will be at group command at 0700. Colonel Adams will address you. Be there! One hour, men. Let's go! Let's go! Let's go!"

The hour passed quickly. One of the cooks was a baker by trade. He made the very best caramel rolls, heaven away from home.

0700 Hours

"Company, attention!" shouted Command Sergeant Major Elkey.

"Gentlemen, I am Colonel Adams. As many of you know, I have taken Colonel Kratz's place as the commander of the 937th Engineer Group, which you are a part of. I would like to first commend you on a job well-done on the bridge you have just completed just east of Pleiku. The time line was extraordinary. Never have we ever completed a project of this magnitude in such a short period of time. The quality of the workmanship is also of the highest standards. The completed structure weighs approximately 120 tons. Again, a job well-done. As a reward, the rest of the day is yours."

"Company, attention!" came the order. "Dismissed."

"Ay, Matty. What ya gonna do today?" came the mischievous voice of Underhill.

"Aww, just hang around the hooch, rest. I don't know."

"How about we go to Pleiku to the Turkish baths?"

"Underdog, I'd go with you, but you insist on going in the officers' side. Man, you're going to get busted yet."

"Aw, come on, I don't want to go by myself."

"OK, OK, but I'm not going in that side with you. Deal?"

"OK, deal."

Within the hour, the 3/4 was rumbling along the road to Pleiku. We entered the secure parking lot of the bathhouse. Underhill quickly slipped through the back door of the officers' side.

Now I have never been a real fan of taking my clothes off and sitting around with a bunch of other guys, naked, sweating in the steam. The bathhouse had a porch running the length of the building, containing several chairs. I chose one of these, plopped myself down for the one-to-two-hour wait for Underhill to return. I hadn't sat there very long when an extremely beautiful young lady came around the corner.

"Hey, GI. Why you sit there? You look *boo coo* number ten. You no want bath?"

"Naww," I replied rather dejectedly.

"How about me give you shave, haircut? Only 250 P. How 'bout?"

"Haircut? There's no barbershop here."

"Oh, yeah silly GI. You come, I show! Come! Come! *Boo coo* number one."

I reluctantly gave up my chair and followed.

The bathhouse was a rather large wooden building that had been constructed by one of the engineering crews. It was a single-story building with the interior ceilings rising to a height of about twenty feet. The noncommissioned and officers' sides were separated by an adjacent wall running the length of the center of the building. A covered porch about fifteen feet wide ran along both sides and the rear of the building. It was the rear porch that contained the barbershop. There were ten to twelve chairs all doing a brisk business.

"Here my chair. You sit. First haircut, then shave. Then I wash your hair. Make you feel *boo coo* number 1."

As I sat down, my mind reverted to some of my previous experiences with barbers. My first haircut in country was with the stiff-necked barber pooping my neck and the barber at Julie whom I had liked so well, only to find him to be a VC.

The haircut went rather well. It wasn't until I was lathered up and she began to sharpen her straight razor that my trepidation quickly became apparent.

"Sarge, what matter with you? You too hot?" A river of sweat poured from my forehead into my eyes. "Here, I turn on fan, make you cooler."

The sight of the razor brought to mind the horror stories and rumors of barbers slitting GI's throats.

"No worry, Sarge, I do good job. I shave long time." With that, she made short work of my scruffy face. She then wheeled a beautician's wash basin over and began the wash job with my head laid back, her supple fingers in my hair, and the cool breeze of the fan in the heat of the day.

"Hey, Sarge, Sarge, all done!"

"Huh," I grunted as reality returned. "What happened?" I mumbled.

"You fall asleep. You feel better?"

"Oh yes," I replied. That was like a breath of fresh air in this hellhole. As I came around the corner, there sat Underhill in my exact same chair, brandishing that mischievous grin whenever things went well.

Monday morning brought a whole new day and a whole new challenge. The second bridge was much larger than the first. This bridge spanned 135 feet with the span being broken into two separate spans by an intermediate pier. The bridge spanned a river instead of a creek. The river flowed from the nearby mountainside with tributaries flowing from the rice paddies that were sculptured in the mountainside in the form of plateaus. The pier had been destroyed, dropping the north end of the southern span into the river.

The balance of our platoon worked on demolishing the bridge. I remained in the ASP yard to finish bending the steel and to form and pour the new deck. These slabs were eleven feet wide and fifteen feet long. The procedure was the same as before.

"Hey, Matty."

"Hey, Sarge."

"You about finished with the slabs?" Smitty inquired.

"Yea, the last five will go today. That'll be all eighteen of 'em."

"The completed ones really look good."

"Well, the lumber they sent this time was a much-better grade."

"The surveyors are coming tomorrow to set the grades. The southern abutment needs to be rebuilt. I need you to get started on it as soon as you have the elevation."

"Will do, Sarge."

"There is a new, I mean, brand-new mixer over at the ASP yard at Camp Schmidt. That will be your mixer, and you will be in charge of all concrete operations at that location. Go over first thing in the morning and learn the ropes. I want you at the bridge by 0830."

"Will do, see you in the morning."

"Ten-four."

The afternoon passed quickly as the remaining slabs were poured and finished. Yet another task completed.

ASP Yard, Camp Schmidt

What a different operation. The yard was huge. The concrete operation was apart from the rest of the yard. It consisted of three large buildings, each about one hundred feet long and thirty to forty feet deep. Each building had three closed sides with the front being open. The buildings were placed in a horseshoe or U formation with the open fronting to a courtyard. At the mouth of the courtyard were the mixing bins containing gravel and sand, a pull-chain yoke, which controlled the mixers, and lastly a raised platformlike shed, which held a pallet of cement (fifty ninety-pound bags).

"Sergeant Travis, I am Bill Mattatall. You are to show me the ropes to the cement plant."

"Yeah, I've been expectin' ya. They told me you'd be here this morning. Those stripes look new, you just get E-5?"

"Yep, sewed 'em on yesterday."

"Good luck. The operation is really simple. These three sheds, as you can see, are fairly full of bags of cement, about seventy-five thousand bags all told. Each month, five semis come in from Quinhon, each carrying one thousand bags. There is more cement here than we could use in the next ten years. But every month, five more truckfuls are shipped. They come in every month on the first Monday. Your job is to check 'em in. One of the trucks always loses his load before he gets here. Don't worry about it, just sign the manifest and go on.

"This is how the batch plant works. Step 1: pull the truck under the hopper. The first thing you do, and always the first thing, is to put the water in the truck. This new truck of yours holds 7 yards of mix. You need 35 gallons per yard. Full truck, 250 gallons. Pull the chain, water goes in. Flip the lever on the hopper shoot left, gravel goes in, flip it to the right and sand goes in. Put the gravel in first, set the scale to 1,650 pounds for each yard, pull the chain, gravel in. After all the gravel is in, flip the lever to the right, and you're in the sand business. Set the scale to 1,150 pounds per yard. Make sure the mixer is turning at full speed. After all gravel and sand is in, pull the truck forward to the yellow line. This will line you up with the cement platform. You will need 7 bags of cement per yard mixed. That's 49 bags for 7 yards. Any questions?"

"Nope, got it."

The drive from Camp Schmidt to the bridge took me through Pleiku, the joy of ten thousand motorcycles and Lambrettas all jockeying for their part of the road at once.

"Well, Matty, how'd it go at Camp Schmidt? Everything under control? What did ya think about Travis? Are ya ready for this project?"

"Smitty! Smitty! What's up? You're goin' a mile a minute."

"Yeah, I know. But I'm down to one hundred days. Just a little excited, I guess. The surveyors aren't here yet. How about you helpin' the guys break up that piece in the river?"

"Where did that thing come from? It ain't part of this bridge."

"It was part of the abutment."

A concrete stone lay in the river shallows. It was about four square feet and nearly as tall. As I went down to the work site, Fair, Underhill, and Holman were struggling with two ninety-pound jackhammers in about two feet of water, trying to break up the stone.

"Ho, Matty, take this thing, will ya? This rock is harder than ten days in the county jail. The hammer and the water's wearing me out." The look of agony all over Fair's face, I gladly took the hammer over. The water current and the slick river bottom made the hammer very difficult to handle. One minute I was fine hammering away, the next minute I was on the river bottom, that damn heavy hammer lying on top of me, holding me down. I felt hands first groping in the murky water, then the weight of the hammer was gone with me being pulled to the surface.

"What's the matter with you, Matty?" Holman laughed. "You're here to work, not go swimmin'."

The whole morning was spent breaking up that rock and getting it out of the water. Just before lunch, along came the same two boys that I had run off at the last bridge.

"*Chow-ong*," Holman called to the boys.

"*Chow-ong*," replied the boys.

"What ya gonna do with those poles?" queried Holman.

"*Boo coo* fish," replied the boys.

"No, no fish here. Too much poop from rice paddies," replied Smitty, who was now getting into the conversation.

"Oh no, you watch. You got biscuit C rations?" came the reply.

"I gotta see this." I came back, quickly grabbing a C rat from the 3/4, pulling the biscuit can from the box. The can was opened. The biscuit was cut into pieces by the ARVN interpreter's bush knife. I gave the boys the biscuit fragments. They quickly threaded the pieces onto their fishing hook (open safety pin tied to a string hooked to a pole). The baited hook barely hit the water. The string went taut, the pole bent slightly, a flick of the wrist, and a fish came out. *A real, live fish!* Soon there were makeshift poles up and down the riverbank. Bootlaces were tied together to form lines. M16s became poles as well as shovel and rake handles. Every available resource was used. There was always an abundance of safety pins as every bandolier of M16 ammo had a safety pin attached to it. Soon catfish littered the shoreline. No C rations for lunch that day. Every man in Third Platoon feasted on fried catfish, knowing full well that the rice paddies that fed the river above were fertilized with human feces.

Right after lunch, the surveyors from the 584th arrived. The elevation for the abutment was established, and I quickly went to work, setting the forms and setting the steel reinforcement. It took the next two days to complete.

"Are you ready to pour?"

"All ready, Sarge. Figure we'll start the pour in the morning."

"Well, I will need to hold ya up for one day. We have to deliver the debris from the bridge to a fill site just about four clicks north of Holloway. It will take the whole platoon. The shake and bakes will be at the front of the convoy, and I want you to be NCOIC. You and Fair will be in the last truck. I have some other business to take care of. Can you handle it, Sergeant?" snickered Smitty.

"Piece of cake. No problem."

"I figure it will take at least five or six trips to haul all that stuff up there. We absolutely need the job completed tomorrow, so you'll have to push on the guys just a little bit. I told Sergeant Ditto to keep the front end rollin'. Good luck," replied Smitty, giving me a little pat on the shoulder.

Friday Morning

The sky was slightly overcast. The commute from Engineer Hill to the bridge site went as well as ever: motorcycles weaving in and out trying to run dump trucks off the road, young boys trying to strip your vehicle at every stop. By 0830, the trucks were loaded and we were on our way with the first load. Our convoy consisted of fifteen dump trucks, each with a driver and one man riding shotgun for security.

The MPs led the convoy with an amphibious assault vehicle (AV) followed by a war wagon, this being a deuce and a half with a quad 40 mounted in the bed (a two-and-a-half-ton cargo truck with a forty-millimeter, four-barrel ack-ack gun mounted in the bed). Sergeants Ditto and Felty were in the lead truck with Lemrise somewhere in the middle, and Fair and I were in the last truck. The day went well with our little convoy moving between the sites about every three hours.

"Hey, Matt. How we doin'?" the radio crackled as Fair and I were taking our position in the convoy.

"This is Sierra Bravo Zebra," I replied. "Come in."

"What the hell is a matter with them?" snapped Fair. "They tryin' to get us all killed?"

"Delta Bravo Alpha, come in! Delta Bravo Alpha, radio protocol!" I replied in my most authoritative voice.

"Delta Bravo Alpha here. Sierra Bravo Zebra, come in. Are we ready?"

"Ten-four. We are all loaded and ready to go. It's almost 1800 hours. Keep sharp."

"Ten-four," came the reply.

The sun was low in the sky. Long shadows draped the free-fire zone between the jungle and the road, causing the jungle and the zone to blend together. Truck by truck rumbled onward, causing the convoy to slowly move forward.

"I'm glad this is the last run of the day. I've had a bad feeling all day about this convoy," said Fair as our truck moved forward.

"Yeah, I know what ya mean, I've been uneasy all day too. Maybe it's just those new NCOs up front."

Kaboom! The truck seemed to explode on Fair's side. The truck careened toward the ditch. Fair quickly corrected, keeping our truck on the road. A warm mist sprayed over my face, filling my eyes. *Rat-tat-tat* came the report of small arms fire from the jungle. *Boom, boom, boom, boom* came the reply from the quad 40 on the war wagon. I quickly cleared my eyes. The truck windshield was covered with blood. A spray of blood was erupting from a wound on Fair's forehead. Fair was half slumped over the steering wheel.

"Fair! Fair! You OK? You OK, man?"

The truck came to a stop as several of the trucks ahead of us tried to pass one another, causing a bottleneck, stopping the convoy.

Tang-tang-tang come the sound of bullets hitting the side of our truck. Fair's eyes were sort of glazed over. He wasn't moving. Blood continued to pour from the wound in his forehead. "Damn you, Fair! Damn you, Fair! Don't you die. You gotta drive this truck!"

I shoved my M79 through Fair's window and began firing, not knowing what I was firing at. "Get this convoy moving!" I bellowed over the radio. "I think Fair's dead. It's really hot back here."

"Ten-four, ten-four." The convoy slowly started moving.

Heavy fire continued, appearing to concentrate on our truck. I kept firing out the window one round after another. As the truck in front of ours began to move forward, our truck also began to move. Soon we were moving at a brisk pace.

"You ain't dead!' I shouted, still firing M79 rounds out the window. Fair, still slumped over the wheel, seemed to have all his facilities at least enough to drive the truck. *Tat-atat-tat-tat, pook-pook-pook, boom-boom-boom* came the report as a Cobra from Holloway flew over us, its landing strut barely missing the top of our truck. It was all over just as quickly as it began.

We arrived at the dump site fifteen minutes later. Fair's head finally stopped bleeding. I had tied my bandanna around his head. "Fair, you haven't said a word since all this began. You need to say something. You're scarin' me!"

"How bad is it?" He turned his head, looking at me. "How bad is it? Am I going to die?"

"I don't know. Blood is all over everywhere." As the convoy came to a stop, a corpsman came running up to the truck.

"Take it easy, take it easy. Can you get out of the truck?"

With that, Fair kicked the door open and jumped out. Minutes later, Fair's face was cleaned up and his wound dressed. The quart or so of Fair's blood sprayed all over the inside of the truck came from a very small flesh wound on his forehead.

The loads were dumped posthaste. The trip back to the hill was filled with anticipation even though we were escorted by two Cobra attack helicopters leading the way and two Huey UH-1 gunships bringing up the rear.

"Hey, man, my speedometer ain't workin'," commented Fair on the return trip.

The next day, Fair's truck was checked out for damage. The shell that had initially hit the truck was one of our own M79 high explosive rounds. The round hit the running board with the fuel tank and the door, absorbing most of the shrapnel. One fragment, however, found its way to Fair's forehead. Numerous AK-47 rounds hit the dump bed, leaving silver pockmarks on the plate steel. One .50-caliber round pierced the side of the truck four to six inches in front of the driver's door, chest high; its path continued through the vehicle, hitting the steering column, ricocheting upward from the impact, and lodging in the speedometer. If the enemy gunner had fired his shot one-half of one second later or if we had been moving a half a second faster, the round would have pierced the door, striking both Fair and myself in the torso, surely killing the both of us.

The next morning, as always, came much too quickly. Underhill and I went to the ASP yard at Camp Schmidt at 0630. I readied the mixer as Underhill went to the mess hall to get us some breakfast. He returned just as I was beginning to put the forty-nine needed bags of cement into the truck. Ten minutes later, he said, "Well, that's the last of 'em."

"Yeah, what a job. Let's see what the baby will do." I shoved the gearshift and tromped on the accelerator. The truck lurched forward, and we were on our way.

"Wow, this thing really runs smooth for a Chevy. Even an automatic. Don't even need to shift." The trip through Pleiku went smoothly as our shiny new toy bullied its way through traffic. The day passed as we made trip after trip from the ASP yard to the bridge site. Load after load poured, forming the abutment. "Finally, she's all done. What time ya got?"

"Hmmm, three thirty."

"Hey, guys, name's Grimes, I'm your new platoon leader," stated a young lieutenant, emerging from the jeep. "You about got it done?"

"Yep, just finished."

"Sure looks good. Job well-done. Job well-done, guys. Need any help loading up?"

"Naw, we're pretty much ready. Thanks. Underdog put the balance of the water from the storage tank into the drum. It'll wash out the drum as we are going home if we keep the drum turnin'."

The traffic through Pleiku was heavy as usual, but again, we bullied our way through.

"Matty, look through your rearview mirror. See that guy on a bike hanging on the ladder?" exclaimed Underhill as we exited the northwest corner of the city.

A fellow on a bicycle decided to hitch a free ride. He was clinging to the drum access ladder at the rear of the truck.

"The MPs see him back thee we'll be in a lot of trouble!"

"Watch this," I snickered, hitting the drum-control lever. Slowly the turning drum stopped. It then began to turn in the opposite direction. Suddenly, a rush of water came out the top of the drum, shot down the chute, hitting our hitchhiking friend squarely in the face, knocking him off his bicycle and shooting him completely across the oncoming traffic lane, narrowly avoiding a swerving deuce and a half. His bike was not as fortunate; in trying to avoid a collision with the downed rider, the deuce and a half swerved directly into the path of the bicycle. Three army tires and a crunch later, the bicycle lay mortally wounded on QL-14.

"Underhill, did you see how much water came outta the drum? What was left anyway?"

"Oh, about 260 gallons," replied Underhill with his all-too-infamous grin.

The next phase of the bridge was to set the pier. The 584th drove pilings into the river bottom to bedrock, which was only about ten feet. The pilings formed a cofferdam, a round tubelike structure extending from the bedrock to about twelve inches above the water. The pieces interlocked, forming a watertight barrier. The water that was left in the cofferdam was mixed with the mud of the river bottom, forming a slurry. This slurry was then pumped out. After several additions of water and mixing and pumping, the bedrock was finally exposed low and dry. One-inch holes twelve inches deep were then drilled into the rock. Fourteen-foot-long number 8 (one-inch) rebars were then inserted into the holes. The entire cofferdam was filled with concrete, forming a footing for the pier. The rebar protruded about two feet above the top of the pier footing. Additional steel (rebar) would later be tied to these pieces extending to the top of the pier, forming a steel connection from the top of the pier through the footing into the bedrock.

It was late March. My first eight and a half months in country were finished! Through! Kaput! The time had finally arrived for my R & R, a full week out of country. My choices had been Australia, Hong Kong, Japan, Thailand, and Hawaii. I had chosen to meet my wife in Hawaii as it was the least expensive plane fare for my wife. She did get a military discount. The five days in Hawaii with hotel and her plane fare was $450. My plane left Cam Ranh Bay on Monday, flew to Okinawa, then on to Hawaii. Sue was there to meet me Tuesday morning as she had arrived the day before. The five days passed like a freight train in the night. It was then back on the plane, heading back to war again. The flight from Hawaii to Okinawa was really, really long. I ended up passing much of the ten-hour trip playing chess with one of the stewardesses.

"Hey, Matty, have a good time? We really missed ya! You low dog," sneered Underhill and Holman as I emerged from a C-130 at Pleiku Air Base. The evening passed with the whole platoon teasing me about being in Hawaii with my wife for a whole week while they had to stay back and carry on with the war.

The next morning, it was off to the ASP yard (Engineer Hill). As I arrived, I noticed two large stacks of rebar that Underhill and I had bent. *Hmmm,* I thought. *The pier must not be poured yet. All the steel isn't tied yet.* My train of thought was broken as a jeep from the 584th pulled up. A very portly middle-aged E-6 crawled out.

"You Mattatall?" he grunted.

"I am."

"I'm Sergeant Osborn. I was assigned to take your place while you were on R & R."

"Well, I'm back."

"Yeah, I can see that. She's all yours. I'll go back to my unit."

"The pier hasn't been poured yet?" I quietly asked.

"Why, hell yes, it's poured! We poured it Wednesday!" he bellowed.

"Well, how about this steel?" I questioned.

"Aww, we didn't need it. You all cut way too much."

"But those are the collar pieces for the arms," I objected.

"Yeah, yeah, yeah, I know. You snot-nosed kids are all alike. I've been in this man's army twenty-one years. I sure know what the hell I'm doin'!" he screamed, his jowls taking on a bright red color and pulsating like two steam turbines.

With a roar of the engine and a hail of gravel, he was gone.

And they wonder why we call 'em lifers, I thought. "Hey, Smitty! Smitty!" I called as he emerged from the CO's office.

"Hey, Matty. I knew you'd be lookin' me up as soon as you got back. Underdog told me about that E-6 from the 584th leaving all that steel out. He tried to tell the guy, but he outranked Underdog and would have no part of it, and by the time he got back here to me, the pier was poured. It was too late."

"There's no steel in the pier?" I questioned.

"Yeah, there is," interjected Underhill, coming up from behind. "All the vertical pieces are in as well as all the collar pieces in the column.

The platoon put those pieces in and tied 'em. We were going to bring the horizontal collar pieces in the morning and place them and tie them, but that sergeant lifer Osborn was in a hurry and was already pouring the pier when we arrived. We were able to set a few of the collars in, but he wouldn't stop long enough for us to tie 'em. We were also able to throw the twenty-foot horizontal rods in but didn't have time to tie them."

All in all, the bridge pier consisted of a vertical column rising twenty-one feet from the top of the footing. The column was eight feet wide (roughly one-third the width of the bridge) and four feet deep from front to back. At the twenty-one-foot mark, the column grew two horizontal arms each extending seven feet from the face of the column. Each arm was six feet tall and four feet thick. When completed, the pier was twenty-seven feet tall and resembled a capital T with the bottom of the arms rounded off. The horizontal portion of the pier measured twenty-two feet from side to side. Forty-four pieces of the number 6 rebar had been cut and bent into rectangles measuring three-feet-six-inches-by-five-feet-six-inches. These rectangular collars were to be placed six inches on center throughout the horizontal portion of the pier with the first and the last piece being three inches from the outside edge. Fourteen horizontal rods were to be tied to the inside of the collars, three on top and bottom and four on each side. Ten of the forty-four pieces had made it into the pier along with the fourteen horizontal pieces. However, none of the pieces had been tied together. Each collar piece weighed 40 pounds. Thus, 1,360 pounds of reinforcement had been left out.

"Our platoon is stripping the forms this morning, let's go see what she looks like," said Smitty, rather annoyed.

We arrived at the bridge site just as the last forms were coming off.

"Hey, Matty!"

"Hey, Lemrise!"

"Well, how was your trip? Sorry I didn't get to see ya last night, I was CQ on guard duty."

"Good. Good. The trip was good. Don't worry about last night, there were enough guys givin' me a hard time about Hawaii."

"Well," said Smitty, "let's see what kind of job they did on pouring this thing."

"Looks good to me, Smitty. Smooth, no honeycombs, little bit of stoning and she'll be first class. Good job, guys, really good job. Hey, Underhill! Back to the ASP, we need to get the forms off our slabs. Oh, oh, something ain't right," I replied as I turned back to look at the pier from a distance. "Hey, Smitty, look at the pier and the two abutments."

"Yeah, looks like the pier is too high. Hey, Felty!" called Smitty. "You did set the top of the form to the elevation the surveyors from the 584th gave you, right?"

"Yes, Sergeant Smith, we did. Here is the elevation right here in the book. Sergeant Ditto and I checked it numerous times."

"Get the instrument out, let's check it."

In minutes, the surveyor's level was set up and leveled. Monroe, a new guy just in the country from New York, scrambled up the pier like a sticky-toed frog. The elevation of the pier was shot, followed by the elevation of the north abutment and, lastly, the south abutment.

"Yep, you're right, Matty. The top of the north abutment and the top of the pier are the same. That's exactly what the surveyors told us to do. The south abutment, however, is two feet lower than the north."

"Well, what do we do now?"

"I don't know," replied Smitty. "Have to check with the old man and see if he wants us to take 'er down and start over. You don't need to worry though, the CO at Camp Schmidt has a rush job for you. Next week, two new mobile communication units are coming in. They need to set perfectly level. He wants you to pour a slab 124-by-64 feet, 6 inches thick. I need the platoon to get this bridge finished up. All we have left is to set the steel and weld the slabs in place. Camp Schmidt will provide all the laborers you'll need."

Camp Schmidt, 0700, the Next Day

"Sergeant Mattatall?"

"Yes."

"I'm Gordon," a tall very thin specialist 4 introduced himself. "There are twenty of us, and Colonel Jansen told us to give you all the help you need to get these slabs poured."

"Well, the first thing we need to do is get rid of these piles of dirt and get the area leveled out. We'll then need a couple trucks of gravel, then we'll start setting forms."

"Ten-four, we're on it."

Specialist Gordon began barking orders. The day passed without incident. By 4:00 p.m., the first slab was ready to pour. I had figured on pouring ten slabs 64-by-12.6-feet. This would ensure expansion and would make it easier to keep the overall slab level. The next four days yielded four slabs. Total pour was 50-by-64-feet.

It was the morning of the sixth day. I had cut the crew down to four helpers as there wasn't enough work for all twenty. It was shortly after seven. Specialist Gordon and I were checking the form elevations just prior to our next pour. His men were busy drilling one-half-by-three-inch holes in vertical face of yesterday's pour. One-half-by-twelve-inch rebar would be inserted in these holes. During the next pour, the concrete would cover the exposed end of the rebar, forming a permanent connection between the two slabs.

Shhhhhhhhhhhhh! Kaboom! Kaboom!

Oh no! I thought as I tried picking myself up off the ground.

Shhhhhhhh, thud.

"B-22s!" yelled Gordon. I looked to the source of the thud and saw a rather ominous tail fin sticking out of the ground. It was about ten feet from a Quonset hut. Two GIs were standing in the doorway, observing the commotion. The rocket had buried about four feet of its six feet of length in the ground. *Kaboom!* was the report as the rocket exploded. The sound was deafening. My head felt like there was a siren going off inside; my ears were ringing so loudly. This time, instead of trying to get up, I actually tried to burrow under the slab.

Shhhhhh, kaboom! came another report. This one was one hundred feet to my rear. The explosion was followed by a creaking sound and then a great crash as the armed forces television tower came to rest twenty feet to my right. Large chunks of dirt and gravel began to beat me about the head and shoulders as debris from the tail fin express returned to earth. One large piece scored a direct hit to my helmet liner, relieving me of it in two pieces.

Shhhhhhhhhhhhhhh.

"Oh no!"

Kaboom! This one hit the guard tower that was next to the TV tower. When the dust cleared, the guard tower was nowhere to be seen. There wasn't a pile of rubble, not a timber, not even a sandbag left.

The next sixty minutes were a flurry of activity. Cobra attack helicopters and Huey gunships searched the surrounding area for the perpetrators. MPs scoured the camp, checking for casualties.

"Sergeant Mattatall, anyone in your group hurt?"

"No," I replied. "I've got a lump on my head and some scratches. The rest of the guys are fine. You might check that Quonset hut, there were two guys standing in the doorway when a delayed fuse went off."

When the dust cleared, a total of five B-22 rockets had hit Camp Schmidt. The first two had fallen harmlessly; the third landed fifty-four feet from my position and buried itself in the ground. This rocket contained a delayed fuse and was used to destroy bunkers as it would detonate after penetrating its target. It was because of this delayed detonation that the lives of my crew, the guys in the Quonset hut, and my own life were spared. A B-22 rocket was six feet long and carried a forty-pound payload of TNT. The very fact that the projectile was buried four feet in the ground was its undoing. Upon detonation, the explosion was forced more upward than outward. The falling debris, however, had left me a little lumpy. The concussion from the explosion had thrown the two GIs to the rear of the hut, slamming them into the wall. They too received only minor injuries. It was later determined that the attack had been launched from the hills of a nearby tea plantation.

Tea plantations in II Corps were strictly and totally off limits to allied forces activity. All the plantations were privately owned. We were not allowed to enter or even shoot into a plantation. The enemy often used these restrictions to launch their attacks.

The rest of the day was spent cleaning up the mess. It was surprising to me to see how quickly the television tower was re-erected. By the end of the day, there was no evidence that five rockets had hit the camp. That is, with the exception of the missing guard tower. The next four days were fruitful; four more slabs were completed.

"Hey, Matty, we workin' tomorrow?"

"Nah, it's Sunday. We need a break. We can pour the last two on Monday and Tuesday. The trailers are to arrive a week from Tuesday. This will give the slabs plenty of time to cure. The units go on the end we poured first."

By Monday evening, slab number 9 was set, poured, and finished.

"Sergeant Mattatall," came a loud booming voice just as I was about to mount my trusty steed for home. I turned to see a gentleman, midforties, a grin beaming from ear to ear.

"I'm Colonel Jansen. I see you have almost finished this assignment."

"Yes, sir!" I reported, coming to attention and saluting all at the same time. "The last pour will go in in the morning. Then you will then be ready for business, sir."

"I just wanted to come down and thank you personally, son. You have done an excellent job with all the adversity going on around us. A letter of commendation will go to your CO and be placed in your file. Thanks again, Sergeant."

"No problem, sir. All in a day's work."

Tuesday Morning, 7:02 a.m.

"Hey, Gordon! Are we ready to button up this job?"

"We sure are, Sarge. Carry's puttin' in the last of the pins."

Shhhhhhhh.

"Oh no! Hell no! Not again!" yelled Gordon, diving for cover.

Kaboom! The first rocket hit the VIP lodge a block to our west. *Kaboom! Kaboom! Kaboom!*

"Oh man, I'm goin' to get it for sure this time."

Shhhhhhhh, kaboom! Again a storm of debris fell on me as I tried again to blend into the ground, lying as flat as possible. The chop of blades was heard as a Cobra gunship passed overhead. *Tat-atat-tat* came the report from his twenty-millimeter cannons. *Pukapukapuka-boom-boom-boom* as he fired the grenade launcher. *Woosh-woosh,* the sound of missiles being launched. *Boom-boom* as they found their targets.

The Cobra had spotted the attackers and was launching a full-blown attack on them. They were again in the hills of the tea plantation. When the smoke cleared and the dust settled, twenty-three VC had been killed, leaving a cache of nine unfired B-22 rockets along with numerous B-40 rockets. Only a few trees in the plantation had been lost. Camp Schmidt was not so lucky. The first rocket left the VIP lodge a pile of sticks, killing a journalist. Three of the four remaining rounds had direct hits, one striking the officers' latrine, a brick-and-stucco structure left behind by the French. The explosion completely removed the tile roof and the front wall as well as every toilet partition and fixture on the inside, leaving only the two sidewalls and the rear wall standing. Another hit the mess hall, another former French structure, blowing a twenty-foot hole in the roof. The third hit a supply shed, destroying it. The last rocket—whether it was the second, third, fourth, or fifth, I know not—hit the exact same spot where the guard tower used to be. It was later determined that the VC were using the TV tower as an aiming point. My position was in a direct line between the TV tower and the plantation.

This time I had no mess to clean up. A little debris was removed from the form, the slab was poured, completing the project on time.

"Hey, Sarge! I'm back."

"Yeah, I know that. Colonel Jansen has called the CO several times about the job you did. I see all the rounds falling over there did not affect ya much."

Quad 40

Setting the Bridge Deck

"Naww, just a lump on the noggin. But, Smitty, I gotta tell ya I was pretty damn scared. Both times I was right in the middle of 'em. I know for sure that Cobra pilot was all that saved my bacon. He took 'em out before they were through."

"Yeah, well, he's up for a court-martial for firing into that tea plantation."

"Awww, man, you gotta be kiddin' me. The guy saved countless lives, takes out twenty-three VC, and they want to bust him?"

"Well, orders are orders, and they need to be followed."

"Well, I'm glad he didn't follow 'em this time."

"Ditto finished the bridge a couple of days ago, your slabs fit like clockwork. The 584th was to finish the railing yesterday. Let's go take a look."

"Oh, they decided to finish it just like it was?"

"Yeah, the big brass said it was really needed and to go on with it."

An hour later, we were at the bridge site. "Smitty, that thing really looks peculiar."

"Yeah, but it works OK."

The bridge from the north abutment to the pier was perfectly level. From the pier to the south abutment, it had a definite slant as if the southern abutment had sunk. Nevertheless, Lambrettas, bikes, and trucks were zipping across in their usual hodgepodge manner. A month later, two large vertical cracks appeared in the pier. Between each horizontal arm and the vertical column, two large metal bands were installed horizontally around the top of the pier, holding the arms in place, not allowing the cracks to get worse. The horizontal rods and collars Underhill managed to get in would keep the arms of the pier from literally falling off.

"Here's to you, Sergeant Osborn!"

Lightning

"Yo, Matty, the CO wants me to go over to the air base and pick up some VIP and take him over to group command. Wanna go?"

"Yeah, might as well. It's raining on our only day off."

The whole day had been consumed by a series of violent thunderstorms, and as you know, when it rains in a rain forest, it really rains.

As we approached Pleiku, the storm seemed all the more threatening. The rain caused the traffic to slow to a crawl. Right in front of our 3/4, there was a jeep without a top full of ARVNs. Those poor fellows looked like six little drowned rats. Our forward movement seemed to be nonexistent. As we approached, lightning struck a 105 telephone pole.

A 105 pole was constructed of empty 105 steel shipping containers welded together. The containers were about twenty-four inches long and approximately eight inches in diameter. One end was larger and belled out to accommodate the lid. The belled-out end was just large enough for the small end of another canister to slide in. They were fitted together and looked like a series of sewer pipes standing on end. The lightning bolt jumped instantly to the jeep, turning it upside down, spurting ARVN soldiers all over the countryside. In that same instant, I had this awful copper taste in my mouth. The hair on my arms began to stand on end, and a tingling sensation coursed through my forearm and elbow that was resting on the door. I noticed a blue hazy fog or fire moving up the outside of the truck door and then the lights went out and the world came to an end. As I came to, cold rain danced over my face; I could hear Underhill moaning. The truck was in the ditch. Both Underhill and I had been ejected and were lying on the pavement, one on each side of the truck.

"Underdog, are you OK?" I questioned.

"My head feels like it exploded. What happened?"

"I'm not sure, but I think we were struck by the lightning," I replied.

Over turned ARVN Jeep, lightening strike

"Hey, man, your eyebrows look fuzzy. They're all curly and melted looking."

Underhill's eyebrows were singed and all but burned off. The hair on my arm had also been singed along with a burn on my forearm where it had rested on the truck door.

Underhill and I were none the worse for wear. The ARVN soldiers, however, had not fared as well. One had been killed, and the other five were all inured with broken limbs, head traumas, cuts, and bruises in addition to receiving very serious burns. The ARVNs were carted to the hospital, the jeep was righted, and our truck was pulled out of the ditch. We were on our way as if nothing had ever happened.

The Quarry at Pleiku

As QL-19 passes by the eastern edge of Pleiku on its journey toward Cambodia, the terrain becomes flatter and less mountainous. Three clicks southwest of Pleiku, just to the south of QL-14 on Route 509, on the top of a large hill lay the Pleiku quarry. The primary function of the quarry was to furnish gravel for the paving of QL-14 from Pleiku to Kontum. Once the twenty-five miles of road paving was completed, the quarry was no longer needed. As the war began to de-escalate, the rock-crushing equipment was needed elsewhere. Company B received the assignment to dismantle the quarry.

The primary assignment of the Third Platoon was to pull guard around the perimeter, manning the twelve towers encircling the compound. The tower closest to the entrance faced northeast, overlooking the city of Pleiku. The hill at that point dropped abruptly into a long valley. From the bottom of the hill, rice paddies stretched almost to the outskirts of the city. The hazy days of summer passed as we manned the towers day after day while the other platoons were busily dismantling the heavy equipment. Ditto and I or Felty and I were usually found in tower one as we were in charge of the perimeter security. Every day we would watch the men and women working in the rice paddies below.

"Hey, Ditto! How long we been in this tower?"

"Oh, I don't know. Couple weeks, I guess."

"Yeah, it seems like months."

"I know what ya mean, not much at all to do all day. Just go and check the other towers several times a day."

"Ya see those people out there in the paddy? How far away do ya think they are?"

"Hmmm, I don't know, maybe 1,000 yards."

"They do look like ants scurrying around. I wonder if my 79 can reach that far."

"Nah-nah, too far away. That thing's range is only about 350 yards."

"I know, but we are at least 500 feet above 'em. Let's see just how close we can get," I said, slipping a round into the barrel of my M79.

"Whoa! Whoa! Whoa! You can't shoot at those people. Ya might get close and hurt or even kill one of those poor souls down there!" came back Ditto, his voice escalating.

"Relax, Larry," I grinned as I pulled the trigger. *Pook!* reported the M79 as the round left the barrel. "Do ya really think I'd shoot an HE round at 'em?" We watched as the round traveling at about 250 feet a second plummeted down the valley. "I can't see it. Can you?"

"Naw, too far." The paddy erupted with a splash and a puff of white smoke as the round hit home.

"Ahhh, didn't even get halfway," I groaned.

"What ya shootin', a smoke round?"

"Nope, CS gas. Might make their eyes water a little bit, but it's really harmless. Let me try again. This time I'll give it a little more elevation." Again the 79 reported as the round left the barrel. This time the round landed about 150 feet short of the group of workers. Again, a splash and a puff of smoke. We watched anxiously as the cloud of smoke drifted to one side of the group.

"Hmmm, wind blowing to the northeast. Need to shoot more toward the ARVN base."

Pook called round 3 as it left the barrel. Quietly we watched as the round left our sight. This time there was no splash, just a puff of smoke. The cloud slowly moved toward the group as we watched. Suddenly, people were running every which way to avoid the CS gas (tear gas).

In minutes, the cloud was gone as quickly as it had appeared. Slowly, the workers returned first one and then another. "What do ya see?" I queried as Ditto observed using binoculars.

"They, mmmph, are talking among themselves and looking around. I imagine they are trying to see just where the gas came from."

Soon it was back to work as usual. The group consisted of twelve to fifteen workers, mostly women dressed in the usual black pajamas and coolie hats. Again and again the 79 reported, the white cloud appeared, and the workers made their escape. Each time, it would take a little longer to return. Finally, after five or six rounds, we became bored and the M79 fell silent.

The Next Afternoon

"Hey, Matty, what do ya say we go over to Holloway and have lunch in the cafeteria?" called Underhill, grinning sheepishly.

"Sounds good to me," I replied, "but Ditto's the NCOIC here."

"That is a good idea. These C rations are getting old." The green Cadillac and the 3/4 was loaded, and we were off.

"Boy, that was really good," commented Ditto as we made our way back to the quarry.

"Whoa!" yelled Underhill as we approached the main gate. The 3/4 came to an abrupt stop. "There's someone behind those rocks. I saw a metal flash."

"Where ya lookin'?" I came back.

"Halfway up the hill on the left," replied Underhill.

"Don't see nothin'," replied Ditto.

"Let's go slow! Let's go slow! We're kinda in the open here."

Slowly we emerged from the 3/4 being joined by the others as the green Cadillac pulled up behind us.

"What's up?" called Felty as he and the others approached.

"Underhill saw a flash up on the hillside. We need to spread out and check it out."

"Arghhh!" groaned Glenn White, falling on his back as a muzzle flash and a loud crack erupted from the hillside. M16s responded instantly as we dragged White to cover.

"Ahhh," moaned White, rolling his head from side to side, his face grimacing in pain.

"How bad is it?" asked Felty as I opened White's flak jacket.

"Don't know, bud, but we'd better call for a DUSTOFF. What the?" I replied as the flak jacket came open. "No blood. Any wounds anywhere else?" I asked, checking White frantically.

A large red mark appeared right in the middle of his chest as I opened his shirt. "Well, I'll be. No Purple Heart for you, Whitey my boy. Your flak jacket kept that 47 round outta your heart. You livin' right or what, bro?"

"Humph, humph," White grimaced, trying to catch his breath. "Feels like a tank sitting on my chest."

"Just take it easy. I'm sure you'll have a shiner right under your dog tags."

"I'm goin' to get that gook," snorted Underhill, jamming a round in his M79.

Simultaneously I concurred. *Pooka, pooka*, two 79s chimed. *Boom! Boom!* called the twin sisters as they found their mark somewhere behind the large boulder that harbored the sniper. Instantly, an AK-47 flew over the boulder and rattled down the hillside.

"*Khong ban! Khong ban!*" came a voice from behind the rock.

"What's he saying?" queried Ditto.

"He wants to surrender," replied the ARVN interpreter.

"Tell 'im to come out," replied Ditto rather sternly.

The interpreter called to the man. After a lengthy dialogue between the two, two hands appeared from the left side of the rock. A torn-looking man followed, his face and clothing covered with dirt. Blood-spotted pimples appeared to be covering his face and unclothed extremities. His black pajamas were soaked from the waist down as he had wet himself. Soon the QCs arrived, and the prisoner was swept away, never to be heard from or seen again.

The day was warm and breezy, the afternoon passing rather lazily. That evening found us back at the quarry this time pulling our share of guard duty. I was CQ (noncommissioned officer in charge). As usual, when in the field, there was no officer of the day. So it was me and the guys on our own. As usual, two or three Lambrettas pulled up just as the daylight faded completely. Mama-san emerged from the front vehicle.

"Hey, Sarge Matty!" she called as she approached. "You number 1 tonight? You in charge?" she asked eagerly.

"Hey, Mama-san. What's up?" I replied.

"I know you no want, but GIs want girl?"

"Don't know. You'll have to ask 'em." Soon, both Lambrettas were void of passengers.

As the girls had gone to the bunkers with the guys, only Mama-san, myself, and the Lambretta drivers were left at the gate. Mama-san was vigorously eating what appeared to be raw fish from a rice bowl.

"Mama-san, what are you eating? That really looks awful."

"Oh no, Matty Sarge, *boo coo* number one. Here, you try. You like," she cried. "Take bite." She shoved a piece of her feast in my face with her chopsticks.

Gingerly I tasted her cherished delicacy. Instantly I began to choke and cough. "What is that?" I complained while gagging.

"Raw squid. What, you no like? What matter you, Sarge? Want more?"

"Nahh, I'll pass," I snorted. "Too strong for me."

At 0700 hours next morning, we were on our way back to Camp Schmidt for breakfast. As we approached the mess hall, a definite stench greeted us. The grease Dumpster had somehow been overturned; its contents flowed down the hill between the barracks. The smell was not of rancid grease but totally worse and indescribable. The stench was so bad it made me nauseous as I walked to the mess hall that morning. Now the mess sergeant was from Puerto Rico, Sergeant Vega Believe. Whenever a new man would come to the camp, if he was from Puerto Rico, the mess sergeant would draft him to mess duty, making him a cook. That particular morning as I went through the chow line, the server slapped a pile of yellowish brown goop on my plate.

"What is that?" I asked rather dejectedly.

"French toast!" was the reply.

Hmmm, I thought, looking at the grease-laden goop. *Not like any French toast I have ever had.* I thrust the tray through the dirty plate window, goop and all. By 0800 hours, it was back to the quarry. As the green Cadillac approached the outskirts of Pleiku, we came upon a woman pushing a four-wheel cart.

"Fair, stop the truck!" I yelled, jumping from the five-ton dump as it came to a screeching halt. "*Chao thuy,*" I called to the lady with the cart.

"*Chao ong,*" she replied. "You want food! *Boo coo* number one? Here, you taste. You want? You want?" she asked eagerly, thrusting a slice of meat in my direction.

Cautiously I tasted the sample. "Hmmm, not bad," I replied. "What kinda meat is that?"

"Number one, number one" was her only reply.

"Come on, Mama-san, if you want me to buy sandwich, you have to tell me what kinda meat that is."

"It, ughhh, it from *danh tu.*"

"You mean monkey?"

"No! No! No monkey. Live on top mountain. No climb trees, live on ground."

"Oh, you mean rock ape?"

"Ugh, ugh," she replied.

"OK! OK! One sandwich. How much?"

"For you, Sarge, two hundred P."

"No no, I give you one hundred P. I come every day, you make sandwich?" At first she disagreed, but after a bit of thought, she made me a really great sandwich.

"Hey, what ya got, Sarge?" called a PFC from the back of the truck, which had just arrived in country. "Wow, look at that sandwich, what's in it?"

"Well," I replied, "the bread is made from rice flour. It tastes a little bit different, but you'll get used to it. Look close, you see those specs in the bread?" I said, opening the sandwich.

"Aghhh! Those aren't specs, those are bugs, man!"

"Yeah, they're weevils, but don't worry, they're cooked."

"Yeah, just little extra protein," added Underhill. "They won't eat much."

The PFC's name was Stebbons. At first, his face began to blush. "Well, ah, what kinda meat is that?" he asked, his voice trailing.

"That there, my friend, is genuine rock ape."

"You, you mean, monkey meat?" Stebbons asked, his voice faltering.

"Yup, and the greens are bamboo shoots." I grinned, pulling a bottle of mustard from my vest.

"You really gonna eat that?" His face was now totally green, and his cheeks were bulging.

"Yep, *boo coo* number one." I grinned, taking a big bite.

"How do ya know she won't poison you or put a razor blade in there?" His voice barely audible as he hung over the side of the truck and vomited.

"Well, she wants that one hundred P every day. Ten to twelve sandwiches, and that's a month's pay, and its way better than the mess hall."

Every day for the next two weeks or so, we stopped and I got my sandwich. Every day, the meat would taste different; sometimes it would be of a red color, other times it would be darker or lighter, sometimes almost white. Some I could identify from past experiences (snake, dog, monkey, water buffalo), some I could not. However, after ten to eleven months in country, it all tasted good.

Steaks, Rats, 'n' Rockets

Saturday night, Holman had brought in our monthly ration of steak. Once again, the sweet smell of cooking beef wafted through the barracks. This time we added fried potatoes, fresh tomatoes (from whence they came, I know not), cold soda, and beer. A good time was had by all. As the night wore on, the barracks slowly became quiet.

"Wow, what a night. Great meal, Matty."

"Hey, all I did was cook it. Ya need to thank Holman for the supplies. Speaking of which, just where did you get those tomatoes?"

"Ask me no questions, and I tell ya no lies. Jesse James is still alive!" chimed Holman.

About 2330 hours, that crazy kid from New York, Monroe, entered our room.

"OK. OK, the gig is up. I know ya got extra steaks, and I want some!"

"Awww, beat it, kid, ya got all you're gonna get," drawled Underhill rather disgustedly. "Man, ya just can't please some guys. What, what are you doin' back? I told ya before to scram. Now SCRAM!" Without saying a word, Monroe stepped aside, allowing Sergeant Claude Lemrise to enter the room.

"You got extra meat?" snapped Lemrise. Underhill nodded.

"Give it up."

"Whoa, whoa, whoa," I interceded. "You might be the patrol leader, but to us you're as green as grass. Acting like that around people that have been in combat and been hurt or seen their buddies hurt or even killed will surely get ya fragged. If I were you, I would reconsider my demands. We've been there, and I guarantee you'll want us around if the goin' gets tough."

"Yeah, yeah, you're right, and I'm sorry. But I'm the patrol leader, and you guys seem to run the show. I just don't feel I get any respect."

"Respect is something you will have to earn. I know that you are a sergeant, that you have more time in grade than I do and you fulfilled all the requirements to fill the position you hold. However, to guys like Fair, Bomarito, Underhill, and me, you are untested. How will you react, not if but when we get ambushed on the road or tracers, gooks in the wire one night while on guard? When those things happen, everyone, and I mean everyone, gets mesmerized by fear. The question is, just what will you do with that fear? Just how well will you be able to lead your patrol? Only time will tell. If you want to be respected by us, you need to be one of us. Put your rank aside and be willing to learn those things that will help keep ya alive while you're here. Deal?" I asked, putting forth my hand in friendship.

"Deal," replied Lemrise, his eyes welling up with tears as he took my hand and embraced me.

"Ahhh, give 'em another steak, but only on one condition. Mum's the word. You tell anyone, and the deals off. Got that, kid?" I barked, grabbing Monroe, putting him in a playful headlock.

"Yeah, yeah, got it," replied Monroe, his eyes gleaming.

Sunday was a no-duty day in base camp. Everyone who wished had the pleasure of an extra hour or even a whole day of sleep. This particular Sunday followed our Saturday night's steak feast. When I awoke, the sun was up. It was already daylight. Underhill and Holman were gone. *Probably on a rations run,* I thought.

It was then I was greeted by a strange noise, *plop, splash.* At first I ignored it, but it continued. Again and again, *plop, splash, plop, splash, pop, splash.* Finally I began to look around to see from where the sound was coming. Still in my bunk, I scrutinized the room. There it was, at the foot of Underhill's bed sat a five-gallon bucket. The night before, it had been filled with ice, which had since melted. Out of the corner of my eye, I saw a brown figure rise above the rim of the bucket only to hit the side and fall back into the water. I quietly watched. Again the figure appeared, and again it hit the side of the bucket and fell back into the water. Again and again it attempted to free itself from the watery depths of the bucket but still remained its prisoner.

How does this compare to our lives? I thought as I lay there. *We get into ruts, and try as we may to get out, it is not until a greater authority comes along that we are able to be freed.* The rat, I imagine, having been enticed by the smell of the cooking meat, came to investigate. Somehow he had fallen into the bucket and was unable to get out. I decided to get up and let him go as he wasn't going to let me sleep any longer. Putting my feet on the crossbar of my bed, I pushed, arching my back, stretching to my full length.

Elephant near Plei Me

Scree! Scree! Scree! came a shrill voice in my ear. Before I could react, I felt a piercing pain in the same ear. Instantly I jumped up, only to see another brown companion fleeing the scene. The rat had taken refuge under my pillow during the night. My stretching antics had caught him between my head and the headboard of the bed. He nipped my ear in retaliation prior to fleeing to safety. I immediately went to the medic, thinking I would have to take rabies shots. The medic assured me that there was no danger as there was no rabies on record. That night, I carefully checked my bed and its contents, making sure there weren't any more uninvited visitors about.

The night was cool; sleep came quickly. At 12:35 a.m., *kaboom!*

"Incoming!" yelled Underhill as I awoke from a dead sleep.

Kaboom! came the second report. This one's concussion turned my bed over on top of me.

"Matty! Matty! You OK?" queried Underhill as I groped in the dark, trying to free myself.

"Yeah, yeah. I think so, just got this stinkin' bed lying on top of me!" Next came the whoosh of a mortar. The room exploded, pelting us with wooden shards as the round landed just outside our barracks. The sandbag retaining wall took the brunt of the explosion, but the barracks wall above the sandbags wasn't so lucky. The explosion and the resulting shrapnel left the wall mortally wounded. The shrapnel ripped through the wall, destroying everything in our room above the sandbag wall. My TV took a direct hit and lay lifeless on its back in the middle of the floor with a fist-size hole in the plastic safety shield that covered the screen.

It was over as quickly as it started. The first round was a B-22 rocket landing several blocks away; the second, also a B-22, landed less than a block away. The concussion from the explosion of its forty-pound TNT payload somehow turned my bed over. The flat spring caught my arm and left a nasty cut on my wrist. Several eighty-millimeter mortars were next, the one landing about four feet from the outside wall of the hooch. Once again we were blessed as Holman, Underhill, and I were spared as we were below the sandbag wall when the round hit.

Camp Holloway

It was early April; the monsoon season was in full swing. At 0600 hours, the rain would come hard for five to ten minutes and then stop just as quickly as it came. Around 1000 hours, the rain would return but only as a drizzle that continued most of the day, only to be added by another real soaking around 1330 to 1400. By 1600, all was calm, then at about 1800 hours, the real rain would come. The raindrops pelting the metal roof of the hooch were much louder than the thundering hoofbeats of a herd of wild mustang. This deluge would last maybe ten to fifteen minutes. Many times this evening rain would fill the five-foot-deep, twelve-foot-wide ditch that ran along the road at the bottom of Engineer Hill to overflow. At times there would be up to eight inches of water on the road. The volcanic soil on the hill was so porous that five minutes after the rain had stopped, one could hardly tell it had rained.

Sunday Afternoon, Staff Meeting

"Hey, Matty," called Sergeant Smith as he entered the dayroom at company headquarters.

"Hey, Smitty."

"Here's your next assignment." He placed a folder on the table in front of me. "This one's close to home. Camp Holloway to be exact. We need to regrade and gravel the roads as well as build several head walls around some new culverts the 584th has just installed."

With our platoon at thirty-eight men strong, about every two weeks, someone would go home only to be replaced by a new guy. It appeared to me that the new guys coming in seemed to have a different attitude. They lacked team spirit and were more anti-establishment than in the past, almost as if the antiwar protesters were being sent to Vietnam. Now there was a PFC from Chicago, new in country, assigned to our platoon, my patrol. His name was Sylvest. Now Private First Class Sylvest seemed to go out of his way to get under my skin.

Payday, April 1970

"Sarge Matty! Sarge Matty!" screamed Mai, the hooch girl that took care of our end of the barracks. "Sarge Matty, you help me! You help me!" she pleaded, clutching at my arms, tears streaming down her face.

"Calm down, calm down. What's going on?" I asked.

"New GI, new GI," she stammered, trying to catch her breath between words. "He try take me to his room for boom boom. Sarge Matty, you know I number 1 girl. I no do number ten! I no do number ten! I no do number ten!" She sobbed.

"OK, you show me GI, I'll take care of him. Come on, Underdog, let's get this straightened out."

Halfway down the hall, we met Sylvest coming toward us, a wad of MPC in his hand.

"Hey, honey," he called as we approached. "You change your mind? I got the money right here." He shoved the cash toward her.

"I NO DO THAT!" Mai shrieked. "You *boo coo* number ten!"

"Hold it, hold it," I interjected, staying between them. "Holman, take Mai down to our end of the hooch while we straighten this out, will ya?"

"Yeah, sure." He took Mai by the shoulder.

"Sylvest, what the hell you think you're doin'?"

"Hey, I know you guys think she's your girl, but where I come from, money talks."

"Well, you ain't in Chicago, and you ain't goin' to convince any of these girls to go to bed with ya. The way I see it, ya got two problems here. Number one, the hooch girls are not whores. The prostitutes are a whole different society. They even live separately from everyone else. There's a neighborhood in Pleiku called Sin City, one street about two to three blocks long. All the prostitutes live right there.

"Problem number two, not to hurt your feelings, but you're black."

"Humph, you think I don't know that?"

"Most of the prostitutes won't have anything to do with a black guy. However, the first three houses on the block, left side of the street, cater only to black guys. About twenty or so of the girls are from Cambodia, too beautiful to be in that profession."

"Yeah, yeah, yeah, well, we'll just see if one of those girls won't play. Like I said, money talks."

"Yeah, well, just be warned, pretty boy, stay away from Mai. She's too good a maid and too good a friend for us to let you run her off."

Sylvest gave me a hideous look and shuffled to his room.

The Following Monday

The grading and graveling at Holloway were in full force. The ten o'clock rain had started. The clouds lay low, touching the ground in most places, shrouding the camp in a hideous fog. The morning was almost cold unlike most days in the rain forest. Sylvest was pulling security at the end of the road near the wire. Barely a hundred feet away, he was enshrouded by the fog.

"Hey, Sarge," he called.

I turned to see him lock and load his M16, an action that was only sanctioned when one was in imminent danger from the enemy. I quickly scrutinized the perimeter, seeking the cause of the action, not seeing a problem.

"Hey, Sarge, ya know what?" shouted Sylvest. "I'm just gonna shoot you right here!"

"Good luck!" I shouted, moving toward him. "You'd better shoot good 'cause when I get to ya, I'm gonna shove that rifle down your throat!"

As I approached, I could actually see Sylvest's knees shaking, beads of sweat forming on his forehead. The closer I got, the weaker he became. He looked as if he would collapse before I got to him.

"I . . . I was just kiddin'," he stammered, his voice cracking as I approached taking the gun from his hand.

"Never! Ever! Lock and load your weapon in base camp unless you're gonna use it!" I snapped, ejecting the shell from the chamber. "Next time, it'll be an Article 15, and ya won't have so much money to throw around."

"Hey, Matty, problem here?" called Lieutenant Sanders, driving up in his jeep.

"No, sir," I returned. "Just educatin' PFC Sylvest here on weapons protocol in base camp."

"Very well, carry on." He saluted as he pulled away. Sylvest became a pretty good soldier after that incident.

The work went smoothly at Holloway. The head walls and grading completed, we moved on to one of several concrete ammo bunkers and began replacing the reinforced block walls around the doorways. Holloway was basically a helicopter base housing Cobra assault helicopters, Hueys, and several Chinooks as well as one or two cranes. At the east end of the base, there were eight to ten reinforced concrete buildings built in the hillside. These were the ammo bunkers that housed the munitions for the choppers as well as the troops in the Pleiku area. New roll-up doors were also installed on several of the bunkers. During the course of this action, one of the new replacements decided to play with a trip-line trigger. (Trip lines were used basically to alert U.S. forces that the enemy had infiltrated the perimeter wire of a camp. This particular type was attached to a flare.)

"What are ya doing there, Aguillero?" I asked as he toyed with the triggered flare.

"Ahh, nothing. I just found this thing in a box over there. Just wondering what it is?"

Before I could respond, the trigger went off, igniting the flare's propellant.

"Whooh! Yeow!" yelled Aguillero as the flare's propellant ignited, showering sparks over the pallets of ammunition, shooting the flare the length of the building's interior.

After hitting the opposite exterior wall, the flare lay on the floor, shooting a trail of sparks across the room. Instantly the door crew fled, fearing the flare would set off the stored ammo. Without thinking, I grabbed a shovel and ran toward the fizzing mimi, knowing full well the white phosphorous flare itself would ignite, surely causing the whole place to go up. *Pop* called the flare just as I scooped it up, flinging it into an empty corner of the building.

The day was heavily overcast due to the rain. The light of the burning flare filled the building, spilling out through the doorway.

"Nanananana . . . __________ *The Twilight Zone*, whooooo," chirped Holman.

As I exited the bunker, I found Aguillero running around in circles, holding one hand in the other.

"Hey, Aguillero!" I called as he continued to run, his face grimacing in pain. No answer.

"Hey!" I called again. "Hey! Hey!" Still no acknowledgment.

"We gotta stop him!" yelled Underhill, running after him.

A flying tackle later, we all converged.

"What the hell's wrong?" I shouted as we tried to restrain him.

"M-m-my hand, my hand," he whispered, ceasing to struggle.

His right hand between the thumb and forefinger was covered with small blisters; a long gray streak burnished itself. The burning propellant had left its mark; a quick trip to the first aid kit, and he was fine. Another classic example of how a little bit of ignorance can get you into an awful lot of trouble, or even killed.

Several Days Later As the Work at Camp Holloway Was Coming to a Close

The morning was beautiful. The sun was shining for the first time in what seemed like a year. The air was crisp. It was great to be alive.

"Hey, Matty," called the CO as his jeep pulled up.

"Morning, sir. What can I do for you?"

"Well," he replied, pointing to the rear of his jeep, "I traded us putting some paneling up in the officers' dayroom for that, and I would like it mounted back there. Is it doable?"

"Wow! Is that a?"

"Yup, a genuine minigun. It came off one of the Cobras. Had some kinda problems."

"We'll get right on it, sir."

That afternoon, Underhill and I cut a base for the gun out of three-eighth-inch steel wall plate. We welded a two-inch pipe atop the base followed by a mounting bracket. By evening, we were ready for our first test fire.

"What makes this thing work?" asked Bomarito.

"Battery," replied Underhill. "I'll get one from the motor pool."

"Naw, don't bother. Takes a twenty-eight-volt battery, you know, like the ones they got in the choppers. Guess we'll have to acquire one tomorrow at Holloway."

Two cartons of cigarettes and a handshake later, there were two brand-new batteries in the 3/4. The day dragged by as we eagerly awaited the testing of our new toy.

Finally, at 1730 hours (5:30 p.m.), Underhill, the CO, I, and twenty boxes of ammo were off in his jeep to the jungle for the big test.

"Well, sir, the honor's all yours," I snickered, snapping the ammo chain into place. The captain took his place behind the piece, grinnin' like a fox in the henhouse. Instantly, the six barrels of the gun came to life. *Burrrrrrup!*

yelled the gun's barrels as the chains of ammo screamed from their boxes. The hail of bullets tore holes in the jungle's foliage 250 yards away. The gun went silent just as quickly as it had started.

"What's wrong?" asked the CO, a puzzled look on his face.

"Hmmm, don't know," I replied, examining the weapon. "Hmmm, looks like the batteries are dead. Yup, must be some sort of short in the electronics. That's probably why they junked it."

"Think we can fix it?" asked the CO eagerly.

"Got any ideas?" Underhill asked.

"Don't know. Let me sleep on it, we'll come up with something," I replied.

I thought about the situation as we headed home.

"Hey, Underhill," I called as we entered the gates at the entrance to the hill. "Drop me off at the ASP yard, will ya?"

"You got something?" quizzed the CO.

"Well, sir, that minigun is nothing more than an electric Gatling gun, just like the manual ones used by the infantry in the 1800s. If this gun's ancestors could be cranked by hand, so can this one."

"Soooo what's the plan, Matty?" asked the CO.

"Well, the way I see it, the big disk on the back of the gun spins, causing the barrels to rotate and fire. If we install a crank on that disk, we can accomplish the same thing."

"Sounds good to me. What are ya gonna use for a crank, and how ya gonna mount it?" the CO questioned, looking a bit confused.

"I, uhahhh, got an idea, Underhill, will you bring the jeep back to the ASP yard after ya drop off the CO?"

"You got it, Matty."

Hmmm, there must be one here somewhere, I thought as I sorted through the tools in the crib. "Ah, here it is," I mused as I picked up a carpenter's brace. Now a brace is the forerunner to the electric drill. At one end is the chuck that holds the drill bit, at the other end a round wooden handle that spins. Now let's see, how do I explain this? The steel shank between the chuck and the handle is U shaped. The chuck is attached to one of the U's protruding vertical legs, the handle to the other vertical leg; both are at a ninety-degree angle to the top and the bottom of the U. The middle vertical leg of the U has a metal or wooden tube wrapped around it. The tool works by grasping the tube with one hand and the wooden handle with the other. One then rotates the brace by turning the U, drilling a hole with the bit attached at the chuck end, the handle or knob is used to hold the tool steady. Now I needed a crank. So first order of business was to cut the brace in two right in the center of the middle vertical leg, discarding the chuck end of the tool. Step 2 was to weld the remaining part of the brace to the disk on the back of the minigun. With the help of Underhill, the task was completed just before supper.

"Well, that's the last of it."

"Looks good. Do ya think it'll work?"

"Hmm, let's see. I wouldn't want to get the CO's hopes up just to disappoint him."

After double-checking the gun's chamber to make sure no live rounds were lurking around and also making sure the ammo chain was disconnected, Underhill grabbed the handle and gave it a spin. As the crank turned, spinning the disk, the barrels rotated, the firing pin clicked as each barrel came into place.

"Wow! That's smooth!" exclaimed Underhill.

After supper, we picked up the CO and were on our way back to the jungle. Not a word was spoken as we drove along the dirt road to the test site. Finally, Lieutenant Reel broke the silence as the jeep came to a halt.

"Well! Think it will work?" There was not a bit of confidence in his voice.

"Give her a try." I smiled as Underhill locked the ammunition chain in place.

"Just turn the wooden handle in a clockwise direction."

"Here goes!" The CO turned the crank rather slowly.

Bam! Bam! Bam! Bam! Bam! Bam! cried the gun as the rounds fired.

"It works! It really works!" screamed the CO over the noise of the firing rounds.

The faster he cranked, the faster the piece fired.

"Well, what do ya think?" I asked as the crank stopped and the minigun became silent.

"It's great! It's great!" The CO beamed. "Not six thousand rounds a minute, but still an awful lot of firepower."

In the next several weeks, the new mini Gatling gun would prove a lifesaver, thwarting sniper attacks by the enemy, surely saving the lives of Underhill and the CO.

Culverts at Camp Halloway

Camp Schmidt: The Move

Sunday Afternoon Operation Meeting

"Well, gentlemen, the time has finally come. It's our turn to follow the 167th [a signal battalion that had been located right next to our company. One afternoon they just packed up and left.] Co. B will be the next to go!" said First Sergeant Gilbert. "Sergeant Baluta will give you platoon sergeants your assignments."

The next Saturday would be the big day. Several units had left Camp Schmidt due to the de-escalation of the war. Eventually the entire hill would be abandoned, turning the compound over to the ARVNs (Army of the Republic of Vietnam).

"Hey, Matty!" called Smitty after the meeting. "Ya wanna take a ride, go look at our new home?"

"Sure, why not?" I smiled.

Soon we were over at Camp Schmidt, looking for barracks that would be our new base camp home. Finally there it sat, a two-story hooch sitting right behind the mess hall, right in line with the television tower and right in line with the tea plantation across the highway. My memory overflowed with thoughts of the B-22 rockets taking out the TV tower and part of the mess hall in the month or so past.

Each floor of the barracks consisted of one open bay end to end with a row of bunks on each side.

"Can ya work your magic by next Saturday?" asked Smitty with his usual humorous look on his face.

"What do ya want?"

"Same as before, but this time, there's enough room for everyone to have their own room if they want."

"Who've I got?"

"Just your patrol, need everybody else for the move."

"What about materials?"

"There's plenty over at the ASP yard. Have 'em delivered first thing in the morning."

Smitty and I pulled up to a terrible ruckus at Company B's hooch. Bomarito was in a rage; he was screaming and yelling, kickin' the wooden walls with his feet, smackin' the walls with his fists.

"What's with Bomarito?" Smitty asked Ditto.

"He got a 'Dear John' letter from his wife. Seems she's pregnant."

"Yeah, and he's only got about sixty days left in country."

"Well, we better getta hold of 'im before he hurts himself or one of us."

Smitty, Ditto, Felty, and I moved in. Six-foot-eight Ditto was the first to make contact. Bomarito threw him off like a rag doll. The remaining three of us jumped him at once. It was like having a tiger by the tail. Ditto jumped back in as well as several other members of our platoon. Once subdued, he continued to scream bloody murder. Finally a medic came and gave him a sedative. The chaplain from group command also came over. Bomarito went home shortly thereafter on a hardship leave through the Red Cross.

Monday morning, with a few notes from the platoon, we were ready to go. By Friday evening, the barracks were finished, each floor had partitioned walls from one end to the other. A six-foot corridor ran the length of the barracks with ten rooms on each side. Forty rooms total. Saturday saw the big move. By the end of the day, we were settled in our new home, never to return to Engineer Hill. Saturday night, it was work as usual.

Several months passed. A GI asked one to pull guard for him so he could attend one of the shows at base camp. Once the word got out, I had a booming side business. I made $15 a month, more than my army salary pulling guard at $20 per shift. This Saturday night would be just a little different. I pulled the first two-hour shift. Upon being relieved by my fellow guard, I retired to the bunker's interior below the guard tower for some much-needed sleep. I unrolled my sleeping bag atop the sandbag mattress, climbed in, closed my eyes. Minutes later, as sleep began to overcome me, I felt a *tap-tap* at my feet. I lay there on my back, my arm crossed on my chest. The next tap was just below my knees, instantly awakening me to my full senses.

Oh no, not a rat again! I thought.

The next tap hit my belt. *OK, here we go, just one more.*

Sure enough, the next jump and the rat landed right on my crossed arms. Both arms shot out toward the sides of the bunker, flinging the rat against the wall, causing a loud squeal and a quick retreat.

Again I settled down for my four-hour nap. Sometime later (ten minutes), a familiar sound awoke me, footsteps up the back of the tower then down again. As the footsteps moved around the right side of the bunker, I was up, weapon in hand. The footsteps then moved around to the front of the tower. Then suddenly, two army boots appeared in the gun port of the bunker. *Time to go,* I thought. Out the bunker door I went only to find a very green second lieutenant waking the guard who had fallen asleep. He had walked around to the front of the tower just to make sure; protocol calls for anything in front of the tower to be fair game. If the lieutenant hadn't stepped into the gun port while trying to boost himself up for a better look, exposing his jungle boots, I would have shot him thinking he was a sapper about to throw a satchel charge.

New lieutenants had a very short life expectancy. These young men would be thrust into combat, trying to lead a platoon without any actual combat experience. About the time a platoon would get one trained, the army would rotate them out, and the process would start all over again with a new guy.

The day was unusually hot and had been spent clearing the new growth jungle from the free-fire zone along QL-19 east of Pleiku. I had just showered that evening. As I reached for the door handle at the top of the steps of our hooch, I heard what sounded like an automatic burst from an M16. I immediately turned to face the perimeter wire, all quiet there.

"Arrhh," a groan came from within.

I opened the door to be greeted by Snyder, holding his neck, his face laced with pain.

"Sarge, something hit me in the neck. It burns like heck."

"Here, let me take a look."

Snyder turned, revealing a large lump on the back of his neck covered in what looked like silver paint. By this time, that end of the barracks was astir. Finally, Ditto emerged from the room below left.

"What happened? There's feathers floating all over my room."

Monroe was next, top room left above Ditto.

"Hey, something just knocked my radio off the shelf."

First we got Snyder over to the dispensary. Next we checked Ditto's room. The investigation revealed eight rounds had penetrated the hooch's outer wall, creating a pattern extending the width of his room, spaced about eighteen inches apart. The last round passed over Ditto's head, devouring a pillow on the upper bunk. Larry had been sitting on the lower bunk. If he would have been anywhere else in the room, he would have been wounded.

Two rounds penetrated Monroe's room, one round knocking the radio off the shelf and lodging into the doorjamb. The second round penetrated the outer wall, passed through Monroe's room, entering the door, crossing the hall, penetrating the inside wall of Snyder's room. The round then hit the steel bar of the head of Snyder's bed, causing the bullet to disintegrate. The silver spray and the lump were caused by the momentum of that bullet. The bed's head bar was about three inches in diameter. The impact of the round hitting the bar left a very big dent in Snyder's bed. Snyder lay with his head on the bar exactly where the bullet hit. The bar literally saved Snyder's life. As the round passed through the hall, it missed hitting me by less than twenty-four inches. One more time, saved by my guardian angel.

By this time, there was a lot of commotion over at Second Platoon's hooch. One of the GIs with whom we had a lot of trouble was high on speed and lost it and shot a half a clip at the wall. The rounds naturally went through the walls of his hooch as well as ours, causing all the commotion. The next morning he was just gone, never to be seen again. The Army CID most likely collected him sometime during the night and hauled him off to get some help. There was another guy in the First Platoon who would get high on heroin, would run through the barracks with his weapon locked and loaded, screaming, "They're after me! They're after me!" He too disappeared one night.

Heavy drug use such as heroin or hashish was not commonplace; however, the use of marijuana was a different story. The pot in Vietnam was so strong that the dealers would cut it by mixing it with Kool cigarette tobacco. Even in its cut state, one drag from a marijuana-loaded cigarette (joint) would instantly turn the user's eyes bloodred. One night, I was awakened from a sound sleep. Several GIs were in the room across the hall, partying. My head throbbed and ached incredibly. Not knowing what was wrong, I tried to get up. Down I went, flat on the floor. I was so dizzy I couldn't even walk. Painfully, I crawled over to the outer louvered wall of the hooch. The cool, fresh air coming through the louvers relieved some of the throbbing and pain. Finally, my head began to clear. The rest of the night was spent on the floor. By morning, only a small headache remained. This was my one and only encounter with cannabis (except for Wooly Bully), a contact high.

Shortly before the move to Camp Schmidt, Holman and I, along with several of the cooks, were off to the supply depot over at the air base to pick up rations for the mess hall. On the return trip, as we neared the entrance to the hill, the truck came to an abrupt stop. Holman and the cooks, who were sitting up front, were out of the truck and running full blast toward the Montagnard village. Not knowing the situation, I too followed, my 79 at the ready. Not long after alighting from the rear of the deuce and a half, I saw a large black mamba snake heading toward the village at full speed, with the cooks and Holman in hot pursuit. The snake was in excess of six feet long and three or four inches in diameter.

As the snake neared the entrance of the village, the cooks surrounded the snake, poking at it with large sticks. A group of villagers had gathered by this time to investigate the commotion caused by the yelling of the cooks. As the cooks fought for an advantage to subdue the snake—which was fast and agile, parrying their every move—a voice came from the crowd.

"You really shouldn't be playing with that snake," came the voice. "That is a black mamba. And very, very poisonous."

Instantly I looked around to see from whence came the voice as only villagers were present in addition to the four GIs.

Again the voice. "You are really playing with fire."

Again I searched the crowd. This time, one of the villagers came forward and spoke to me.

"You really need to stop those guys from playing with that snake, if it bites one of them they won't have a chance," he continued.

At that moment, one of the strikes of the cooks connected. The snake was no more. The cooks immediately skinned the snake, giving the skin to one of the villagers. The meat they also shared with the villagers, taking about half of the meat for themselves. As the villagers turned to return to their homes, I turned to the fellow with the voice.

"How is it you speak perfect English?" I asked the man clothed only in a loincloth.

"Well, it's a long story," he replied. "You see, I was educated in the United States, Yale to be exact. After finishing my education, I returned here to my people to try and make a difference."

"Who would have thought?" I replied, shaking the man's hand as I left.

Holman and I were walking from the motor pool to our barracks, having delivered the rations to the mess hall. Holman was carrying a large box. Somehow, he had acquisitioned an additional case of T-bone steaks.

Convoy stopped after lead truck (foreground) hit mine

"Boy, are we goin' to party tonight," snickered Holman.

"Hey, you there, Specialist, Specialist," called a second louie, coming up from the rear. "What ya got in that box, Specialist? Looks like contraband."

"Just some rations for the mess hall," replied Holman disgustedly.

"Yeah, well, you're goin' the wrong way, the mess hall is over there." The lieutenant pointed in the opposite direction. "Let's have a look." He took the box from Holman.

"Yep, just as I thought, contraband," suggested the lieutenant, opening the box, revealing its contents. "Now I will just relieve you of this contraband, and we'll just pretend this never happened. Understood?"

Holman nor I said a word as the lieutenant departed with our booty. Shortly thereafter, the smell of cooking steaks wafted through the compound. "Man, I was really planning on those babies, they really smell good," replied Holman, a tear in the corner of his eye. "We need to get even with those bums, taking our supper like that."

"You got that right. We need to teach those guys not to mess with us."

"Hmmmmm," remarked Underhill. "Looky what I got here." He pulled a baseball grenade from his tunic pocket. "Just what can we do with this thing? Hmmmmmm."

"Gimmie that thing, I'll show ya what we can do with it. Hey, Monroe, those bums took our steaks and are cooking 'em right there in front of our very own eyes, what do ya think?"

"That a gas grenade?"

"Yep."

"I'll fix 'em."

Monroe took the baseball grenade and stealthily headed toward the lieutenant's quarters where they were barbecuing our meat. He pulled the pin and launched the grenade. A white cloud emerged as the grenade popped. The cloud began to move slowly toward the lieutenant's position; all of a sudden, the wind changed, pushing the cloud away from its target and toward Company C's barracks. Soon GIs were running in every direction, trying to escape the gas. Needless to say, we thought it best just to keep our mouths shut and lie low, knowing another day would offer another opportunity.

Du-Co

May 1, 1970

With the deployment of the U.S. forces back to the United States having begun, the allied forces decided to invade or in surge into Cambodia. Until now, the countries of Cambodia and Laos were listed as neutral territories and were off-limits to the allied forces. The allied forces in our theater of operations consisted of the U.S. forces (army, air force, and navy along the coastal areas) along with a few companies of Aussies (Australian troops) and Korean ROKS (South Korean army). The Aussies were scattered around with the U.S. Army. The ROKS were used mainly to guard the bridges as they were unmerciful to the VC or NVA that tried to destroy their bridges as they called them.

Once the insurgence began, there was very little opposition from the VC and NVA forces. They were just lying back, biding their time as they knew the U.S. boys were heading home. Huge caches of weapons and foodstuffs were found.

Two gathering points in Vietnam were established in the II Corps area. The first was near a Montagnard village (CIDG camp) named Du-Co. The other was fourteen miles to the north and called Plei Dejereng. Du-Co was located three clicks from the Cambodian border. Lieutenant Simmons, platoon leader, Company B, Twentieth Engineers, was in charge of establishing our presence in these two areas.

"Matty."

"Hey, Smitty, what's up?" I replied.

"We need two trailers fashioned into tank sprayers. Co. A has welded us a couple of eight-by-eight-by-eight foot steel boxes to use as tanks. You're a farm boy from the Midwest, design us some kind of spray nozzle that will distribute a spray path as wide as the trailers that we can attach to the rear of the trailers."

"The hell I'm a farm boy. I don't know the first thing about farming."

"Awwwwww, you're from the area. You've seen those things. Do it anyway."

"OK! OK! I'll go over to A Co. and see what they've got."

"Mattatall, are you the sergeant from B Company?"

"Yeah, that's me."

"What do you think, will the cans work?"

"Looks fine to me."

The eight-square-inch, eight-inch-tall tanks were welded to a two-wheel trailer chassis.

"Have you guys got any six-inch pipe and fittings to go along?" I asked.

"Sure, what ya need?"

"Well, if we can cut a hole right here in the middle of the tank chassis at the bottom, weld in a nipple about ten inches long, screw on a valve, followed by another nipple about three long, a tee, two forty-eight-inch sections capped at each end, I think we can make it."

"Give us an hour, and we'll have her done."

I returned an hour later, and the first tank was completed.

"Well, Sarge, she's all done, but how is it going to spray?"

"Now I need you to drill a series of holes, one every four inches along the entire length of the pipe. Include the tee so the pattern will be even."

"Can do. How big around do you want the holes?"

"Ohhh, a quarter inch should do fine."

"Stand back, this is a piece of cake for Northcutt. Northcutt, cut me one-fourth-inch holes in that pipe, one every four inches."

Within minutes, Northcutt had all the holes completed. I thought he would use a drill. He used a cutting torch instead and made short work of the project.

"Looks great, Lenny," I replied. "Let's test it."

We filled the tank about a quarter full of water (about one thousand gallons), hooked the trailer to a dump truck, opened the valve, and took off. The spray worked just fine, evenly covering an eight-foot-wide track of ground behind the trailer.

"Lenny! The thing works great! Can you have the other one ready tomorrow?"

"Sure thing, Sarge. Take that one back with you, and we will deliver the other one tomorrow morning."

"Smitty, here's your sprayer. Signed, sealed, and delivered."

"Hmm," replied Smitty. "Does it work?"

"Smitty, what do you think I am? Do you really think I would give you something that wouldn't work? We tested it with a thousand gallons of water. The thing's nifty. Lenny will have the other one ready in the morning."

"Good. We have a briefing this evening and will pull out tomorrow. The CO will give you all the information tonight right after supper."

2 May 1970, 1830 (6:30 p.m.)

"Lieutenant Simmons, is your platoon here?"

"All present and accounted for, sir."

"Gentlemen, I have called you here as this platoon, Third Platoon Co. B, has been selected for a very important mission. As most of you know, we went into Cambodia this week. A problem has arisen, and we are needed to solve it. There are over two hundred sorties being flown into Du-Co each day. Plei Dejereng has at least that many, if not more. The Hueys flying the sorties are bringing back weapons and foodstuffs. The terrain in those two areas is so dry, great clouds of dust are being stirred up as the Hueys hover while unloading. These dust clouds are causing unseen problems with the next choppers in line, and several collisions have occurred. Your first mission will be dust control.

"You will fill the tanks with penta prime [a type of road oil] mixed with Agent Orange. Our hope is that this mixture sprayed in the drop-off area will solve the dust problem. Once the dust is under control, your mission will be to go into Cambodia and destroy the supply bunkers from which the weapons and foodstuffs are being taken.

"As you know, Smitty is short and won't be going out in the field anymore. The platoon will be broken up into two units. Lieutenant Simmons will take one unit to Plei Dejereng, and Sergeant Mattatall will take the other unit to Du-Co. Sergeant Mattatall will be acting platoon sergeant. Ditto and Felty's squads will go with Lieutenant Simmons. Underhill will take over Mattatall's squad. Lemrise's squad will also go to Du-Co. Tomorrow you will go to supply and draw five bandoliers of ammunition each. Those of you who are carrying M79s will draw a .45-caliber sidearm and ammo along with a case each of M79 rounds, all HE [high explosives]. You will also draw five uniforms each, all DX goods. As you know, DX goods are already worn-out, but they will all be laundered. The oil you will be working with will ruin your clothes.

"There are bunkers and wall tents at Plei Dejereng. There are no facilities of any kind at Du-Co. Sergeant Mattatall, at the end of each day you will need to go to Plei Dejereng for the night."

"Beggin' your pardon, sir, I don't feel comfortable driving fourteen miles through the jungle in late evening. If it is all the same to you, we will bivouac in the dump trucks. The air force and the Montagnards are close by."

"Suit yourself, but Plei Dejereng will be open to you if you so desire. Mattatall, you will be the first to leave, your spray tanks are ready. You will pull out right after breakfast tomorrow. The 584th is building a perimeter to secure the weapons cache. Trucks from the other platoons will be in and out all day hauling the bags of rice back to Pleiku. Lieutenant Simmons, do you have anything?"

"No, sir."

"How about you, Sergeant Smith?"

"Well, sir, we haven't quite figured out how we will get the penta prime into the tanks, but I am sure we will."

3 May 1970, 0830 Hours

Our two-to-five-ton dump convoy joined the main convoy going to Plei Dejereng. Du-Co is located about twenty-five miles southeast of Pleiku. The terrain flattens out after leaving Pleiku and is mainly rolling hills. We passed several of the dreaded tea plantations along the way (tea plantations were sacred, protected hiding place for the VC). As we approached the second tea plantation, a Huey passed over, banked sharply, and returned. The side door was open, and I could see a fellow in the chopper patting his head with his hand.

"What's that all about?" asked Fair.

"Don't know," I replied. Again the chopper flew over, again the fellow patted his head with his hand, this time the chopper was a little closer. The next pass, the chopper dropped down and landed right in the road directly in front of us. *Uh-oh, what now?* I thought as an officer jumped from the helicopter. I quickly exited the dump and ran toward the waiting officer.

"Sergeant Mattatall reporting, sir!" I shouted as I approached, saluting. There in front of me stood General Glenn Walker, commander of the Fourth Division.

"Soldier, do you realize we are in a war here?"

"Yes, sir!" I replied.

"Then tell me why not one of your men have their flak jackets or helmets on! Not four clicks up this very road a convoy was hit not ten minutes ago, I lost an entire motorized infantry patrol. Now get your men in line and be at the ready! UNDERSTOOD!"

"Yes, sir" was my reply, saluting.

The general returned to his chopper and I to my men. As I alerted them of the situation, several of the new guys turned almost white with fear. As we approached, the convoy had been ambushed as they passed the second tea plantation. A great fight had ensued. F4 Phantoms had to be dispatched to dispose the perpetrators.

As we passed the ambush site, the first thing to come into our view was an APC (armored personnel carrier) setting off the side of the road in a skewed position. A B-40 rocket had hit the hatch door, blowing an eighteen-inch hole dead smack center. All inside were KIA. The entire machine looked as if it had been in a bonfire. Just beyond the APC lay a fuel tanker. It too was burned to a crisp. As we passed, the intense heat scalded us, reminding me just how fragile life was, just how close the enemy and death really were.

A few more miles and the main convoy turned north, leaving our two trailer-laden dump trucks on our own. "Underdog, have everyone on the ready, but don't let 'em shoot any of the locals. There are too many with us who are new in country." Of the twenty guys in our half of the platoon, eight were in country less than a month and had no combat experience.

We arrived in Du-Co in late afternoon.

"Wow, man, there ain't nothin' here but a runway!" bellowed Fair, my trusted truck-driving friend.

"Look down at the other end of the runway. What is that, a building? Head down there, Fair, let's check it out."

The runway was partially constructed of landing mats, but most of it was just red clay. The actual runway was about three thousand feet long. As we approached the end of the runway, the building was a thatched roofed pavilion. The floor was dirt. There were wall-to-wall hammocks inside. The pavilion measured about twenty-four-by-thirty. Every hammock was occupied as it was the barracks for the Montagnard soldiers guarding the runway. Some had uniforms, most wore only loincloths.

To the rear of the pavilion sat a 105 pull-behind howitzer.

"What do ya want to do?" queried Fair.

"Well, I guess the best thing is to park here near the Montagnards. It should be safe enough. We'll just sleep in the back of the dumps. This should protect us from a mortar attack."

It was early evening by the time we got settled. The sun had gone down, leaving a reddish hue reflecting off the clouds.

"Lemrise, post a guard. Make sure they look sharp. We don't want to wake up with our throats slit."

Darkness fell quickly. A cool breeze came in, pushing out the hot stickiness of the jungle afternoon. Everyone fell asleep quickly. About 2130, it began to sprinkle. As part of our supplies, we had several boxes of very large clear plastic bags. They were about thirty-six inches wide, eighty-four inches long. Everyone quickly grabbed one and used it for a bivy sack.

The rain continued steady but not too hard. At 0023 a.m., "Gulp, cough! Cough! What the hell is going on? I'm drowning!" I quickly rose up to find I was lying in about six inches of water. The floor of the dump was slightly tilted toward the front. The truck was also parked on a slight incline, rear wheels first. The steady rain had filled the truck bed with water. When the water depth reached my mouth and nose, it woke me immediately.

"Everyone, out of the truck! Try the pavilion."

All twenty of us converged on the pavilion only to find the dirt floor was a sea of mud. That's why there's all the hammocks. By now the rain was pouring down, a typical Vietnam monsoon. Our only choice was under the trucks as we had moved all the supplies to the cab area to keep them dry. The trucks offered little or no assistance. The rain was blowing. The volcanic soil turned to a deep, very red mud. The entire unit was soaked to the bone. The rain continued till almost dawn. The morning found twenty GIs wet, tired, and irritable.

"What's for breakfast?" grumbled Dominique, a PFC from New York not long in country.

"Wellllll," replied Holman, our rations driver, "ya all see those big boxes in the truck? Well, they got scrambled eggs and ham or beef and potatoes, turkey loaf, or how about some space-age spaghetti?" He snickered as he looked at Underhill and me.

"You're kiddin' me, Holman. There ain't no ham and eggs in those boxes."

"Oh yeah! Oh yeah! Not only are there ham and eggs, but there's a biscuit and jelly in that box too."

"Oh yea, right. Okay, Holman, put up or shut up."

Holman moved to the truck and shortly emerged with a box about six inches square and two inches thick.

"Here ya are, boys, eat well."

"Wait a minute. What's this? The box says 1945!"

"Those are C rations, you dummy. Where did you take basic training?"

"Fort Dix, New Jersey, and we never had anything like this. What about the date, 1945?"

"That's the year they were packed!" snapped Holman. "I thought we had used up all the WWII leftovers, but I guess not."

"I ain't eatin' these things, they're twenty-five years old! They can't be any good."

"Suit yourself, give 'em to me, I'm hungry."

"What else is there to eat?"

"That's it, pretty boy, this ain't no Howard Johnson's."

Dominique kept the box, opened the various cans, and cautiously ate the contents. "Hey, these aren't half bad."

"Yeah, they taste better if you warm 'em up."

"Okay, let's build a fire. I'll gather some wood."

"Save your breath, pretty boy." Underhill chuckled. "All the wood you see at the edge of the jungle is mahogany. You would need a blowtorch to get it lit, and there's probably a VC in the undercover just waitin' to snatch your scrawny butt."

"I ain't afraid of no VC. I enlisted. I came here to fight 'em."

"Yeah, you ain't afraid until you see one."

All of us had a good laugh.

"Here, let me show you how to do this," suggested Underhill. "Take that biscuit can and punch some holes in it with your can opener. Now cut a piece of C-4 off a block. Roll it up into a ball, put it under the can, and light it. Presto, a cooking stove."

"I know you're pulling my leg now. C-4 is highly explosive."

"It burns fine as long as you don't stomp on it while it's on fire. Just remember, always, and I do mean always, stir your food up before you heat it up."

"Right, Matty."

"Yep, you'll launch your lunch to the moon if you don't."

After breakfast, we began to plan our operation. A convoy of flatbeds came in at about 1030 hours carrying fifty-five-gallon drums of penta prime and Agent Orange. The barrels we literally rolled off the trucks. There were one thousand barrels in that first shipment.

The first plan of attack was to use a piece of landing mat for a ramp and roll the barrel up to the top of the trailer using an additional landing mat to span the width of the top of the trailer. Then the contents of the barrel could be dumped in. We quickly discovered this plan wouldn't work. The top of the trailer was ten and a half feet above the ground. The landing mat was only twelve feet long and the barrel weighed 450 pounds. We also found removing the plugs from the barrels and allowing the contents to empty into the trailer took much too long.

"Matty, this just isn't going to work. The trailer is too high. The landing mat is almost straight up. The barrels are too heavy. We need a new plan."

"Okay, plan B. Lemrise, call HQ. Tell 'em to send us a D-9 Cat and seven or eight pickaxes."

"Matty, HQ says there's a D-9 and the other stuff at Plei Dejereng. They can have it here with a driver in about an hour."

"Sergeant Mattatall, Spec. 4 Ramieriz reporting. I have a D-9 as you can see and about a dozen picks and axes."

"Good. This is what I would like you to do. See all those fifty-five-gallon barrels lined up about halfway down the runway? I want you to dig me a trench ten feet deep with both ends at ground level. My plan is to pull a dump truck and trailer down into the trench, roll the barrels out onto the trailer, and dump 'em in. The bottom of the trench needs to be level. About thirty feet of the trench needs to be ten feet deep before it starts to shallow up, OK?"

"Gotch ya, Sarge."

It took Ramieriz about three hours to dig the trench. By 1400 hours, we were rolling barrels across the landing mat two at a time, punching holes in them with the pickaxes. The total capacity of each trailer was about 4,000 gallons. The first trailer was loaded with 70 barrels, 3,850 gallons. The movement of the truck and trailer caused a lot of the mixture to slush out. The trailer worked best about half full, at 35 barrels, 1,925 gallons.

The operation took one hour to fill and about thirty minutes to spray the load. By the end of the day, we had sprayed four loads between the two trailers, 140 barrels in all.

"Hey, GI. Come smoke, we talk." One of the Montagnard soldiers approached, speaking some English. "Sit, we smoke, we talk."

"What is your name?" I asked.

"Name Phong-Tran. Want b-u-k-e-t-s."

"Buckets? I'm sorry, Phong, we don't have any buckets."

"No want buckets. Those buckets." He pointed to the empty barrels. "Trade *boo coo* number one for buckets."

What could he possibly have to trade? I thought. "Okay, we trade."

I had no idea as to what to do with the empty barrels. In a very short period of time, a large group of Montagnard women and children arrived, bringing baskets of cucumbers and corn. Every day, the empty barrels just seemed to disappear. I told the Montagnard chief that the first baskets of food were enough to cover all the barrels. I didn't want to eat up their only food supply. I never could speak to the chief well enough to know what they did with the barrels.

5 May 1970, 1055 Hours

"Hey, Sarge, there's a convoy comin'. Hey! It's Lieutenant Simmons."

"How's it going, Matty?"

"Going real well, sir, had to dig a trench to get the barrels in the trailers. We're running about two thousand gallons an hour. We sprayed the area where the choppers are dropping their loads first. No dust, but I think we will have to keep spraying until the operation is over. The soil is loose and deep."

"Looks like you are doing OK. I am going on to Plei Dejereng, if you need anything, just call."

"Yes, sir."

"I'll drop by about every third day just to make sure I'm doing my job."

"Good. See you in a few days."

"Hey, Matty, we need a way to clean up. I've seen the Montagnards going off in that direction. Let's take a look," suggested Zieggy (Spec. 4 Robert Zeigler).

"Underhill, bring your patrol. Lock and load just in case."

About one hundred yards north of the end of the runway, we came to a river that was fairly wide. Everyone almost immediately jumped in, clothes and all. How refreshing. For the next few days, we bathed in the river. Ten guys bathed while ten guys stood guard. However, the bathing slowed as we learned the river was severely polluted. Human waste is used to fertilize the rice paddies, which in turn drained into the river system.

One morning, the air force came to our rescue. A crane helicopter delivered a long metal box, which looked to be made of aluminum. Actually, it was made of magnesium. The chopper dropped the box right at the end of the runway. Within a few minutes, a deuce and a half and a tank truck arrived. A crew immediately disembarked the deuce and a half and started removing the bolts that held the box's lid on. The tank truck filled with water began to spray an area about fifty-by-one-hundred-feet, and 2.5-ton stake bed trucks arrived, carrying more men as well as filled sandbags. The men built a sandbag wall in the fifty-by-one-hundred-foot area. Upon completion, an additional wall was built, dividing the area into two fifty-foot squares. The wall was only three sandbags tall, about twelve inches. The crews then pulled two rubber mats from the box and placed one each in the fifty-feet square. When completely flat, the mats covered the interior of the squares.

"What are those things?" asked Gomeric.

"I don't have a clue," I replied. "But I'm sure we'll find out if we just watch."

Large tank trucks began to arrive. A hose was attached to each of the mats, and presto, the contents went in, blowing the mats up like giant flat green water balloons. They were huge fuel bladders. Pump nozzles were attached, and the gas station was complete. The water-truck driver was the station attendant. I saw an opportunity and went into action.

"Hey, Sarge, just how much fuel does each one of those bladders hold?"

"Oh, about fifteen thousand gallons."

"Is that gasoline?"

"Oh, no," he said. "Matter-of-factly, that is JP-4. Its fuel for the choppers."

"What do you do with the box the bladders came in?"

"Uh, I don't know. Just discard it, I guess."

"Do you mind if we take it?"

"Naaa, I ain't got no use for it."

"How long will that tank truck be here?"

"Well, I have to have it here. Every day, the bladders need to be sprayed. They can't be allowed to get too hot."

"Can we get you to fill the box up with water once we move it?"

"Got any beer?"

"Yeah, we got some beer but no ice."

"I don't care as long as it's wet."

"We got a six-pack if that will help."

"That will be fine."

There was no beer in our supplies, but Holman and Fair had brought several cases between them. The box was hooked up to one of the dumps and hauled to our area about halfway down the runway. We put the spare tire under one end to level it, brought in the tank truck, filled it with water, and voilà, we had a six-man bathtub. We were able to get the tub refilled every three days.

Life got a lot better. Lieutenant Simmons kept us supplied in DX clothes and beer. At the end of every day, our pants would be covered with penta prime. We would discard them only to find they would mysteriously disappear by the end of the next day. I imagined the Montagnards would take them along with the barrels.

We found mixing fifty gallons of JP-4 along with penta prime and Agent Orange made it spread much easier. The Montagnards, along with a set of MACV advisors, erected a fence six feet tall around a two-acre plot that was later used to store the weapons brought back from Cambodia.

The way the Montagnards set the fence posts was quite interesting. They would send the women for buckets of water (buckets were five-gallon metal buckets supplied by Special Forces advisors). At the location where the post was to be set, water was poured on the ground. One of the Montagnard men would then insert one end of a steel pipe into the muddy soil. The pipe had been bent in the middle at about a forty-five-degree angle. The Montagnard would then walk in a circle holding the bent end of the pipe, causing it to burrow deeper into the wet soil. More water was added, more spinning, and soon, the pipe was down to the bend. The bent pipe was removed, leaving a hole about six inches in diameter and thirty-six inches deep. The fence post was then inserted and the earth tamped around it, and it was on to the next. The Montagnards could set a post about every five minutes using only the bent pipe and a bucket of water.

The Hueys were flying sorties from first light until dusk. A chopper would fly in, hover while everything was being unloaded, then fly off for another load. For the entire day, the choppers would be lined up five, six, seven deep, waiting for their turn to dump their goods. The caches were barely across the border in Cambodia not more than four clicks away. As the weapons arrived, they were sorted and neatly lined up inside the fenced-in area. After about two weeks, so many weapons were brought in. They just began stacking them up.

Eventually, the weapons completely filled the area, forming a mound about twenty feet tall. There were thousands and thousands of SKs, AK-47s, and various types of machine guns. Some were beyond imagination, and some looked as though they were used against the French operations some twenty-five years prior.

A weld broke on the spray nozzle of one our trailers, allowing the whole spray bar to flop around. I was frantically trying to lash the spray bar to the trailer so it wouldn't break off completely, resulting in the loss of the whole trailer.

"Good morning, soldier," came a gruff but kind voice.

I looked up, and there, standing in front of me, was a three-star general.

"Sir! I'm sorry. Sergeant Mattatall reporting, sir!" I blurted out while jumping to my feet.

"Oh, you're fine, son, as you were. I'm General Smith. Just wanted to check with you to see how things were going. Your operation is working out really well. Is there anything I can do to help the morale of your men?"

"A hot meal once in a while would really help, sir."

"You're with the 937th Engineers?"

"Yes, sir, Company B of the Twentieth."

"I'll see what I can do. Carry on, soldier."

The next day, at about 1700 hours, a helicopter we had not seen before landed. It was smaller and slimmer than a Huey.

"Are you Sergeant Mattatall?" asked a specialist 5, emerging from the chopper.

"I am."

"We've brought you supper, compliments of the Fourth Division."

We quickly began to unload Bessemer coolers filled with roast beef, mashed potatoes and gravy, corn, green beans, bread and butter, along with two coolers full of cold soda. Specialist 5 Nichols set up two portable tables, and the feast was on. I was sure I was in heaven. After everyone had eaten, the chopper was loaded up and they were off. One of the coolers of cold soda was left behind for us to enjoy later.

The warrant officer flying the chopper told me it was a brand-new model replacing the LOCH (light observation helicopter). It was called a Ranger. That one hot meal really did a lot for the morale of the guys.

The next morning, Lieutenant Simmons came into camp.

"Heard you had a hot meal catered in yesterday."

"Yes, sir, really helped everyone's morale."

"Well, get ready for the next surprise. Lieutenant Colonel Cole will be coming in this morning. He has heard a lot about your operation and wants to come see for himself."

"We'll be ready, sir."

The morning wore on with more problems with the broken trailer. Penta prime poured from the broken weld left heavy puddles of oil in the work area.

"Fair, let's see what will happen if we drive the truck faster."

In and away we went. The increased speed of the truck eliminated the puddles as we were flying around the area at a breakneck speed of thirty miles an hour, spraying the second load of the day with the crippled trailer. A Huey landed behind us. As we turned and made our return pass, a fellow ran from the Huey at top speed and leaped onto the running board of the truck.

"Why are you going so fast? You see! You see! You were driving so fast you have broken the sprayer on the back." It was Lieutenant Colonel Cole.

"No, sir, we didn't," I meekly replied.

"Yes, you did! Yes, you did. Just take a look."

It was at this moment Lieutenant Simmons pulled up and came to my rescue. "Colonel Cole, Lieutenant Simmons reporting, sir."

"You see! You see what your men have done? When I came in, they were driving around the field like scared rabbits and have broken the sprayer."

"I'm sorry, sir, but the sprayer has been broken for several days. Sergeant Mattatall found if the trailer was pulled a little faster, the trailer could still be used, eliminating oil puddles."

"Sergeant Mattatall, I apologize for scolding you so in front of your men. I know you better than that. I would like for you to give me and the others a tour of your operation."

Upon completion of the tour and a briefing of our operation, Colonel Cole spoke to me privately as we walked back to his chopper.

"It's good to see you again, Matty. I kinda miss our Sunday afternoon hunting trips. You look well. How are you holding up?"

"I'm fine, sir."

"Yeah, you always find the excitement. You are doing a great job here, you really impressed General Smith. He wanted to put you in for an army commendation medal. I told him you already had two."

"Awww, just doing my job, sir."

As Colonel Cole's chopper lifted off and disappeared to the north, I came to realize just how close Colonel Cole and I had become. The colonel, fifteen years my elder, had become my big brother. Tears began to well up in my eyes as his chopper disappeared from view.

The next week passed almost without incident. Four large tarps were requisitioned from the rifle company overseeing the weapons cache. One tarp was fashioned to each side of our two dumps, creating four lean-to tents. This addition worked very well. However, a number of us preferred the dump beds to the dusty earth. Every night, I posted guards as we had no perimeter defense.

Tuesday, 12 May 1970

The operation of spraying Agent Orange and penta prime was moving forward rather smoothly. The two-acre site that had been fenced off to store the weapons being brought back from Cambodia was already looking like a junkyard. The neat rows of categorized armament had become piles of metal filling up the entire area with many more weapons stockpiled than originally anticipated.

Lieutenant Simmons's jeep pulled up at about 0830 hours.

"Morning, sir!" I said as I saluted.

"Morning, Sergeant. I'm here to let you know that Colonel Cole, Sergeant Major Elkey, and others will be here to observe your progress. I know you will be glad to see Colonel Cole. General Dillard and General Adams will also be in the group, so look sharp. They are scheduled to arrive here about 1300 hours. I need to get back to Plei Dejereng, they'll be there about 1130 hours."

I waved as the lieutenant's jeep pulled away. It was back to work as usual. The morning and afternoon passed quickly. I hadn't noticed the lateness of the hour, figuring Colonel Cole and the group had probably been sidetracked.

As the day's activities were drawing to a close, Lieutenant Simmons's jeep reappeared on the scene.

"Matty, get in the jeep. We need to talk," he commanded rather solemnly.

We drove a short distance away from the platoon's activities. The jeep came to a halt. It seemed minutes passed. The lieutenant said nothing. Finally he turned toward me, tears welling up in his eyes.

"I don't know quite how to tell you this, Matty." He forced back the tears. "Colonel Cole was killed today along with General Dillard, General Adams, Captain Dulak, Captain Booth, Mr. Adams, First Lieutenant

Rogers, Sergeant Jones, Spec. 5 Renner, and Spec. 4 Rawson. Sergeant Major Elkey was the only one to survive."

Terror swept over me. *Fred, Fred, Fred. Oh, Lord, my brother Fred, why? Why? Why?* were the first thoughts through my mind.

"Matty, I know how close you were to almost everyone on that chopper. If you need to go back to base camp for a while, I can arrange for someone to come and take over this operation."

"No," I replied. "This mission is too important. I'll be fine."

"One more thing. I don't want you to think not even for a moment that any of this is your fault. You know they were coming to visit my operation as well. Are you sure you'll be OK?"

"I'm fine, sir. I've been here a long time."

Every day for the next five days, Lieutenant Simmons made the fourteen-mile drive from Plei Dejereng to Du-Co to check on me, making sure I was OK.

About two weeks later, I had the opportunity to return to Pleiku to secure supplies for the men. I stopped at the hospital to see Sergeant Major Elkey. As I entered his room, he lay in his bed in what looked to be a full-body cast. He had two broken legs, a broken arm, broken sternum, and a broken pelvis. As our eyes met, I broke into an uncontrollable laugh. This caused the sergeant major to laugh also.

"You have got to stop laughing, you're killing me," he interjected between his outbursts.

"You jumped out of the plane, didn't you?" I sputtered, still in an uncontrollable state.

"You know that I did" was his reply. "When the chopper started going down, I waited until we were about treetop level, open went the door, and out I went."

The Huey, a UH-1, left Pleiku about 1000 hours, carrying 1,200 pounds of JP-4. The first mission was to visit a bridge just southeast of the city limits of Pleiku that had been devastated by a VC attack at an earlier date. As the Huey approached the bridge on Route 509, it turned and began to circle the site. Colonel Cole was conversing with General Dillard and General Adams concerning our rebuilding that bridge as we had been successful in reconstructing the two bridges on the east side of Pleiku. A Soviet-made .51-caliber radar-controlled machine gun burst into fire at the tree line. The first round penetrated the side-door window of the Huey, striking General Dillard in the forehead, killing him instantly. He was sitting in the jump seat situated just behind the aircraft commander's seat facing the port (left) side of the aircraft. Additional rounds penetrated the aircraft engine, causing the craft to be inoperable. Mr. Adams (WO-3), the AC pilot, tried setting the Huey down for an emergency landing. As the aircraft skids contacted the ground, the forward motion was too great, causing the craft to turn over headfirst on the main rotor blades. The JP-4 burst into flames, cremating everyone inside. Everyone on the aircraft had put their dog tags in their mouths. It was by this action they were able to be identified correctly.

Sergeant Major Elkey did survive this life-threatening experience; however, he did have to retire after twenty-eight years in the Army. That was the last time I saw my infamous sergeant major Elkey. He passed away in 1998.

CSM Robert W. Elkey

Brigade Sergeant Major

Command Sgt. Major Robert W. Elkey

Snakes, Lieutenants, and Charlie

The days and weeks passed as the spraying went on. The red dust runway was transformed, taking on a black asphalt look. The sidewalls and the bottom of the trench had become saturated with penta prime. One morning after breakfast, Dominique decided he would sneak off for a smoke as smoking wasn't allowed in or around the work area due to the flammability of the penta prime and JP-4. Without warning, a huge ball of flame erupted from the trench in an explosive manner. Dominique, who was standing at the edge of the trench, was thrown head over heels, landing in a heap some twenty feet from the trench. The flames quickly crawled out of the trench, engulfing the entire area around the magnesium bathtub.

"Oh! Oh! Dominique is not moving! We need to get him out of there now!" I yelled. Half the platoon went into action. The flames were barely two feet from Dominique.

"I got 'im! I got 'im!" Underhill snorted. "Fair, help me drag him out!"

As we helped Underhill, the magnesium box caught fire. The intense heat seared and singed us. Thick black clouds of smoke engulfed the rescue team, taking the very breath from our lungs.

"OK! OK! I think we're safe now. Set him down! Somebody get some water!" I commanded, fearing Dominique had been killed either by the concussion of the fireball or his headfirst landing after being plummeted through the air.

"Here, give him this!" called Zieggy, running up with a fresh canteen of water.

As the first drops of water touched his lips, he began to cough violently. Slowly he opened his eyes. "What happened?" Dominique queried weakly.

"You blew yourself up," I said softly.

"Wow! The things people do to get a smoke."

"How ya feeling? Can you move? Can you get up?" I asked.

"Yeah, I think I can. I got one hell of a headache, but the rest of me feels okay," Dominique replied, rubbing a large lump just above his forehead.

In just minutes, our bathtub was gone, not even an ash left. The fifty gallons or so of water that was in the tank boiled away as the magnesium burned, actually adding oxygen to the fire. It took the fire about an hour to burn itself out. Then it was back to work as usual, and it was back to the river to bathe.

"Hey, Matty, how are things?" called Lieutenant Simmons, his jeep coming to a stop at my side.

"Good, sir, good. The sorties are starting to slow down. There seems to be more time between flights."

"Yeah, this will be the last week. The operation will be completed by Thursday or Friday. The week after will be spent blowing the bunkers."

"The crew is functioning smoothly, sir. Underhill and I are going to Pleiku this morning. It's getting pretty hot, about 105 degrees on the runway in the afternoon. I figure we'll pick up, oh, about ten cases of soda and five cases of beer along with some more DX uniforms."

"Sounds good. I'll see you around midweek to brief you on blowing the bunkers. The C-4 will be here Thursday afternoon. Keep it dry and safe. See ya Wednesday," replied the lieutenant, his jeep pulling away.

"Lemrise, I'm takin' Fair and Underdog back to Pleiku. We need some soda and beer. It's just getting too hot out here. See ya this afternoon."

"Okay, we'll be here." Lemrise smiled.

Fair, Underhill, and I piled into Fair's five-ton dump and were off. The trip was uneventful; that is, until we neared the tea plantation. "Fair, Fair, slow down. What is that in the road?"

"Don't know!" replied Underhill. "Looks like a fire hose lying across the road."

"Better stop, might be some sort of a mine."

As the five-ton jerked to a stop, the hose slowly began to move. As we cleared the truck and the door slammed, a king cobra raised his head a good four feet above the ground.

"Look at that thing, it's huge!" I stammered with the snake slowly moving its caped head from side to side in a menacing manner.

"Yep," said Underhill, taking Fair's M16, drawing a bead on the snake. "This one's mine." He squeezing off a round.

The snake's bonnet twitched at the report of the M16. The report of the M16 came again and then again, a total of five rounds. Each time the snake's head barely moved, yet the snake was unscathed.

"I'm outta here, let's go!" came Fair's shaking voice.

"Yeah, I'm with you. That thing's about thirty feet long. If he comes, we won't be able to get away."

As the diesel of the five-ton started, the snake began to crawl off toward the jungle. "Do you see the size of that thing? Look! Look! It's actually two snakes, one intertwined with the other."

The three of us let out a sigh of relief as we passed the tea plantation. This was the same plantation where the earlier convoy had been ambushed. Just past the plantation, a muzzle flashed on the hillside to our left, at about ten o'clock, A B-40 passed over the hood of the truck inches in front of the windshield. Fair instantly floored it, large beads of sweat forming on his forehead.

"Look! Look! Look!" yelled Underhill. "There's a guy on the hillside pulling his M79 to the ready."

"Wait, he's waving at us!" I replied just as Underhill was ready to fire. The roaring truck quickly took us out of range. Charlie would live to fight another day. The rest of the trip to Pleiku was uneventful.

"Underhill, you and Fair go to supply and draw us some DX fatigues. I'll go and brief the CO." The green Cadillac pulled up to Co. B HQ As I alighted from the truck, I was met at the front door by a second lieutenant I didn't know.

"Soldier!" he yelled as I tried to pass. "I am an officer! You will come to attention and you will salute! Understand?"

"Yes, sir! Sorry, sir." I came back, came to attention, prompting a salute. *Oh boy!* I thought. *Who is this idiot?*

"Just who are you? And what kind of uniform is that? A holey shirt, pants cut off at the knees, no name tag. You're on report, soldier! Consider yourself under arrest under an Article 15 court-martial. Now let's go see the CO." The lieutenant turned on a heel and followed me to the CO's office.

First Lieutenant Raymond Reel rose from his desk as I entered the room. He smiled and started toward me. "How ya doing, Matty?"

The lieutenant entered the office before I could reply. "Sir, I found this soldier outside in this ragtag uniform and not following military protocol. I'm recommending him for an Article 15," the lieutenant retorted with a smirk on his face.

"Well," replied the CO rather calmly, "I see you've met Lieutenant Combes."

I just smiled.

"Lieutenant, this is Sergeant Mattatall. He is running a special ops in Du-Co about three clicks from Cambodia. Matty's uniform is authorized due to the fact of the work his unit is doing. The penta prime ruins the uniforms, so a new one is needed every day. DX uniforms are being gathered from all over the country. Matty's pants are cut off at the knees because the pants were becoming so saturated the added weight interfered and hindered the work. We found it was easier to wash the legs than to deal with safety hazard of the saturated pants.

"Point number 2: In case you haven't noticed, we are in a war zone! Saluting is not warranted or recommended. I guarantee you that if you pursue this, you will be the prime target for a sniper. As far as the Article 15, an 01 can't court-martial an E-5. Now, if you will excuse us, Lieutenant, Sergeant Mattatall has a report to file. I need to be briefed on his operation. That will be all."

"Yes, sir," replied Combes, sulking away.

"Well, how's it going?" asked the CO as the door closed behind the lieutenant.

"Good, good. Dominique all but blew himself up, sneaking a smoke in the work area."

"Well, does he need to be reprimanded?"

"Naah, the explosion threw him about twenty feet, blew up our bathtub and spare tire. I think he learned his lesson. Who is this Lieutenant Combes? I have never seen him before."

"Oh, he's new in country, just graduated from an ROTC program, some college back east."

"I hope he makes it. Just seems to have a bit of an attitude."

"Yeah, he's green. Just give him some time, he'll be okay."

"I hope you're right. I need to get back, any special instructions? Oh, I almost forgot, a gook took a shot at us with a B-40 at the tea plantation, near miss, and then he waved at us."

"Oh really, be safe. General Walker was really impressed with what you're doing out there. Just thought you'd like to know. See ya next time."

"Yes, sir."

As I left HQ, Underhill and Fair were waiting. Our next stop was the PX. After loading ten cases of soda, five cases of beer, ten cartons of cigarettes, and several bags of candy, we were on our way.

"You know, if we could get that beer and soda cold, it sure would be nice," interjected Underhill, licking his lips.

"Yeah, sure would," replied Fair, his eyes lighting up.

"Fair, are you drooling over there?"

"Yeah, yeah, might be."

"Well, that settles it. Fair, to the icehouse in Pleiku."

The icehouse sat next to the Turkish bath in Pleiku, a large antiquated building built by the French. The Fourth Division had taken over the ice-making process, providing ice for all the allied forces in the Pleiku area. A young PFC barely raised his eyes as we entered the dingy ten-foot-square office of the ice plant.

"How can I help?" he asked, not looking up from the Green Lantern comic book.

"Yeah, I'm Sergeant Mattatall, Company B of the Twentieth Engineers. I've got a platoon of men bivouacked near the Cambodian border. The heat is pushing 120 plus. I want to get a block of ice so the guys can at least have a cold drink."

"Hmmmm, got a chit?" replied the private first class, still not looking up from his book.

"No, we don't, just came in for supplies and thought the ice would be nice."

"No chit! No ice!" he replied, still not looking up.

"Hey, listen, we got guys dying out there in the heat while you're sitting here with the Green Lantern in your air-conditioned office. We need a little help here."

"Now you're aggravatin' me!" replied the PFC, jumping up from his chair. "As I said, NO CHIT, NO ICE!"

I turned. "Fair."

Without a word, he handed me his M16. *Clip clop* reported the weapon as I chambered a shell. Instantly, I shoved the muzzle of the M16 into his chest, backing him up against the plate-glass window behind his desk. "Now, Mister PRIVATE FIRST CLASS, understand this! Either I get ice, or you won't see the sunrise in the morning."

"The . . . the . . . the keys are in the top drawer. Don't shoot, don't shoot!" Tears welled up in his eyes.

Underhill snatched up the keys. He and Fair were out the door loading up the block, which measured 18" x 18" x 42" and weighed about three hundred pounds.

"Look, kid, take some advice," I offered, lowering the weapon and stepping back. "We are all on the same team. No chunk of ice is worth dying for."

"Would . . . would you have pulled the trigger," he stammered, still shaking, his voice cracking, "if I if I hadn't given you the keys?"

"In a New York second," I moaned as I walked out the door.

After spending enough time in a situation where people are continually trying to kill you, after seeing close comrades fall, life just doesn't mean as much as it once did, and death means even less.

The ride back to Du-Co was uneventful; that is, until we neared the tea plantation.

"Hey, look, there's that guy on the hill and he's still waving."

As we drew closer, his waving arm turned into a tube.

"Uh-oh! Here we go again! Floor it, Fair!" I yelled as an orange flash erupted from the tube held by our new friend.

Woosh—kaboom. The B-40 rocket passed well in front of the truck, leaving a white smoke trail and exploding harmlessly in the jungle. Fair jammed the brakes as the rocket passed, bringing the dump to an almost screeching halt.

"Look, Charlie is taking off!" Fair jumped out of the truck and ran to the edge of the road. "A A A, Charlie. A, come back. Let's talk. A, come on back!" shouted Fair as Charlie disappeared into the jungle.

Fair turned, shrugged his shoulders, and came back to the truck. "Why ya think he ran off?"

"Mmm, don't know. Probably only had one shell. Was usin' a piece of bamboo as a launcher. Probably by himself, and one rocket is all he can carry."

We finally arrived back at Du-Co about supper time. Another day, another dollar.

1000 Hours the Next Morning

"Hey, isn't that the CO's jeep comin' up the runway?"

"Yeah, looks like him. Wonder what he's up to all the way out here?"

"Mornin', sir, what brings you out here so early?"

"Well, seems that General Walker over at the Fourth Division's got a burr under his saddle. Someone kinda roughed up one of his men over at the icehouse, and the kid got the numbers off the dump truck. He called me last night and insisted I investigate. Well, he is a general and I'm a lieutenant, so here I am. Let's see. There were three guys: an Indian, a black guy, and a skinny white guy. Just for the record, you, Fair, and Underhill don't know anything about the incident, do ya?"

"Incident? Incident? Why, of course not. We stopped by the icehouse and picked up a block for the guys back here on our way out. But incident? Roughing the guy up? Sir, we never laid a hand on the guy."

"Yeah, well, I know you guys well enough. You wouldn't leave any loose ends hangin'. As far as I'm concerned, case closed. However, next time, stop by HQ and pick up a chit. You know, an 'authorized request.'"

"Roger that, sir."

"See ya in a couple of days."

"Careful goin' home, sir," called Fair. "Charlie's in the tea plantation with a B-40 launcher."

"Really?"

"Yeah, but his aim ain't nothin'," snickered Fair. "He couldn't hit a barn let alone your jeep." With a cloud of dust and a "Hi ho silver," the CO was gone.

That afternoon, Lieutenant Simmons arrived in camp.

"Hey, Matty."

"Well, Lieutenant Simmons, how ya doin? What brings you here?"

"Just checkin' in to see how your operation's doing?"

"The last of the barrels will be gone tomorrow. The sorties are down to two or three a day."

"I have to tell ya, Matty, your guys did a great job. We'll be about three more days at Plei Dejereng finishing up. Your C-4 and supplies are coming up from Long Binh and should arrive tomorrow. I'd like you to go back to Pleiku day after tomorrow and bring back two D-9 Cats as we will need them in Cambodia. The 584th will have 'em ready. You just need to show 'em the way. I'll send some of my guys down to pick up the Cats when ya get 'em here."

"Ten-four, sir, we'll have 'em here about three p.m. That'll give you plenty of time to get 'em to Plei Dejereng before dark."

"Keep safe, Matty, and no incidents," the lieutenant said laughingly as he drove away.

The Next Morning

"Sarge, that's the last of the barrels. The truck's full and ready to go. We thought it would only be right if you spread the last load."

"Underdog, what's this sarge stuff? You and I been in this together since AIT. We came together, we'll leave together. Now let's get this load on the ground so we can have the rest of the day off."

"That's it, there ain't no more, Matty. How many barrels were there in all?"

"Ten thousand, 550,000 gallons total. Not bad for forty-two days on the job."

The next morning, we were on the road bright and early.

"Will he be there?" asked Underhill mysteriously.

"Humph . . . I don't know, but I'm ready for 'em." I came back, brandishing my M79 and four bandoliers of ammo.

The next fifteen minutes passed quietly. The air grew tense as we neared the plantation. "Here we go! Keep a sharp eye." Seconds dragged by. "Phew! There's his spot where he usually fires. See anything?"

"Nope, looks like nobody's home."

Seconds later, an orange flame erupted from the hillside, followed by a white telltale smoke trail. The rocket passed twenty feet or more above the top of the truck.

"Wow! What's he shooting at?" remarked Fair, stretching his neck to see where the missile landed. Charlie then waved as usual and disappeared into the jungle.

"Do ya think he is really that bad of an aim or do ya think he's missing us on purpose?" asked Underhill as we rolled into Pleiku.

"I really don't know. It's hard to believe his aim is so crummy."

An hour and a half later, we were loaded: soda, beer, cigs, snacks, and two D-9 Cats. Fair had traded his dump truck for a ten-ton, eighteen-wheel flatbed semi. Two trucks were needed to haul both cats. Frank James, a specialist 4 from the 584th, had the honors of chauffeuring the second truck. He too had two companions to increase security. Twenty-five minutes out of Pleiku, the air again became very tense as we approached the attack zone. "James, we're gettin' close. Keep your eye on the hillside just north of the tea plantation," I barked into the mike over the roar of the trucks' engines.

"Look! Look! There he is, a little lower than usual. Oh! Oh! He's got the launcher up!" screamed Underhill, shoving the barrel of his M79 out the window.

Pooka! called Underhill's weapon as the .40-millimeter shell cleared the barrel. Simultaneously, the familiar orange flame erupted from the hillside.

"Watch it! That thing's heading right at us!" bellowed Underhill, jamming another shell in the breach of his 79.

"We bought it this time!" I yelled as the rocket bore down on us. *Shoooo* called the B-40 as it passed the backlight of the truck cab, splitting the sixty-inch space between the cab of the truck and the upright tandem of the trailer. The rocket then smashed into the burned-out hulk of the previously hit tanker. The explosion was deafening. Shrapnel plummeted on the side of our truck, smashing the driver's-side window, showering us with glass.

"Hey, you guys OK? That thing hit your truck. I saw it! Come back!" the radio crackled.

"Ohhhh!" groaned Fair, again slumped over the wheel with the truck still smoothly moving. The truck finally came to a stop about 150 yards from the attack site. The smoke and dust in the cab started to settle. My eyes just wouldn't quite focus. I tried to access the situation, concentrating beyond the throbbing of my head. Underhill lay in the floor of the truck, curled up like an armadillo, head down, butt up.

"Underdog! Fair! You guys hurt? You OK? Say something!"

"Am I dead? Ahhayy! I am dead," groaned Underhill.

Fair just lay there, his face buried in the steering wheel, his fingers tapping on the dashboard. Slowly, Underhill rose from his upside-down fetal position, his mustache twitching. Fair finally raised his head and turned toward me. The left side of his uniform shirt was all but shredded from the flying glass shrapnel and whatever else came through the window.

"You OK, buddy?"

"Yeah, my arm hurts like hell and I got a few scratches, but I'm OK."

"Well, ya know you've used up about seven. I figure ya got two left."

"What do I look like, a cat?" snapped Fair.

"Yeah," Underhill snickered. "You do look like a cat, a big black cat, a big black holey cat," Underhill came back, laughing uncontrollably.

Fair turned and looked at his tunic. He too began to laugh. "Oh, the stresses of war."

The remaining ten miles or so to Du-Co were totally uneventful. We were sure glad of that.

As we approached the Plei Dejereng / Du-Co fork in the road, there sat a jeep and a 3/4 pickup.

"Yep, there's the lieutenant," hollered Underhill. The two-truck convoy pulled in behind the 3/4.

"Well, how was the trip?"

"Well, ten o'clock, Charlie almost got us this time."

"Yeah, he sure wasn't wavin'," Underhill chuckled.

"Fair took the worst of it."

"Yeah, but I'm OK. Got nine lives, ya know."

"Whoa, you sure are a mess!"

"Yeah, the window blew out, cutting up my shirt, but I only got a few scratches."

"How about you guys, Matty? Underhill?"

"Ah, we're OK. Got a few glass splinters here and there and one heck of a headache."

"Second truck take any damage?"

"Naah, he only had one rocket."

"Good, good. Glad to hear it. Matty, we'll take your truck and Cat on to Plei Dejereng and leave James with you. Tomorrow the fireworks begin. Are you ready?"

"I believe we are, sir."

The stress of command

The Capture

The road from Du-Co to the Cambodian border was barely more than an animal path. Heavily rutted and barely passable, the trucks would actually brush back the jungle as they passed. The D-9 had to be used on several occasions to smooth out the road in order for the trucks to pass. The distance from Du-Co to the border was about three clicks (three thousand yards) or one and a half miles. The bunker complexes were located from just inside the Cambodian border to about one thousand yards inland. A north-south dirt road passed close by with bunkers on one side of the road in places and on both sides of the road in other places. The next few days saw hundreds of pounds of C-4 detonated as huge underground cities were destroyed.

The Morning of the Fourth Day, 8:00 a.m.

Underhill and I were bouncing along the road on our way to the job site. The ten-ton flatbed crawled along with James at the wheel.

"What is that?" gasped Underhill as we passed a large clump of what looked like giant split-leaved philodendrons.

"I don't know," I replied. "This area is said to be secure. We'd better check it out." Cautiously, we exited the truck and approached a strange-looking vehicle blocking the road.

"What is that thing?" James asked.

"Don't know, kinda looks like a German half-track from World War II, and listen, sounds like the motor's runnin'."

"Yep, it is."

Russian Troop Carrier captured near Cambodia

There in front of us sat the oddest truck I had ever seen. It was about thirty feet long. The front of the truck was long, almost looking like the snout of a rat. The cab was enclosed with the cab height about seven feet. The rear structure was kinda cylindrical like a tanker trailer. The sides came up to the height of the cab. The top of the rear section was open. Along each side there was a long bench extending from the front to the back. A single door in the rear allowed access to the interior. Two enormous rubber-tired wheels graced the front. Four large wheels filled out the rear. Somehow we got the ten-ton turned around. We soon learned the truck was abandoned as it had lost its clutch, becoming undrivable. Surprisingly enough, the behemoth rolled rather easily. With a little bit of effort, we were able to winch the vehicle to the flatbed. Upon arriving back at camp in Du-Co, we examined the vehicle more closely. Lying on one of the rear seats were an RPG launcher and a belt of .51-caliber ammunition. The tires were clearly marked with the Russian hammer and sickle molded into the rubber. The same symbol was found on the steering wheel, horn button, and the dashboard. The army CID came and relieved us of our trophy. Several weeks later, there was an article in the *Stars and Stripes* newspaper telling how a Russian personnel carrier had been captured near the Cambodian border.

Kontum Helicopter Base

21 June 1970

With the completion of the project at Du-Co, my platoon was given several days at base camp to refresh and regroup.

Sunday Afternoon, Company Operations Meeting

"Matty, you really impressed the brass upstairs the way you handled things. General Walker [Maj. Gen. Glenn D. Walker, CO, Fourth Division] has asked that you take the Third Platoon to Kontum. He wants you to give the base the same dust control treatment that was used at Du-Co."

Monday morning, we were on our way. The blacktopping of the Pleiku-Kontum sector of QL-14 had just been completed, a joint operation of several of the engineer units. *Wow, look at this!* I thought. No more dust, no more mines. *Bet Co. A would really appreciate that.* My mind continued to wander.

Just as we rounded a curve at a blistering twenty-five miles an hour, I saw it—an ARVN deuce and a half lying on its side. "Stop the truck!" I bellowed, seeing what looked like a trench across the road. While my new driver locked up the brakes—too late—the truck hit the ditch with a jolt, throwing everyone in the rear of the truck out, pasting Underhill and myself against the windshield. As the dust settled, GIs were picking themselves from the surrounding countryside. Again no serious injuries, just a few cuts and bruises with an occasional lump or bump here or there. During the night, the enemy, whoever they might be in this sector, had dug a trench across the road right where the road negotiated a sharp curve. Several hours passed as we had to be pulled from the trench. A Cat had to be brought down from Wooly Bully to fill the hole so traffic could pass.

As the green Cadillacs arrived at the chopper base just on the outskirts of Kontum City, we were greeted to an eerie sight.

"Hmmmm, what a dump," Underhill mused as we entered the base.

The hooches were dilapidated and covered with a thick layer of red dust. None of the roads were paved or even graveled. No wonder they needed our help.

The next week passed as we spread our magic potion, covering every square inch of bare earth. Every morning, a fleet of gunships along with DUSTOFFs would leave. As the days wore on, it seemed that fewer ships returned.

1 July 1970

As another project was coming to a close, I wondered what would be next.

"Sergeant Matty! Sergeant Matty!" called one of the clerks from HQ, breaking my train of thought.

"Yes, what is it, Specialist?" I replied.

"The CO sent me to get you, today is payday, and you're needed to assist the paymaster in paying your men."

As I entered the HQ hooch, the paymaster and the CO were just finishing the compound's payroll.

"What shall we do with these?" asked the CO, holding up fifty to sixty pay envelopes.

"We'll just send them back. They will be forwarded to the families."

The envelopes represented twenty-five chopper crews that hadn't returned that month. Some of the crew members had been rescued; however, fifty to sixty just didn't make it.

Soon all the men were paid, and it was back to work as usual.

"Hey, Sarge!" one of the men called. "I need a haircut, how about it?"

"Yeah, go on, we are about finished here," I replied, not looking up.

A few minutes later, I emerged from the interior of the spray tank to find Underhill and one or two others at the job at hand.

"Hey, where did everyone go?"

"Who knows." Underhill shrugged, looking up from his raking.

Soon Underhill and I were roaming around the compound looking for my crew. As we approached the barbershop there they were—a long line of my men filled the small shop and spilled out into the street. I moved toward the front of the line to see what the commotion was about. As I neared the front of the line, a very old toothless mama-san looked up from her work, smiled, and replied, "You want one hundred P?"

I turned and left immediately.

"What's up?" snickered Underhill, knowing full well what was going on. All I can say is boys will be boys.

Sixteen Days

2 August 1970

After not having done much in the last week as I was extremely short (a short timer being one with ninety days or less in country), I figured the next seventeen days in country would be a walk in the park, and I would be on my way home.

"The CO wants to see you at HQ right away," replied Ditto, a shake and bake E-6, as he entered my room.

"I know you are really short," replied the CO as he returned my salute. "I have a problem, and only you can help me. The rock crusher over at Pleiku quarry is needed in Buon Me Thuot [Bam Me Thuoy, GI pronunciation] posthaste."

Buon Me Thuot is a city consisting mostly of rubber plantations. It is located in III Corps, about 105 miles due south, over the mountains through the jungle.

"What do you need me for, sir? All you have to do is go to Qui Nhon and then over to Highway 101, and you are there."

"Well, it isn't that easy. If we go through the jungle, it will cut a day off the drive time."

"Why me? I've only got seventeen days left in country."

"I know, but you are the only one that can run a minesweep. Ditto and the others are all shake and bakes and have no experience in this sort of thing. I will send Felty with you so you can show him the ropes. You will report to Lieutenant Grover in the morning, over at Camp Hollowacs."

"Sir, with all due respects, that idiot tried to kill his whole platoon at Ben Het last year when a tank attacked them. I mean, calling artillery on yourself is not exactly the smartest thing in the world."

"I know, I know, but you have been requested, and that is that. You leave at 1600 hours today, is that clear, soldier?"

"Yes, sir!"

"Hey, Billy, what's up?" asked Underhill as I sulked by.

"Ahhh, I've gotta go and report to our old buddy Grover at Hollowacs this afternoon. The CO wants me to go to Buon Me Thuot with a convoy. They need the rock crusher down there."

"Hey, man, can I go too?"

"What, are you nuts?"

"Well, we've been together almost our whole army life." Soon Underhill came back all mad. "That bum Combes . . . He said I couldn't go, said I was too short. I'll just go and ask the CO."

Now Underhill was the CO's jeep driver, and being close to the same age, they were good friends. Shortly, Underhill came back all smiles. "When do we leave?"

That afternoon Underhill, Felty, and I—along with three semis, a deuce and a half, and a D-9 bulldozer—went over to Camp Hollowacs, an engineer base that contained a portable asphalt plant much like the one at Wooly Bully. It was located just off Highway 19, a couple of miles east of Pleiku. About a block off the highway on a gravel road, the engineers had built an engineer castle. This is the symbol of the Corp of Engineers of the U.S. Army. This castle was about ten feet long, five feet wide, and four feet tall, all solid reinforced concrete. I always wondered why the Vietcong never blew it up. After reporting to the CO at the camp and settling in a wall tent home for the night, I went over to HQ and asked the sarge how that castle had survived, being it was about a quarter of a mile from the camp entrance.

"Vietcong think they own that castle," he replied. "I have been here for ten months, and every morning when we go out, there is a North Vietnamese flag stuck in the center of the castle."

While speaking to the sarge, I noticed several TV monitors across the room. Each monitor showed different views of the perimeter of the camp outside the wire. There were five total, and every one showed a lot of activity, people moving about, all armed and looking very suspicious.

"Who are they?" I asked.

"Those are just our local Vietcong," replied the sergeant.

"All those Vietcong?" I queried. "Why don't you do something about it?"

"Well," said the sarge, "we don't bother them, and they don't bother us. We know they're there, and they know we're here."

Seventeen days left, and I knew I was going to get killed. I just knew it.

3 August 1970

Morning came much too early. Much of the night before had been spent thinking about the past fourteen months and all that Underhill and I had been through. We had almost made it and would surely be killed traipsing through the jungle with only two weeks left until it was home forever. Every mission had a certain amount of fear attached to it. When you are first in country, you are really afraid of everything. Then after a few weeks, the fear passes and you do okay until that ninety-day mark. Then it all starts over again and magnifies itself until you go home. Most of the guys who were killed in my unit (Twentieth Engineers) were either lost in that first two weeks or in the last few weeks of their tour.

The convoy was all lined up and ready to leave by 0730 hours. Lieutenant Grover was first in his jeep, followed by a ten-ton semi loaded with the D-9 Cat. A deuce and a half was next, carrying a patrol of eight for security. It was followed by an empty semi that was to be a backup in case anything happened. The rock crusher was next, using two five-ton semis to carry all the parts, and finally, an additional deuce and a half with yet another security patrol.

Felty, the driver, and I were in the first truck with the D-9. Underhill was pulling shotgun in the second truck. At 0800, the convoy was on its way. As we pulled out onto Highway QL-14, the paved road soon turned into a dirt road. A bird-dog spotter plane was also accompanying the convoy.

A mile down the road, I spotted a trail marker. "Stop the truck!" I shouted.

The semi came lumbering to a stop. In front of us, at the roadside, there was a branch stuck in the ground. The top had been split and a smaller stick inserted in an almost perpendicular manner, more or less pointing to the ground. Quickly, Lieutenant Grover came backing up.

"Who stopped this convoy?" he spurted.

"I did, sir," I replied.

"We have got to get to Buon Me Thuot." Frustration poured out of his face.

"Sir, don't take another step, there is a mine in the middle of the road, right between your jeep tracks."

Felty, Underhill, and I quickly went into action to detonate one of our own 105 artillery shell turned into a land mine.

Lieutenant Grover said, "You really saved our bacon. How did you know the mine was there?"

"I saw that stick in the ground, sir. The VC leave signs for the villagers so they won't stumble into the mines, especially in areas that are VC friendly." The rest of the afternoon went by without a hitch.

1200 Hours

We came to the Van-Vleck Bridge (Voun Vleck).

"Wow, look at that bridge," Felty replied as he went for a closer look.

The center pier of the bridge had been blown, dropping the center section of the bridge into the river. The villagers, needing to cross, had filled the fallen center with mahogany logs, branches, and dirt, bringing the center to almost level. However, one lumber truck was not so lucky. It lay in the river upside down, still loaded with logs. We spent a half hour there eating lunch, the ohhh-soooo-wonderful C rations. After lunch, we headed up the trail. Two hundred yards up the road, there was a huge tree someone had dropped across the road, blocking our way. The D-9 made short work of pushing the tree out of the way.

1400 Hours

The little convoy came to the Van-Vleck MACV compound. Grover stopped the convoy.

"I think we'll stay here for the night. The bird dog is getting nervous. I'll check with the MACVs, see if we can stay here for the night. Lieutenant!"

"There's no way we can get all these trucks up there," I objected. The MACV camp was located on the top of a very small hill, more like a knoll.

"Oh yeah," he replied, "plenty of room."

After a short conversation on the radio, the bird dog was soon out of sight. The jeep leading the way, we slowly turned off the road and headed for the compound.

"Wow, what is that?" yelled Felty.

Just as we turned onto the lane, a tiger jumped out of the ditch and headed toward the village that sat at the foot of the hill. He was running just fast enough to stay in front of our truck as the jeep was already in the village. The tiger ran right into the village. The villagers were waiting for him and shot him on the spot. The village consisted of Montagnard Indians. As we approached the village, they already had the tiger skinned.

We parked the trucks just outside the village. The lieutenant went and spoke with the commander of the compound.

"Hey, guys, I've got good news and bad news, which do you want first?"

Everyone let out a simultaneous moan.

"The CO said it would be fine for us to stay the night here, but we can't get the trucks through the gate and up the hill."

"Well, that is just great," suggested Underhill. "What will we do now? The bird dog is long gone, it is getting dark, and we are surrounded by VC."

Lieutenant Grover said, "I guess we will just have to circle the trucks and do the best we can."

"Yeah, right. Hey, Lieutenant, we ain't no covered wagon train," remarked one of the truck drivers.

After circling the trucks just below the compound, not too far from the village, we decided to have some supper before it got too dark. As we were getting ready to dive into another case of C rations, it was decided that we would mix them all together, making a mulligan stew. Having completed the task, waiting for the concoction to boil, a small village boy came by riding a water buffalo. Several of the guys thought that they would try their hand at riding the beast. To their dismay, after nearly getting gored to death, they learned that water buffalos are one-man animals.

Following the boy, a village woman came along carrying a basket of corn. She was an angel, or so we thought. "*Chao em*, can I buy that corn from you?" I asked in my most polite manner.

"*Boo coo* number one" was all that she would say.

"She no understand you, go away, you *boo coo* number ten, go on. *Di, di*," said an old man from the village coming down the path, seriously chastising me.

"Wait a minute. I only want to buy the corn from her. Ask her if she will sell it to us."

"She says she take three hundred piastres for corn."

"Done." I quickly paid the young lady the three hundred piastres. I felt that I had died and gone to heaven. It was very seldom we had any kind of fresh veggies.

"Hey, Matty, put it all in the stew," said Underhill. I did just that and all sat there, mouths watering, waiting for the corn to cook. An hour later, the corn was as hard as when we had put it into the stew.

"What kind of corn is this anyway?" complained Felty. "I have never had any this hard, I think it gets harder the longer we cook it."

Supper finally over with, it was decided that we wouldn't need to post guard with the Montagnards around us. Underhill, Felty, and I sat around talking after supper. We all missed our good friend and comrade Fair. Just before going to the helicopter base in Kontum City, Fair had been shipped to Japan. All the jostling about in army trucks had given him kidney stones, and Japan was the only place he could receive proper treatment.

"Underhill, where you gonna sleep?"

"The canopy [cloth roof of truck cab] looks pretty comfy to me, how about you?"

"I think I'll sleep under the bulldozer, just in case."

The bulldozer was still sitting on the trailer of the ten-ton tractor. Evidently, the local VC or North Vietnamese regulars didn't like the hospitality of the Montagnards.

At 12:02 a.m., *kaboom!*

I'm dead, I'm dead, I thought as I jumped up out of a sound sleep, not remembering where I was, instantly banging my head on the bottom of the trailer.

Underhill was under the trailer in an instant. "We're gonna die, we're gonna die" was all that he could say.

Trying to clear the stars out of my head, still not knowing what had happened, I crawled from under the trailer.

"What, are you crazy?" bellowed Underhill as he grabbed my leg, dragging me back.

"I knew it, I knew it. Fifteen days left, I'm a dead man, I'm a dead man."

The "whoever they were" had shot several artillery rounds at the village. The first one had fallen short, hitting about two hundred feet from our trucks. The rest of the night went without incident; needless to say, Underhill and I spent the rest of the night under the bulldozer, not sleeping a wink.

4 August 1970, 0730 Hours

Breakfast (more C rations and extremely hard corn) being over with, we were on the road again.

"Hey," crackled the radio, "this is your friendly eye in the sky."

It was our buddy, the bird dog. As we left the compound road back onto the dirt highway, we began to climb, gradually at first, then more abruptly as the ten-ton rounded a curve, laboring under the weight of the dozer and the incline.

"Man!" shouted the driver as the truck came to a screeching halt, again stopping the convoy. The road went straight up the mountain, getting narrower as it went. After assessing the situation and a lot of hard-core coaxing from Grover, up we went. The truck was really moaning this time. I kept a lookout through the rearview mirror, knowing the road was too narrow for the truck.

"Hey, Billy," crackled the radio. "Look at your back wheels."

It was Underhill in the truck behind us. Looking in the mirror, I noticed the outside duels were out in thin air with no road at all under them.

"Hey, Scotty, you OK, man?" I asked the driver.

Frustration and determination covered his sweat-laden face. "I'm OK, I'm OK, just a little bit further, just a little bit further," he replied as the big truck groaned up the mountainside. As we crossed the summit, the truck seemed to let out a sigh of relief. Every truck made it without incident.

We arrived in Buon Me Thuot about 1500 hours (3:00 p.m.). Buon Me Thuot is a beautiful town, so well kept. One could hardly tell there was a war waging. Our convoy pulled up in a section of town that was part of a huge rubber plantation. There were sidewalks along a neatly paved road. The trees were planted in a manner of rows that no matter what angle at which you looked at them, they were always in straight rows, kinda like tombstones in a military graveyard.

Young boys were stationed along the road, watching that no one molested the trees. Not having seen a rubber tree up close, I approached one to have a look at the rubber-gathering process. Four or five young boys came running up to me.

"*Di*, DI, no touch tree, *boo coo* numba ten, *boo coo* numba ten."

Not wanting to endure the wrath of all those boys, I quickly retreated. Having delivered the rock crusher, we were treated to a hot meal and a real bed.

5 August 1970, 0730 Hours

The convoy, minus one rock crusher, was ready to go home.

"I want to congratulate you guys for a job well-done," stated Lieutenant Grover. "We'll have to spend one more night at Van-Vleck. I have arranged for extra security from Puff the Magic Dragon. Be careful. Keep your eyes open, especially you, Mattatall. The VC and the NVA regulars would like nothing better than to knock us off."

Several hours into our return trip, "What the heck is that?" exclaimed Felty.

At the end of the fire zone, just at the jungle's edge, there sat a large reddish object.

"Felty! How long you been in country? Ain't you ever seen an elephant before?"

"Does it belong to anyone?" Felty asked.

"Naa, just a wild one, master probably killed by the VC."

Late afternoon, the truck was huffing and puffing going up the mountain again.

"Stop the convoy! Stop the convoy!" the radio crackled just as we crested the summit.

The ten-ton truck came to a jarring halt, rear wheels hopping around. There was complete silence. The lieutenant's jeep was nowhere in sight. The situation became tense very quickly.

"Felty, get the guys out of the trucks," I barked. "Spread them out along the edge of the road away from the trucks."

Underhill and I were huddled in the ditch line, fully armed with our M79s ready for the worst. It wasn't the first time we had been ambushed while being in a convoy. Seconds ticked by like hours. No radio communication. I knew if the lieutenant wanted to speak to us, he would. No word from him meant complete radio silence. The jungle was so quiet, not even a rustle in the trees, sun beating down.

Suddenly, an F-4 flew right over our heads, then another. I knew we were in big trouble. The F-4s made a quick turn and were coming back. As they passed, we could see the silver napalm canisters released. The jungle at the bottom of the mountain became a fiery inferno. Again, another pass, more canisters. The heat of the napalm gas belched up the mountainside, another familiar sight as well as another familiar smell, the smell of burning flesh, one I will never ever forget.

A battalion of NVA regulars had planned a surprise party for us on our way home. The bird dog had spotted them and called in an air strike, lucky for us. The rest of the trip to Pleiku was uneventful. I don't really know how many NVA soldiers were waiting for us; the report was always a battalion. Underhill and I arrived back at base camp with six days left in country, and boy, were we in trouble.

Over turned mahogany truck at Van Vleck Bridge

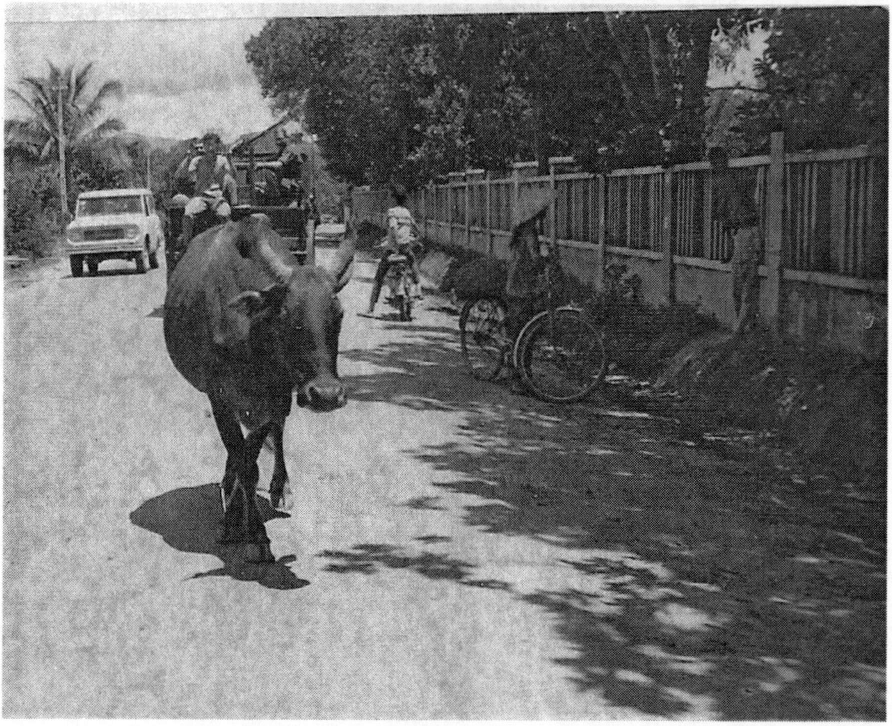

Boy on water buffalo near Kontum

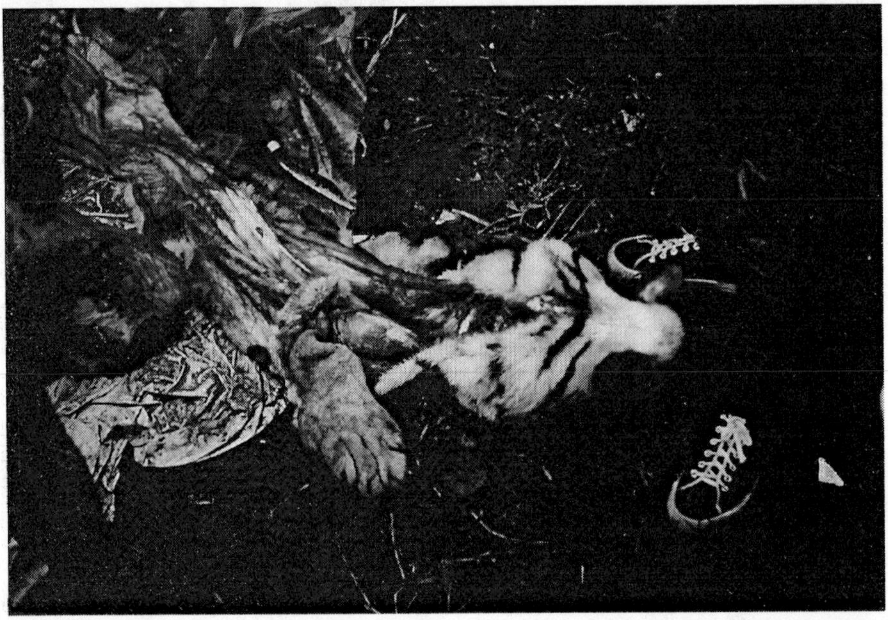

The Tiger at Van Vleck

"Oh, man, I've got guard tonight, six days left and I have to pull guard."

"You got what? What the," I replied, not being able to subdue my laughter.

"Well, don't feel left out, Billy," Underhill came back. "He's got you on CQ [NCO commander of the guard], and he has made himself the OD [officer of the day, commanding officer of the guard detail]."

Our good friend, the platoon leader Lieutenant Combes, was sure PO-ed. He didn't like it a bit that Underhill had gone over his head asking the CO for permission to go with me to Buon Me Thuot. He had put me on CQ and Underhill on guard that night as it was the last day we would be under his command. The last five days were spent clearing country, blood test, etc., in order to go home.

Guard Duty

As the lengthening shadows signaled the approach of evening, I began to muster my troops, those assigned to guard duty for the night. The assignment was once again the infamous Pleiku quarry.

The quarry, now long abandoned with the equipment dismantled and gone, was not threatened by the attack of the VC or the NVA; the threat lay in the nearby ARVN camp and the local nationals carrying away what was left of the place. As mentioned before, the compound sat on a hillside overlooking a large valley that terminated at the outskirts of Pleiku. The north and west sides of the quarry faced that valley. The sheer wall of the quarried hillside formed the compound's south elevation. Route 509 passed the quarry's eastern boundary. The two sides facing the valley were guarded by a ten-foot-tall chain-link fence. The east side by the road had the customary seven-strand concertina perimeter with the rear guarded only by the rock faces of the mountain. Along the three fenced sides of the compound stood twelve guard towers. Each tower required three men each with each man pulling two-hour shifts.

By 1930, two green Cadillacs were loaded along with the 3/4, and we were on our way. Upon arrival, three men were dispersed at each tower as per the guard roster prepared by headquarters company. As evening approached and one could barely see the twinkle of the first star, a jeep pulled up to the front gate where Underhill, I, and Monroe sat talking.

The three of us stood as the driver approached. It was Second Lieutenant Combes.

"Boy, has he got guts!" Underhill whispered under his breath.

"Sergeant Mattatall!" Combes's voice boomed.

"Yes, sir!" I replied quietly.

"I will be your OD tonight [officer of the day]. I know that this is your last night under my command. Now these are my instructions. If I catch so much as one of your guards asleep or if I find as much as one girl on this compound, I will personally court-martial you! Is that understood?"

"Perfectly," I replied.

"I will be in that hooch over by the mess hall if you need me. That will be all."

He retrieved a small laundry bag from the jeep and sauntered toward the hooch.

"Sir!" I called in a voice loud enough to be heard.

The lieutenant stopped, came to attention, did an about-face, and returned to face me.

"Sorry, sir," I replied in the calmest voice I could muster. "But I am afraid you don't have enough shit on your shoulders to court-martial me."

His face flushed; he did an about-face and marched to his hooch without a word. I turned toward Underhill; his face was red, if not redder, than the lieutenant's.

"I'm gonna frag that SOB!" huffed Underhill, moving toward the 3/4 for the armament.

"Hold it! Hold it! Hold it!" Monroe and I both stepped in front of Underhill, blocking his path.

"Tonight. Tonight, man. That's all we got. Just tonight, and it's all over with."

"I don't care. I've had all I can take of that guy. He's been on us since he's been here."

"I know, I know, just let me handle this, OK? No need for you to go to Hotel Long Binh over some stupid lieutenant. OK?"

"Why, what you got in mind?" asked Underhill, his voice a bit calmer and cunning.

"Monroe, you been with us for a few months now, what do ya think, are you with the lieutenant or us?"

"Sarge, you know me, I been with ya all the way."

"Well, then, how about you puttin' an HE round over there in the rafters of the old mess hall. Can ya do that?"

"Think it's far enough, Sarge?"

"Yeah, that's over ninety feet away."

"You got it, Sarge."

With that, Monroe's M79 reported. *Pooka. Kaboom* called the 79's daughter as it collided with one of the trusses of the mess hall, showering the OD's hooch with splinters and broken pieces of two-by-four. Needless to say, Lieutenant Combes did not come out of his hooch the rest of the night. We didn't even see him the next morning; as a matter of fact, neither Underhill nor I ever saw him again.

As darkness overcame the compound, a Lambretta pulled up the front gate. A tall slender, shapely lady emerged from the front passenger's seat.

"Hey, Sarge, you want girls tonight?" she called through the gate. "Oh, Sarge Matty, it's you. I no know who it was."

"Hey, Mama-san, how ya been? Haven't seen ya in a while."

"Number 1. Number 1, Sarge Matty, got pretty girls. You need some?"

"Hmmm." I thought. "How many girls you got, Mama-san? Need a bunch. You got, say, fifteen or twenty?"

"Have here twenty minutes, twenty girls, twenty minutes," she answered, shaking her head. "You want, I get."

"Just wait a minute. What's your price?"

"Sarge Matty, you know price. Five MPC, six P each girl."

"Mama-san, I'm talkin' all night."

"For you, Sarge Matty, one carton Kool per girl."

"Tell ya what, one carton any brand per girl."

"OK, OK. Number 1 deal for you, only be back with twenty girl, twenty minutes, OK?"

"Don't worry, I be here."

With that, Mama-san and the Lambretta quickly disappeared.

"Boy, what a deal," quirked Monroe. "The price is always two cartons per night, and they have to be Kools." (The girls would sell the Kool cigarettes to the dope dealers who would mix the tobacco with marijuana and sell it back to the GIs. The marijuana, uncut with tobacco, was too strong to smoke. The menthol in the Kool cigarettes was also a factor.)

Eighteen minutes later, two Lambrettas pulled up full of girls. Of course, Underhill and Monroe had first choice. We loaded up the 3/4 with girls and made our first round, stopping off at each tower, dropping off one or two girls. I drove with Underhill and Monroe in the front seat, their two girls sitting on their laps. It took two trips to distribute all the girls. At tower number 9, a GI came out and wanted to talk. He was fairly new in country and didn't know me very well nor the original deal I had made with my platoon.

"What's the deal?" he snapped.

"What deal might that be, Private?" I snapped back.

"Just what's in this for you? What do you get out of the deal? A free girl? What?"

Underhill exploded with a burst of laughter. He looked at the girl sitting on his lap and asked, "Tell this stupid GI what Mama-san calls the Sarge here."

The girl instantly began to giggle. "She call him cherry boy. He no boom boom with girls. Him, Mama-san, *boo coo* number one friends. He no chase Mama-san and girls away."

"OK, OK, what's the price?"

"For you, my friend, one carton of cigarettes."

"OK, OK, here's the cigs." He pushed a carton through the truck window.

"Oh no, no, no. You give those to the girls in the back."

With the last girl gone, I drove back to the front gate; Underhill and Monroe kinda melted into the night.

"Well, that's it, Mama-san. All girls gone. See ya in the morning, 0700 hours sharp."

"Sarge Matty, girls be OK?" said Mama-san, almost pleading.

"Yes, Mama-san," I replied. "These guys know I won't allow them to mistreat girls."

"Good, be here seven a.m."

I spent the night in the 3/4 parked near the front gate, knowing I wouldn't have to worry about anyone falling asleep at their post. Sleep would be a stranger this night. I sat there thinking about the past thirteen months in country, what an adventure. Tomorrow would be the start of the end. I thought about the things to come, what it would be like going back to a life that had left me behind over a year ago.

Reality returned as the sun peeked above the horizon to the east. By 0630 hours, the girls, one by one, meandered toward the front gate.

Where did all those cigarettes come from? I thought to myself. Each girl was loaded with several cartons each. Just as we were about to leave, Mama-san pulled up and hurried over to the 3/4.

"Sarge Matty, you give girls ride home. No want MPs to see girls with cigarettes." (The MPs considered American cigarettes contraband and would take them away from the girls if they were to catch them.)

"Sure, put 'em in the dump trucks."

The ride home went without a hitch; that is, until we arrived at the street where the girls lived. They exited the truck, carrying large plastic bags filled with cigarettes. At that moment, a jeep carrying two MPs pulled up behind the rear dump truck. Instantly, the two MPs tried to take the bags of cigarettes from the girls. This brought the families of the girls out of their homes and into the street. Our 3/4 and the two dump trucks quietly left with the MPs surrounded by a mob of angry villagers.

As Underhill and I disembarked the 3/4 at Company B HQ, Lieutenant Reel was there waiting.

"Morning, sir!" I saluted.

"Morning. A major from MP headquarters just called me. Said something about a riot over at Sin City. Seems they got the numbers off of one of our dumps. I don't suppose you and Robert know anything about it?"

"Nope, not a thing, sir."

"Hmm, didn't think so. Oh, and I just wanted to tell you two, good-bye. It's been a real pleasure serving with you, and you both have been good soldiers. Go home proud."

"Yes, sir!" we replied in unison.

"Oh, one more thing, Robert, got any suggestions for a new jeep driver?"

"Well, sir, I think Monroe would do you a great job."

"Thanks, I will look into it. Again, it's been a pleasure."

Underhill and I shortly left for group command and began clearing (the physicals, paper work, etc., needed to leave Vietnam).

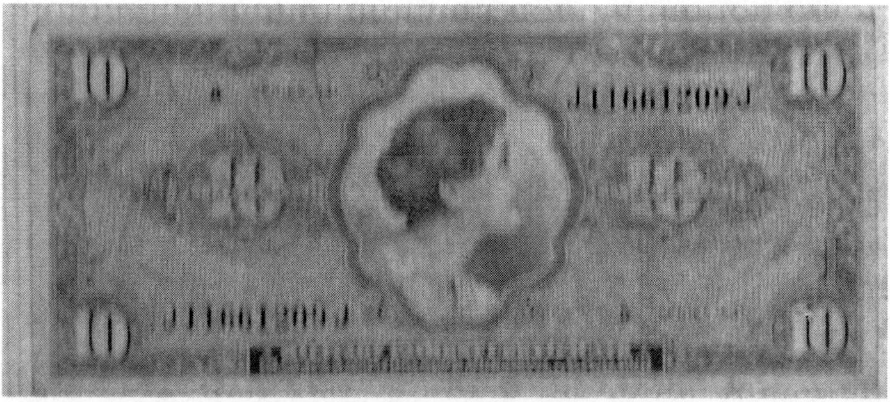

M.P.C. (Military Payment Currency)

Piasters

Homeward Bound

The day was spent first at group HQ, then it was to the dispensary. There they would drain a little blood, and we would be off to the air base and to Cam Ranh Bay. As I waited for my turn, the medic taking the blood was talking to one of his colleagues; he kept poking the needle in the arm of the guy in front of me. It was clear to me that the medic just wasn't paying attention. Finally he hit the vein, and the vial quickly filled. My turn, as the medic wrapped the rubber surgical tube around my arm, I looked him in the eye and gave him the following words of advice:

"Specialist, if you wish to see the sun rise in the morning, you've got one chance to make this work. Understand?" I whispered.

The specialist's eyes grew large as he nodded to the affirmative. Seconds later, my vial was full, and I was on my way.

As Underhill and I arrived at the air base, a C-123 sat on the tarmac warming its engines prior to take off. This would be the plane that carried us to Cam Ranh Bay. The drone of the engine reminded me of that day a C-123 (probably this very plane) brought me here to Pleiku some thirteen and a half months ago. It seemed like a lifetime ago.

Soon the plane was loaded, and we were on our way. There was a row of seats running along each side of the fuselage back to the rear liftgate of the plane. The seats faced toward the center of the plane with the cargo deck running down the middle. All the seats were filled as well as most of the cargo deck. After about twenty minutes in the air, the starboard engine sputtered several times and then quit altogether. Instantly the right side dipped severely, sending everyone aboard to that side of the plane.

"Gentlemen! Gentlemen!" barked the intercom. "I need you to move to the port side of the aircraft. I currently can't bring the wings to level due to your excess weight on the starboard side!"

Now the port side of the aircraft was directly over our heads. About ten feet of smooth aluminum cargo deck rose straight up to the row of seats and then the cargo netting that hung along the sides of the fuselage. At first, everyone tried to clamor up the slick deck floors only to slide back down. Finally, one GI would actually crawl up the back of another and stand on his mate's shoulders. A third would climb up the first two, enabling him to reach the seats and netting. One by one, we reached the port side. As the weight began to shift, the starboard wing began to come up, forcing the port wing down until the pilot was able to right the aircraft, enabling us to land safely.

As the aircraft taxied to a stop, the rear liftgate began to open, letting the sunlight in.

"Yow!" screamed Underhill. "The light is blinding."

Everyone donned sunglasses prior to leaving the C-123. As we exited the plane, we were greeted by the whitest sand I have ever seen.

The army compound at Cam Ranh Bay sat right on the coastline with the South China Sea lapping the shore just a block away. We were moved to the mess hall, fed, and given the rest of the day off; and of course, just about everyone went swimming. With the white beaches and the palm trees, this place was truly a paradise. That evening, we crawled into our barracks totally exhausted. Later that night, I lay in my bunk reflecting on the events of the past several weeks. This afternoon was the first time since R & R (some five months past) that I felt safe, that no one was trying to kill me.

The next morning saw the sun rise over the horizon of the ocean, another spectacular sight. Breakfast was served until 9:00 a.m. If one wished to sleep in, he could have at it. The first debriefing class wasn't until 1000 hours at 1500 hours (3:00 p.m.). We were again released for the day. It was back to the beach until sundown.

18 August 1970

Today, the fourth day of clearing was much like day 3. However, at 1700 hours, we gathered at the training hooch to receive our actual orders home. The CO called Underhill into his office. After several minutes, Underhill burst through the door, slamming it behind him. He brushed past me, not saying a word. After searching the beaches, the PX, and the EM Club, I finally found him lying in his bunk, his arm draped over his face.

"Hey, man, what's up?" I asked, concerned. At first, no answer. "Come on, man, we been together too long. What's goin' on?"

Slowly, Bob moved his arm from his face. There were tears in his eyes.

"I've had it. I've just had it. I just can't deal with it any longer. The CO said I couldn't go home for three more days. If I leave tonight, I won't get an early out. So I gotta stay."

"Hey, no problem, man. We'll just hang out here for three more days."

"Nah, Matty, you need to go. You've done your time. Go on, man."

"Hey, come on, I'll be glad to stay with you."

"No no no. Now go, ya goin' ta miss your plane."

With a heavy heart, I pulled Underhill out of his bunk, embraced him, turned, and walked out the door, never to see him again. An exercise field lay directly behind the barracks. I ran to the center of the field, threw myself on the ground, and sobbed like a baby. Everything I knew was being taken away. I felt as if I were being cast back into a world, a life that had left me behind, gone on without me. As I rolled over my back and I was exposed to the myriad of stars in the heavens above, it seemed as if every star above said to me, "Don't worry. Everything will be OK." I got up, brushed myself off, and off to the airfield I went.

The plane, one of the same Flying Tiger airliners that brought me to Vietnam, lifted off just a few minutes after 3:00 a.m. on 19 August 1970. We flew first to Japan, refueled, and then it was sixteen hours to Fort Lewis, Washington. We landed on U.S. soil just prior to 3:00 a.m. on 19 August 1970, which was about five minutes before we left Vietnam.

Clearing the army began immediately. However, the wheels came to a stop at exactly 1200 hours. Some of the private contractors on base went on strike. The rest of the day was spent idly waiting. Finally, at 2100 hours, all was resolved. By 2345 hours, I was out of the army (active duty) and on my way home.

The plane home left Seattle just before 0100 hours and arrived in St. Louis just after 6:00 a.m. As I moved from the plane to the airport's interior, I noticed a group of people (mostly younger hippie types although some were nicely dressed and clean shaven) protesting the war. They were gathered in front of the USO making quite a ruckus. As I passed, one of the group ran up to me and yelled "BABY KILLER, YOU STINKIN' BABY KILLER!" spitting a wad right at my face. I simply moved aside, the spittle catching my pant leg.

The adjustment to civilian life took well into a year. To all that served, I say unto you, "Welcome home."

Glossary

A.I.T.	Advanced Individual Training
ARVN	Army of the Republic of Viet Nam
ASP Yard	Supply Yard
B-22	A 72 inch long rocket delivering a 40 pound TNT payload
B-40	A rocket about 18 inches long fired by means of a hand launcher similar to a bazooka
Boo Coo	A lot, many
Boom Boom	Sex
C-4	Plastic explosive
C.O.	Commanding Officer (Company Commander)
C.Q.	Charge of Quarters
DiDi	Go! Leave
Dinky Dow	Crazy
Duce and a half	2 ½-ton Cargo truck
Fou Gas	Jellied gasoline used in perimeter defense
50-cal	Fifty caliber machine gun
G.I.	Government Issue (soldiers)
Green Cadillac	5-ton Dump truck
H.E.	High explosive
Hooch	Vietnamese house
Hooch Girl	House maid
Honey Bee	60-mm mortar
Klick(click)	Kilometer or 1000 yards
Lambretta	Taxi, cargo scooter
Law	Light Antitank Weapon
Loach	Light Observation Helicopter

Montangard	Vietnamese Aborigine
MP	Military Police
MPC	Military Payment Certificate or currency. Currency used by GIs.
M-79	U.S. grenade launcher. Shoots a 40-mm projectile at about 250 feet per second. Range is 350 yards. Projectile arms upon traveling a distance of 90 feet. Uses 4 different shells: H.E.(high explosive), CS(Tear Gas), Shotgun(bird shot), and Willie Peter(white phosphorus).
Napalm	Jellied gasoline
NCO	Non-Commissioned Officer
NCOIC	Non-Commissioned Officer in Charge
Number 1	The best
Number 10	The worst
NVA	North Vietnamese Army
OD	Olive Drab
PCS	Permanent Change of Station
Piaster	Vietnamese dollar
PT	Physical training
PX	Post Exchange
Quad Forty	4 barrel 40-mm ack-ack gun
Satchel Charge	An explosive device packed in a canvas bag resembling a book bag
¾	A ¾-ton pickup truck
Underdog	Nickname for Robert A. Underhill
VC	Viet Cong, Charlie, Gook
War Wagon	2 ½-ton cargo truck with a quad 40 mounted in the bed
W.O.	Warrant officer (non-commission pilot)